Peaceful
Revolution

Peaceful Revolution

How We Can Create the Future Needed for Humanity's Survival

by Paul K. Chappell

ESP
easton studio
press

Published by
Easton Studio Press
P.O. Box 3131, Westport, CT 06880
www.eastonsp.com

Print ISBN: 978-1-935212-76-8
eBbook ISBN: 978-1-935212-75-1

Book and cover design by Barbara Aronica-Buck
Front cover photo is of the Greek goddess Eirene, who was the goddess
of peace (eirênê) and of the season of spring (eiar, eiarinos).

www.paulkchappell.com

Printed on recycled paper and paper manufactured
using sustainable production methods.
Printed in Canada
First Printing: February 2012
Second Printing: November 2014
10 9 8 7 6 5 4 3 2

MIX
Paper from
responsible sources
FSC® C004071

ANCIENT FOREST ™
FRIENDLY

FSC
www.fsc.org

For Janice Vaughn, my tenth-grade English teacher,
who told me I should be a writer.
I have been writing ever since.

ACKNOWLEDGMENTS

I would like to begin by thanking Jo Ann Deck. This book would not exist and I would not be alive today if not for her endless compassion and invaluable guidance. I would also like to thank David Wilk, who is the kind of publisher every author dreams of having and the kind of person who embodies many of the ideals I discuss in this book. I would like to thank Gray Cutler, whose thorough copy-edits brought this book to a higher level, and whose tireless attention to detail reminds me why every writer needs an excellent editor. And I would like to thank Leslee Goodman and Vicki Weiland, for helping with the developmental editing of this book and for being great friends and comrades in the struggle for peace. I would like to thank Barbara Aronica-Buck for designing a beautiful book cover that visually conveys the hope, love, and longing for peace that I strive to convey in words. And I must thank Joanne Sprott, who made an important contribution by proofreading this book and compiling a great index. Her professionalism and exceptional ability as an editor remind me that creating a book is truly a group effort. Finally, I would like to thank my new family at the Nuclear Age Peace Foundation. They have saved my life in more ways than one.

CONTENTS

THE GREAT QUESTION
BY
GENERAL DOUGLAS MACARTHUR

The great question is: Can global war now be outlawed
from the world? If so, it would mark the greatest advance in
civilization since the Sermon on the Mount. It would lift at
one stroke the darkest shadow which has engulfed mankind
from the beginning. It would not only remove fear and bring
security—it would not only create new moral and spiritual
values—it would produce an economic wave of prosperity
that would raise the world's standard of living beyond anything ever dreamed of by man.

The hundreds of billions of dollars now spent in mutual
preparedness [for war] could conceivably abolish poverty from
the face of the earth. It would accomplish even more than this;
it would at one stroke reduce the international tensions that
seem to be insurmountable now, to matters of more probable
solution. This would not, of course, mean the abandonment
of all armed forces, but it would reduce them to the simpler
problems of internal order and international police. It would
not mean utopia at one fell stroke, but it would mean that the
great roadblock now existing to the development of civilization would have been cleared.

You will say at once, that although the abolition of war
has been the dream of man for centuries, every proposition
to that end has been promptly discarded as impossible and

fantastic. But that was before the science of the past decade made mass destruction a reality . . . now the tremendous evolution of nuclear and other potentials of destruction has suddenly taken the problem away from its primary consideration as a moral and spiritual question and brought it abreast of scientific realism. [The abolition of war] is no longer an ethical equation to be pondered solely by learned philosophers and ecclesiastics, but a hard-core one for the decision of the masses whose survival is the issue . . .

Many will tell you with mockery and ridicule that the abolition of war can be only a dream—that it is but the vague imagining of a visionary. But we must go on or we will go under. And the great criticism that can be made is that the world lacks a plan that will enable us to go on. We have suffered the blood and the sweat and the tears. Now we seek the way and the truth and the light. We are in a new era. The old methods and solutions for this vital problem no longer suffice. We must have new thoughts, new ideas, new concepts . . . We must have sufficient imagination and courage to translate this universal wish for peace—which is rapidly becoming a universal necessity—into actuality.[1]

General Douglas MacArthur,
1961

Unlocking the Mysteries of Human Nature

I have hope because I am alive. I have hope because my existence shows the impossible can become possible. When people said racial segregation in America must end, those who supported segregation controlled the society, government, military, corporations, many universities, and most of the money. What did the advocates of desegregation have on their side? The truth. Contrary to widely believed myths, it was not true that African Americans were inferior to whites. It was not true that racial harmony was impossible.

When people said women should have equal rights with men, those who opposed women's rights controlled the society, government, military, corporations, many universities, and most of the money. What did the advocates of gender equality have on their side? The truth. Contrary to widely believed myths, it was not true that women were intellectually inferior to men. It was not true that women were less than human.

Today ending war is necessary for the survival of humanity, yet those who perpetuate war control the society, government, military, corporations, many universities, and most of the money. What do we have on our side? The truth. Contrary to widely believed myths, it is not true that human beings are naturally violent. It is not true that war is inevitable. It is not true that war protects our way of life and makes us safe. This book provides the evidence and reasoning necessary to support these claims, and it outlines a path away from war that shows how we can solve our world's most serious problems.

Historical perspective is one ingredient in the recipe for hope, because when people lack perspective they also lack hope. To see how much humanity can achieve, we must recognize how far we have come. Five hundred years ago ideals such as democracy, the right to vote, freedom of speech, freedom of religion, freedom of the press, and women's and civil rights virtually did not exist. And how many democratic countries were there two hundred years ago? By 1810 Napoleon had overthrown the democratic government in France, and the United States was not a democracy for African Americans, women, and even many white people, since owning land was a common requirement for voting. But because people in the past had hope and took action, democracies now exist in many parts of the world, and America has become a place where I can write these words today.

I grew up in Alabama, and although my father was half white, half black and my mother was Korean, I had the opportunity to graduate from West Point because our ancestors who waged peace embodied the highest ideals I learned in the U.S. Army, such as its Warrior Ethos: "I will always place the mission first. I will never accept defeat. I will never quit. I will never leave a fallen comrade."

Whether their mission was ending racial segregation or achieving women's rights, those who struggled for a better world placed the mission first, never accepted defeat, and never quit. When the ship of justice allowed only a few people on board and seemed to disappear over the horizon, they refused to leave behind their comrades, their brothers and sisters, their fellow human beings. This book will explain why the ongoing struggles for justice, peace, women's rights, and racial equality are stagnating and even losing ground in many parts of the world, and what we can do to turn the tide. This book will show how far humanity has come, how much further we can go, and how we can get there.

For hundreds of years my African ancestors were slaves, and my father was drafted into a segregated army. Progress happened not only because people had hope and took action, but because truth is more powerful than lies. Injustice is built on lies, and every lie has a fatal flaw—it isn't true.

State-sanctioned slavery existed on a global scale for thousands of years, but this unjust system could not have existed without the help of lies and myths. For example, many slave owners believed it was in the nature of certain people to live as slaves. They even believed most slaves were happy being slaves. State-sanctioned slavery was supported by the myth that slaves, like domesticated animals, needed masters. The myth also claimed that a slave owner could be a kind and gentle master of his slaves just as a shepherd could be a kind and gentle master of his sheep—and slaves wouldn't know what to do with freedom if you gave it to them.

Today if I said, "It's not in the nature of some races to be slaves. Human beings have an innate yearning for freedom, and to enslave a group of people harsh techniques must be used to break their will and suppress their human nature," most of us would agree it is a self-evident statement that makes common sense. But this was not common sense several hundred years ago. By the eighteenth century, state-sanctioned slavery had existed since the beginning of recorded history and was an integral part of the global economy. Thomas Clarkson and other abolitionists believed all human beings should have the gift of freedom and dedicated their lives to ending slavery. If you think the world looks hopeless today, imagine how it must have looked from Clarkson's perspective, a man ridiculed for thinking slavery was wrong.

Hope allows us to see not only how the world is but also how it can be. Because Americans had hope, in 1848 they organized the first convention for women's rights in Seneca Falls, New York. Approximately three hundred people showed up. They wrote a document called the Declaration of Sentiments, stating women should have the right to vote, the right to own property, and other freedoms often taken for granted today. Many of the women at the convention thought having the right to vote was too radical, but social activist Elizabeth Cady Stanton and Frederick Douglass, the only African American at the convention, spoke in its favor. Despite this, only one hundred signed the document. If you think the world looks hopeless today, imagine how it must have looked from the perspective of Stanton and Douglass. They couldn't even get the women's rights movement to fully support women's right to vote.

Without people like Stanton and Douglass, nothing would ever change for the better. The information in this book will unlock the mystery of hope that made them so powerful. It will also show why writer and human rights activist Victor Hugo was correct when he said: "Nothing can withstand the force of an idea whose time has come."[2]

During the seventeenth century, Galileo Galilei offered scientific evidence showing the earth revolved around the sun. Threatened by his new evidence, the Roman Catholic Church gave him the choice of recanting his ideas or facing execution. Even if he recanted, the church would ban Galileo's books and put him under house arrest for the rest of his life. At this time the church was a superpower that controlled governments, societies, militaries, religious beliefs, educational systems, and much of the wealth worldwide. If you think the world looks hopeless today, imagine how it must have looked to Galileo, who was almost killed for saying the earth revolved around the sun and spent the rest of his life on house arrest after recanting his ideas.

In 2000, Pope John Paul II issued a formal apology on behalf of the Roman Catholic Church for its treatment of Galileo and other mistakes it had made. His apology reveals a lot about the power of truth to overcome deception.

Truth is eternal, but the lies that sustain oppression and injustice have a lifespan. Since the birth of humanity it has always been true that women are not less than human and no race was designed for slavery, but lies suppress these truths. Unlike truth, which can be concealed but never destroyed, a lie can eventually grow old and die. However, unlike the struggles for racial equality, women's rights, intellectual freedom, and the abolition of slavery—primarily moral issues—ending war is a matter of survival. The great question of our era is: What will die first—the myths that support war or the human species? Unlike the movements that furthered racial and gender equality around the world, the struggle to end war is a race against time in which our survival is at stake. During the twentieth century, a cold war between the Soviet Union and United States held the world hostage. Today, if we fail to take action we could face far more dangerous situations: a nuclear arms race might escalate not between two superpowers but among many countries, or nuclear weapons could fall into the hands of terrorists.

This book offers new solutions to help us win this race. To win we must get to the root of the problem by unlocking the mysteries of human nature that have eluded us for far too long. *Peaceful Revolution* will show how terrorism, injustice, oppression, tyranny, racism, sexism, violence, war, genocide, and our destruction of the environment are caused by the same underlying problems. They are features of the same face. Instead of treating surface symptoms we will discuss how to cure the underlying ways of thinking that cause conflicts around the world, violence in our societies, turmoil in our homes, and suffering in our hearts.

West Point, the military, and war have given me a window into the mysteries of human nature. West Point and the military also gave me the training necessary to work for a safer and more peaceful world. To show why and how this happened, *Peaceful Revolution* journeys deeper than my previous two books, *Will War Ever End?* and *The End of War*, and its content is much broader. In *Peaceful Revolution* I will revisit some of the ideas and stories in those first two books, to expand our understanding in new directions. I will also unlock the mysteries of hope, empathy, and the other muscles of our humanity that hold the secrets to our salvation. This is important, because in the twenty-first century our survival depends on our ability to understand and embrace our humanity. This book, by clarifying what it means to be human, is a next step on the road to peace that will help us achieve our highest potential as a global family.

I have been working on *Peaceful Revolution* for ten years. More personal than my previous two books, it journeys into our shared human struggle for meaning. It examines the most painful moments of my life—the times when I lost hope and peace seemed like an impossible dream. It also explains why I nearly committed suicide and why I kept choosing the path of life. These pages explore dark personal experiences and even darker content. But ideas that shine with real hope and empowerment can only rise from the deepest shadows. To unlock the mystery of hope we must also explore our doubts, hopelessness, and despair. To understand peace we must journey into the foreboding source of violence. *Peaceful Revolution* analyzes our destructive behavior in a way that sees through the illusions, stereotypes, and lies—the myths that confuse us and prevent us from solving our problems. We will return from this voyage with new strength, hope, direction, and solutions.

In 1962, two years before his death, General MacArthur gave his final address to the cadets at West Point. He said: "This does not mean that you are warmongers. On the contrary, the soldier above all other people prays for peace, for he must suffer and bear the deepest wounds and scars of war.

But always in our ears ring the ominous words of Plato, that wisest of all philosophers: 'Only the dead have seen the end of war.'"[3]

World peace is necessary in an interconnected global society where technology has given us the means to destroy ourselves. Like General MacArthur, most of us have seen our attitudes toward war and peace change over time. Also, like him, most of us want to believe world peace and human survival are possible, yet we have doubts. Although he had significant doubts about the attainment of world peace, this book reveals what humanity has learned about the possibility of peace since General MacArthur expressed his uncertainties fifty years ago.

We are living during an information revolution that has dramatically changed our understanding in many ways. We discovered more about physics during the twentieth century than every previous century of recorded history combined. We also made more advances in medical technology than all the preceding centuries put together. In 1926, General George Patton wrote: "Despite the years of thought and oceans of ink which have been devoted to the elucidation of war, its secrets still remain shrouded in mystery."[4]

Just as humanity's understanding of physics and medical technology grew more during the twentieth century than the rest of recorded history put together, this book will show that we have learned more about war's true nature since General Patton wrote those words in 1926 than all of the centuries that preceded him. We are living during an exciting time when the deepest secrets of war, which General Patton believed to be shrouded in mystery, are finally being unlocked. One of these secrets is how to end war.

This book explains why we are living in one of the most hopeful eras in human history and why peace is within our grasp. It also shows how I arrived at these conclusions while being a very skeptical person. A degree of skepticism can be healthy because it prevents us from being fooled by quick fixes and shallow solutions that don't address the root causes of our problems. Skepticism should not be confused with cynicism, however; skepticism is the act of questioning while cynicism is the triumph of hopelessness.

We can talk about how tragic war is, but unless we question its underlying assumptions and challenge its prevailing myths, war will continue. A peaceful revolution that dispels the myths of war while lifting our perception of humanity to new heights is crucial. A peaceful revolution that shows what all people can do to create the future needed for humanity's survival is necessary now more than ever. That revolution is alive in these pages, but to truly succeed it must also become alive in you. For the sake of humanity and our planet, I hope this book will help ignite a peaceful revolution within you.

> Paul K. Chappell
> July 14, 2010
> Santa Barbara, CA

CHAPTER 1

The Muscle of Hope

Born Human

Since my earliest memories, I have been obsessed with war. My father served in the Korean and Vietnam Wars, and when I was young I saw how war can ruin families. I grew up as an only child in Alabama and have fond memories of being three years old and watching my father tend to his garden, feed the birds in our backyard, and chase away a spider that almost frightened me to death. But when I was four, everything changed.

I was sleeping peacefully late one night when I felt someone grab my leg and drag me from my bed onto the floor. My leg was pulled so hard I heard my pajama pants rip down the middle. Looking up and seeing my father, I began to panic as he pulled my hair and told me he was going to kill me. His cursing and my screaming woke my mother, who ran into the room and bear-hugged him until he finally calmed down.

When I was four something else occurred that I could not understand at the time, but that I later attributed to my father's war experiences. One evening I heard him screaming at my mother and threatening to shoot himself with his pistol. This was the first time I heard him threaten to commit suicide, but it would not be the last. Throughout my childhood, I watched my father lose his grip on reality, and his frightening behavior caused me to struggle with my own sanity. Rage overshadowed his once peaceful nature, and when I heard him complain about violent nightmares, I realized something called war had taken my gentle father from me.

During these early years, I internalized my father's despair and longed for an escape from his violent behavior. When I was five, this trauma led to my lifelong obsession with war and suffering—when I had a vivid dream that I killed myself. I still remember the dream clearly: I walked through the front door of my house, where I saw both my parents lying dead in coffins. Without thinking, I went to the bathroom cabinet with the intent of stabbing myself in the heart. I opened a drawer and saw a large pair of scissors, but their menacing size frightened me. Next to them, I saw a smaller pair of scissors that my mother used to clip my fingernails. I picked them up, stabbed myself in the chest, and watched as blood covered my hands. Then I walked to my mother's coffin and laid in it with her, where I waited to die so that my anguish would finally end.

When I woke from this dream I was never the same. I realized life was painful and cruel in incomprehensible ways. I had not asked to be born, and I had not chosen to live in these terrifying surroundings. I felt trapped in a prison of helplessness, and my only crime was being born human.

I am not the only one guilty of this crime. As I grew older, I saw that my agony was not unique in the world, for we all suffer as human beings. At times we all feel that life is painful and cruel beyond comprehension. None of us asked to be born nor were any of us allowed to pick our genes or country of birth. Babies are not given the option of selecting the shape of their face, color of their skin, or parents' financial standing. Yet here we are, breathing, thinking, living, and vulnerable to so much pain. We have to do the best with what we have.

During these years, I realized life was full of anguish, but as I was lying in bed late one night a new thought crept into my mind. What if I could escape the prison of my helplessness and overcome my suffering? What if I could heal myself and transform my life into a joyful celebration? As I pondered this possibility, I developed an obsession with pain and its cause. I became determined to discover if happiness was real or just an illusion to be futilely chased. I remembered being happy before my father's violence had transformed me. If I tried to overcome my suffering, couldn't I gradually experience the warmth of happiness again?

As a child I did not yet possess the intellectual capacity necessary to answer these questions, but a seed within me sprouted and grew stronger over the years. It kept me alive long enough to find solutions to our human problems. That seed was hope.

For many years I thought the hope within me had died. Children's minds are fragile and unable to cope with trauma; violence inflicted on them has lasting consequences. Growing up not just as an only child in a violent home, but also experiencing racism as a small boy suppressed my hope for a brighter future. Yet as long as we are alive, the possibility of hope lives within us.

Today hope has become a cliché. We must transcend this cliché, because realistic hope is one of our strongest allies in the struggle to solve our personal, national, and global problems. To harness the power of hope we must explore and understand what it really is. We must recognize that hope is a form of trust. And like trust, hope is not easily gained.

To create the realistic hope that strengthens us during times of adversity, we must increase our understanding. When people lack vital information about the world and what it means to be human, they lack hope. The absence of hope, like losing the ground beneath our feet, causes us to fall into the pit of cynicism, bitterness, and helplessness.

I was born human, but only when I began to understand what it *means* to be human did I realize that life, no matter how painful, is not a prison sentence to be spent behind bars of helplessness and anguish. Hope taught me life is a gift, and in these pages I will share the experiences and ideas that gradually led me to this awareness.

My experiences as a child in Alabama, a student at West Point, and a soldier in the army taught me being born human is not enough. If we are to survive and prosper in the twenty-first century, we must also explore what it means to be human. When we wipe away the myths preventing us from knowing who we truly are, we will see why there is so much reason for hope during these times of great challenge.

The Army's Hope Training

The human mind is not only our greatest strength, but also our greatest weakness. In the struggle for survival, it is our strongest and weakest link. The army understands this and that is why it trains its soldiers to be hopeful.

Army training puts soldiers in difficult situations where hunger, exhaustion, and muscle fatigue push the body to its limits. Soldiers must rely on teamwork and their training to overcome challenges designed to make them want to quit. When I attended basic training at West Point in 1998, every squad of around ten cadets had to complete a twenty-four-hour team event that tested their skills, endurance, and resilience. The day consisted of challenges requiring co-operation, like pushing a heavy vehicle and protecting an area from a simulated attack. This demanded a lot from my eighteen-year-old body and my muscles sometimes begged me to quit, but I kept going with the help and encouragement of my squad mates.

The feeling of accomplishing something you once believed you couldn't do is indescribable. Prior to basic training at West Point, I had never rappelled down a cliff (I was afraid of heights), fired a weapon (let alone passed an army marksmanship test), or marched for fifteen miles while carrying heavy weight on my back. And the list goes on.

After basic training, West Point cadets must continue to overcome a wide variety of challenges that might have once seemed daunting to them. In addition to mandatory gymnastics and swimming classes, every male freshman must take a boxing class (optional for females). Freshmen must also lead their peers, speak in public constantly, and not only write a poem for their English class but also read it out loud. The education at West Point is designed to take cadets out of their normal range of experience in order to build their self-confidence.

The army utilizes the same educational philosophy. Every time soldiers successfully complete a challenge their self-confidence increases. By repeatedly putting soldiers through tough training requiring teamwork, the army develops three kinds of trust.

Trust in yourself. Soldiers are trained to never underestimate themselves and to never be afraid of trying. By having soldiers overcome a wide variety of challenges, army training conditions soldiers to believe in and trust themselves. In my case, this did not lead to the arrogant belief I can do everything, but it did build the self-confident belief that anything is possible if I try my best. This self-confidence is not based on wishful thinking, but on the many training experiences that taught me to trust myself. Since soldiers must be prepared to survive in some of the harshest situations imaginable, lack of self-confidence and low self-esteem are among the worst enemies they can have. To make them resilient in the face of adversity, army training gives soldiers an optimistic perspective that can help them overcome other challenges in their lives as well.

Trust in other people. Because the army cannot function without teamwork and cooperation, the strongest army units are similar to a family. Army training taught me I can rely on others and trust them with my life, and that cooperation is one of the most powerful forces in the world. In the army I learned that nothing worthwhile is possible if we do not trust other people, but all things are possible when we build the bonds that lead to trust.

Trust in your ideals. When people say that selflessness, sacrifice, and service are naive moral ideals, it shows how little they know about the military and humanity. In the army these ideals are not naive, but matters of military necessity. Without them a community cannot survive in extremely difficult circumstances. Imagine if ten greedy people willing to exploit each other for personal gain were transported to the harsh African plains of a million years ago, where they would be hunted by predators and continually faced with starvation and drought. Unless they changed their selfish attitude, they would not survive long.

Now imagine if ten people willing to sacrifice for each other—similar to the bond within an army unit—were transported to the same unforgiving environment. Their chances for survival would be much greater. Our earliest ancestors had to survive in conditions where predators hunted them relentlessly and not even water was guaranteed. Selflessness strengthens teamwork and cooperation by transforming isolated individuals into a strong family unit that functions like a superorganism—something far more difficult for predators to conquer. In the army I learned that greed and selfishness are cancers in this superorganism.

The army gave me a lot of evidence and experience that enabled me to trust in the ideals of selflessness, sacrifice, and service. It taught me that these ideals are necessary for real bonds of friendship and family to exist. When I studied our greatest peacemakers—like Buddha, Jesus, Socrates, Lao Tzu, Susan B. Anthony, Mahatma Gandhi, Albert Schweitzer, Mother Teresa, Martin Luther King Jr., Albert Einstein, and many others—I found they all said the same thing. Are West Point, the army, the peacemakers who contributed so much to humanity, and my own experience, all wrong?

The army also taught me to trust in other ideals: *I will never accept defeat. I will never quit.* Soldiers are required to memorize these lines from the Warrior Ethos, and the army also conditions them through rigorous training to embody these ideals. Sometimes retreat that allows you to fight another day is the best option, but the decision to retreat should be based on good judgment, not fear or lack of resilience. Many of us are so cynical and pessimistic that we quit before even trying. People have told me that attempting to end war is impossible and a waste of my time. But army training gave me trust in my ideals by teaching me that if we never accept defeat and never quit, what once seemed impossible can become possible.

Wishful thinking, unsupported by evidence and experience, is the basis of *naive hope*, but the three kinds of trust—in myself, in others, and in my ideals—are the basis of *realistic hope*. They transform hope from a cliché into a powerful ally. The army trained me to have this trust, and with it I have the strength to wage peace. Military training is not essential though; people like Martin Luther King Jr., Susan B. Anthony, and many others who did not serve in the military demonstrate there are other ways of developing these three kinds of trust. *Peaceful Revolution* will reveal some of those paths.

How Realistic Hope Enables Human Survival

Whenever the world seemed dark and I wanted to give up, the three kinds of trust created light in the darkness. Like a telescope, realistic hope focuses these sources of light into a powerful vision, allowing us to see far. This telescope gives us the vision to see not only how the world is but how it can be. Without the far-reaching vision provided by realistic hope, nothing would ever change for the better. Without the determination created by realistic hope, our ancestors would never have survived.

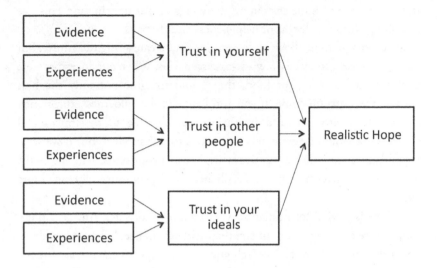

Figure 1.1: Realistic Hope

As I mentioned earlier, the human mind is not only our greatest strength, but also our greatest weakness. In the struggle for survival, it is our strongest and weakest link. Almost all other organisms fight for life as long as their bodies allow, but we humans often give up long before that. No other organism takes premeditated steps to terminate its own existence.[1] No other organism commits suicide out of despair. The will to live may decrease in wild animals held in captivity, but we are the only creatures who commit suicide while still possessing health and freedom. In the army I heard a saying: "A human being can survive for a few weeks without food, a few days without water, but only a few moments without hope." A person with absolutely no hope at all would be depressed and suicidal. If we do not have at least a little hope, it is difficult to get out of bed in the morning.

Our large brains give us a significant survival advantage. Our imagination is an incredible ally in the struggle for survival that allows us to anticipate problems, implement creative solutions, and plan for the future. Like a bird's wings, our imagination gives us the ability to soar, but it also creates the risk of falling. If a bird is flying high and the muscles sustaining its wings fail, it will plunge to its death. In a similar way, if we are faced with adversity and the muscle of hope sustaining the wings of our imagination fails, we will plunge into the depths of helplessness and despair.

Our imagination allows us to envision and create a brighter future, but we can also use it to dwell on worst-case scenarios. When our ancestors were hungry and searching for food, they could imagine not only the best but also the worst outcome. If you and I were in the wilderness, threatened by predators, drought, and starvation, succumbing to pessimism and hopelessness would be extremely dangerous to our survival. But if we were hopeful and maintained a positive attitude when confronted with adversity, we would gain determination and resilience, making our survival much more likely.

Hope is as vital for human survival as food and water. And it is not a coincidence that hope is an inherently joyful experience. When it is realistic rather than naive, hope always feels good, which in turn encourages the behavior that enables our survival. However, it is important to distinguish between realistic hope and naive hope. Naive hope gives us the illusion of joy while realistic hope improves our perspective in a way that gives us a more positive attitude. Naive hope sets us up for a big fall, for disappointment and pain; realistic hope gives us the strength to endure and overcome big falls. Naive hope is built on wishful thinking; realistic hope is built on the trust that comes from evidence and experience.

Similar to the trust that keeps soldiers alive, our ancestors also required realistic hope and the three kinds of trust to survive.

Trust in yourself. Our ancestors who lived on the harsh African plains were threatened by starvation, drought, predators, disease, injury, and death. There were no emergency rooms in the wild, and they had to surmount overwhelming odds to survive in these difficult circumstances. But when they were hungry, they trusted their ability to find food. When they were thirsty, they trusted their ability to find water. When predators threatened their tribe, they trusted their ability to protect their family. This trust was built on evidence and experience. No matter how bleak their situation might have seemed, the fact that they were still alive, and the fact that their ancestors had endured for countless generations, taught them to always have hope, to never accept defeat, and to never quit.

Trust in other people. Cooperation is necessary for human survival, and selflessness, sacrifice, and service forge the most indestructible bonds of cooperation. Early human tribes lived as families, and just as military units rely on cooperation and teamwork for their strength, so did our ancestors. Evidence and experience not only taught our ancestors that people could be trusted, but that they must be trusted if the tribe is going to survive. Every nomadic tribe that has ever been studied relies on cooperation and trust among its members for its survival.

Trust in your ideals. For our nomadic ancestors, nature was not an enemy to be conquered. Despite the many dangers of the wilderness, they trusted nature. They trusted in nature's ability to provide for their needs as long as they respected its ways and never gave up. The fact that nature had provided for their ancestors for countless generations gave them abundant evidence that nature could be trusted.

Just as liberty is an ideal to us, living in harmony with nature was an ideal to our nomadic ancestors and many tribes all over the world. Just as we trust the ideal of liberty to improve our lives, our nomadic ancestors trusted that respecting nature would improve their well-being. The following two Native American quotes express trust in nature and the ideal of treating our environment not as an enemy, but a friend.

A Navaho proverb eloquently says: "I have been to the end of the earth. I have been to the end of the waters. I have been to the end of the sky. I have been to the end of the mountains. I have found none that are not my friends."[2] And in the words of Mohawk Peter Blue Cloud: "Will you ever begin to understand the meaning of the very soil beneath your feet? From a grain of sand to a great mountain, all is sacred. Yesterday and tomorrow exist eternally upon this continent. We natives are guardians of this sacred place."[3]

Surviving Trauma and Betrayal

Throughout *Peaceful Revolution* I will share the evidence and experience that gave me realistic hope. I will also show that realistic hope can survive even when we have suffered enormously and our trust has been betrayed. Descent into cynicism and hopelessness is not inevitable for the person who has experienced unbearable pain. Historian Will Durant said that "those who have suffered much become very bitter or very gentle."[4]

An example of someone who suffered much and became very gentle is the great American folk singer and social activist Woody Guthrie, one of the most hopeful people of the twentieth century. He said: "The note of hope is the only note that can help us or save us from falling to the bottom of the heap of evolution, because, largely, about all a human being is, anyway, is just a hoping machine."[5]

The Rock and Roll Hall of Fame called Guthrie the "original folk hero" who "transformed the folk ballad into a vehicle for social protest and observation." Although he had little formal education and lived during an era of immense racism, Guthrie became a strong advocate for human rights and social justice. He wrote songs to inform people about the injustices ignored by our world. And during the despair of the Great Depression he used his music to remind people they should never give up. Despite his traumatic life experiences, he had hope a brighter future was possible and did not fall into the pit of cynicism, bitterness, and helplessness. Describing his childhood, Guthrie said:

> [When my family's] six bed-room house burned down . . . just a day or two after it was built . . . well right after that, my fourteen-year-old sister either set herself on fire or caught on fire accidentally. There's two different stories got out about it. Anyway, she was having a little difficulty with her school-work, and she had to stay home and do some work, and she caught on fire while she was doing some ironing that afternoon on the old kerosene stove. It was highly unsafe and highly uncertain in them days, and this one blowed up and caught her on fire and she run around the house about twice before anybody could catch her. The next day she died. And my mother, that one was a little too much for her nerves . . . My mother died in the insane asylum at Norman, Oklahoma. Then about that same time, my father mysteriously for some reason or other caught on fire. There's a lot of people say that he set himself on fire, others say that he caught on fire

accidentally. I always will think that he done it on purpose
because he lost all his money.[6]

After those tragic incidents, Guthrie and his siblings became orphans.
He lived with a foster family at first, and then around the age of seventeen
he began wandering across the country and working manual labor jobs. The
Great Depression soon followed. Yet despite all this misfortune, he remained
hopeful about life, humanity, and the future. No one can call him naive
about suffering. His hope was based on a strong foundation of resilience and
deep life experience —and that is why it was so powerful and capable of carrying him through so much adversity. He explained it this way:

> I have hoped as many hopes and dreamed so many
> dreams, seen them swept aside by weather, and blown away
> by men, washed away in my own mistakes, that—I use to
> wonder if it wouldn't be better just to haul off and quit hop-
> ing. Just protect my own inner brain, my own mind and
> heart, by drawing it up into a hard knot, and not having any
> more hopes or dreams at all. Pull in my feelings, and call back
> all of my sentiments—and not let any earthly event move me
> in either direction, either cause me to hate, to fear, to love, to
> care, to take sides, to argue the matter at all—and, yet . . .
> there are certain good times, and pleasures that I never can
> forget, no matter how much I want to, because the pleasures,
> and the displeasures, the good times and the bad, are really all
> there is to me. And these pleasures that you cannot ever forget
> are the yeast that always starts working in your mind again,
> and it gets in your thoughts again, and in your eyes again, and
> then, all at once, no matter what has happened to you, you
> are building a brand new world again, based and built on the
> mistakes, the wreck, the hard luck and trouble of the old one.[7]

Guthrie's hope was even strong enough to help him survive betrayal—
an especially painful and dangerous experience that can shatter our faith in
humanity. Betrayal, whether in friendships or relationships, is among the

most agonizing of human experiences. Can realistic hope survive the dagger of betrayal when it is thrust deep into our heart?

As a child I was terrified of my father. His violent behavior made me fear for my life, and I will never be able to express what it was like to be four years old and have the person I most trusted attack me and threaten to kill me. As my father's psychological trauma consumed him, the person who was supposed to protect me continued to attack me unexpectedly. I felt betrayed by the man I had loved and admired through a child's innocent eyes.

Because this sense of betrayal happened so early in my childhood, I spent most of my life unable to trust people. My experiences taught me the people closest to me will try to kill me. I truly believed trusting others meant putting my life at risk, and for many years I associated trust with being violently attacked. It has not been easy, but my journey has led me to a point where I can trust again.

My life and the lives of many others like Woody Guthrie demonstrate that trust and realistic hope are never beyond our reach, no matter how much we have been hurt. There is no easy answer to recovering from trauma and betrayal. Everyone's path is different, and this book can help you along the path that leads to trust, realistic hope, and healing.

Participation: A Higher Expression of Hope

Beware the dangers of hope. In our society the most common form of hope isn't realistic hope, based on evidence and experience. It is naive hope, which is dangerous for several reasons. When we feel threatened by significant challenges, naive hope leads us to think, *Everything will work itself out. We just have to wait for a miracle to happen.* It also urges us to put all our faith in a "great leader" who will magically solve our problems. Naive hope misleads us into believing that if we just elect the right president, we can sit back and watch all the world's conflicts vanish. Unlike realistic hope, which grows from the trust we have in ourselves, others, and our ideals, naive hope is a result of helplessness.

On the other hand, realistic hope encourages us to think, *Because I believe in myself and trust my abilities, I can do something to help solve this problem. Because I trust others, I can work with them to solve this problem. Because I trust in my ideals, I'm empowered with the determination to persevere, and I have a vision of what a brighter future could look like and how we might get there.*

Unlike realistic hope, which empowers us to take action and make a difference, naive hope causes us to think, *Because I feel helpless and don't know what I can do to make a difference, I need a miracle, great leader, or God to solve these problems for me.* When we feel helpless, our only choices are either naive hope or cynicism. We should not ridicule others for having naive hope, but empower them by revealing what is possible and how they can take action. When we empower people and combat their helplessness, we give them options other than naive hope.

Woody Guthrie wrote the famous song "This Land Is Your Land" because he was irritated by another popular song at the time, "God Bless America." He felt that, in the midst of the suffering of the Great Depression, "God Bless America" promoted apathy and failed to reflect reality. He did not see how God had blessed America for the starving poor and oppressed racial minorities. One of the many verses he wrote for "This Land Is Your Land" was "One bright sunny morning in the shadow of the steeple, / By the relief office I saw my people. / As they stood hungry, / I stood there wondering if God blessed America for me."[8]

During their efforts to build a more humane and peaceful world, religious figures like Martin Luther King Jr., Mother Teresa, and Archbishop Desmond Tutu realized prayer in the form of words is no substitute for action. They knew it is our responsibility to solve society's problems, and action is the highest form of prayer.

During the civil rights movement, people with realistic hope prayed not only with words but also with action by marching, boycotting, and protesting. They prayed not just on their knees but also on their feet. Rabbi Abraham Heschel, who marched with King during the civil rights movement, said: "For many of us the march from Selma to Montgomery was about protest and prayer. Legs are not lips and walking is not kneeling. And yet our legs uttered songs. Even without words, our march was worship. I felt my legs were praying."[9]

These people embraced participation, a higher expression of realistic hope. Participation is realistic hope transformed into action. It is a committed effort to transform our hope into reality. As I mentioned in the last section, the hope something *can* be accomplished is necessary before attempting to accomplish it. Accordingly, if we lack the realistic hope that it is possible to solve our national and global problems, we will quit before we even start trying. What evidence do we have that we can solve these problems and create a brighter future?

Five hundred years ago, democratic countries with the right to vote, freedom of speech, freedom of religion, freedom of the press, women's and civil rights, and the intellectual freedom to say the earth revolves around the sun virtually did not exist. Today these liberties are widespread.

When my father was drafted into the army as an African American in 1949, the military was segregated; the government upheld an official policy that viewed African Americans as inferior and subhuman. Fifty years before then, the government would not allow women to vote, and only fifty years prior to that, the government supported and protected slavery. Because Americans participated in the democratic process of improving their country, America has journeyed from a society where all people except white, male landowners were oppressed, to a country where I could graduate from West Point and write these words today, despite having grown up in Alabama part African American, part Asian.

In addition to the abundant historical evidence that proves people can make a difference, my existence is also evidence that positive change can happen. My life and the lives of so many others demonstrate that progress is possible if people take action. Every woman in America allowed to vote and own property is also living proof that participation can advance us on the road to peace.

Peace is more than just the absence of war. It is also the presence of liberty, justice, opportunity, fairness, environmental sustainability, and other ingredients that create a healthy society. Participation makes peace and its ingredients possible, but not inevitable. The notion that world peace is inevitable derives from naive hope. This makes us complacent, because if a peaceful future is unavoidable then our actions are not needed. I speak with realistic hope, because I do not believe peace is inevitable. It depends on what we do.

People often ask me, "How long will it take us to end war?" I respond by saying, "That's a great question, and I can answer it by posing another question. How long does it take to run a mile? A person can run a mile in under four minutes or walk it in over an hour. A person can also fail to complete the mile because he or she stops halfway through or quits before taking the first step. Similar to running a mile, how long it takes to end war will be determined by what we do. Depending on the quality and quantity of our actions, we might end war in twenty years or two hundred, or we might never end it and humanity will become extinct. It's up to us."

Like the gradual transition from dark to light that occurs at sunrise, our journey on the road to peace is a continuum where change occurs in increments, not all at once. Every step we take on the road to peace represents progress. A world where half the women on the planet can vote is preferable to a world where only a third can. A world with less war is preferable to a world with more. Even if it takes years to reach our destination, every step we take in the direction of peace, universal women's rights, or any worthwhile goal has positive consequences for all of us. Real progress is not an all-or-nothing endeavor. Like gradual steps on a path, it is composed of many small victories that eventually add up to the change our world needs.

The steps on the road to peace require us to dissent from the destructive attitudes that perpetuate violence and war. General Dwight D. Eisenhower believed all worthwhile progress requires dissent and that questioning injustice is the highest form of patriotism. He said: "Here in America we are descended in blood and in spirit from revolutionaries and rebels—men and women who dared to dissent from accepted doctrine. As their heirs, may we never confuse honest dissent with disloyal subversion."[10]

While naive hope tells us that the best way to save our country and planet is to elect a messianic president or great leader who will magically solve all our problems, realistic hope tells us that nothing could be further from the ideal of democracy. One of the most undemocratic things I have ever heard, which I hear often, is that the American president is the leader of the free world. If we understand what the ideal of democracy truly means, we realize that the people are supposed to lead, and the president is supposed to be the administrator of the people's will. Although we live in a representative democracy instead of a direct democracy, we still have methods to pressure our politicians to do what we want. The evidence from American history shows that nothing will change for the better unless Americans tell the president what to do. American history also shows that ordinary citizens, not presidents, are the brightest visionaries and the true engine of progress.

For example, Lyndon Johnson was not a strong advocate for civil rights when he became president, but he later supported racial equality because Martin Luther King Jr. and other members of the civil rights movement pressured him to do so. Franklin Roosevelt was not a strong advocate for workers' rights, which included child labor laws and a five-day workweek, when he became president, but the workers' rights movement changed his viewpoint. Woodrow Wilson opposed women's equality when he became president, but he later supported the constitutional amendment that gave women the right to vote because Alice Paul and other members of the women's rights movement pressured him to do so. Abraham Lincoln was not a visionary who believed slavery should be completely abolished when he began his political career, but his views changed due to the influence of the abolitionist movement.

If we have naive hope that an American president will act as a messiah and magically solve all our problems, we are neglecting the ideal of democracy and setting ourselves up for a big disappointment. As we increase our realistic hope, fortitude replaces disappointment, empowerment replaces helplessness, and participation replaces complacency.

As a child I was taught that voting was the be-all and end-all of citizenship, and if I showed up at the polls to vote I was fulfilling my civic duty. But the women's and civil rights movements created dramatic change, even though many of their participants had little or no voting rights. Voting is just one tool in the democratic toolbox, and we cannot build a house with just a hammer. Realistic hope tells us voting is only one of many ways to participate in democracy. Susan B. Anthony and Martin Luther King Jr. knew that hope for a brighter future is only realistic when we exercise many democratic methods such as protests, petitions, boycotts, pressuring the legal system, and changing people's attitudes for the better. Historian Howard Zinn said: "Democracy doesn't come from the top. It comes from the bottom. Democracy is not what governments do. It's what people do."[11]

If we do not have realistic hope that progress is possible, and if we do not transform our realistic hope into participation, nothing will ever change for the better. Although General Eisenhower believed citizens must be peaceful revolutionaries, we must never forget that citizens must also perform a duty as sacred gardeners.

Peace and justice are similar to gardens that must be nurtured and maintained, and every citizen who wages peace protects humanity's most sacred garden. Victories for peace and justice are not achievements permanently etched in stone. They are similar to living organisms that must be kept healthy through our care, attention, and participation. Victories for peace and justice, like delicate plants, will wilt and die if we take them for granted.

Every liberty and human right can be taken away by an oppressive government, especially during times of crisis when people are desperate. If citizens are complacent, do not be surprised if the victories our ancestors worked so hard for begin to slip away. If citizens do not use participation to protect the peace and justice our ancestors struggled to achieve, do not be shocked if slavery and the oppression of women begin to reemerge in new forms.

Abundant historical evidence and the fact that I exist give me realistic hope that progress is possible if we take action. In addition, my understanding of human nature also gives me a great deal of realistic hope. When we understand who we truly are and look deeply into our hearts and the humanity of others, we will see why hope in the twenty-first century is so realistic.

Realistic Idealism: The Highest Expression of Hope

The muscle of realistic hope gives us the power to climb out of the pit of cynicism, bitterness, and helplessness. When the muscle grows stronger and transforms into participation, the collective action it generates has the power to solve our national and global problems. When the muscle of realistic hope reaches the height of its strength, it becomes realistic idealism.

The highest expression of hope is realistic idealism. Unlike naive idealism, it is based on evidence, experience, and the three kinds of trust (trust in yourself, trust in other people, trust in your ideals). It exists when the cup of hope overflows and spills into the world around us. Realistic idealism is hope that spills into our actions, the way we treat people, our commitment to something larger than ourselves, our determination to make a difference, every corner of our personalities, and every aspect of our lives. Participation is hope transformed into action; realistic idealism is hope that transforms us into the people our world needs most.

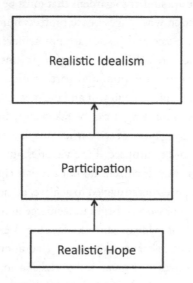

Figure 1.2: The Muscle of Hope

Not all who have realistic hope choose to participate in solving our national and global problems, and not all who participate are realistic idealists. Like any muscle, strengthening the muscle of hope toward its highest expression is not easy. Because most of us are never taught how to exercise the muscle of hope, it has atrophied and left us weak. While my father was on military duty in Germany during the 1960s, he purchased a hand-drawn portrait of Albert Schweitzer, a great idealist of the twentieth century, who transformed his hope into action. Since my earliest memories that picture has hung in the hallway of my parents' house. Schweitzer said:

> In my youth I listened to conversations of grown-ups which wafted to me a breath of melancholy, depressing my heart. My elders looked back at the idealism and enthusiasm of their youth as something precious that they should have

held on to. At the same time, however, they considered it sort of a law of nature that one cannot do that. This talk aroused in me the fear that I, too, would look back upon myself with such nostalgia. I decided never to submit to this tragic reasonableness. What I promised myself in almost boyish defiance I have tried to carry out.

Adults take too much pleasure in the sad duty of preparing the young for a future in which they will regard as illusion all that inspires their hearts and minds now. Deeper life experience, however, talks differently to the inexperienced. It entreats the young to hold on to the ideas that fill them with enthusiasm throughout their lives. In the idealism of his youth, man has a vision of the truth. In it he possesses a treasure which he must not exchange for anything ... [12] So the knowledge about life which we grown-ups must impart to the young is not: "Reality will surely do away with your ideals" but rather: "Grow into your ideals so life cannot take them away from you."[13]

Schweitzer grew into his ideals, and they gave him a vision of the truth that allowed him to help countless people. He said he did not want to preach the ideal of unconditional love taught by Jesus; he wanted to practice it.[14] According to Albert Einstein, Schweitzer "is a great figure who bids for the moral leadership of the world ... He is the only Westerner who has had a moral effect on this generation comparable to Gandhi's. As in the case of Gandhi, the extent of this effect is overwhelmingly due to the example he gave by his own life's work."[15]

Following the cruelty and devastation of World War II, Schweitzer showed the world how we can all embrace humanity's highest ideals such as compassion, service, and peace. By embodying the ideals many had forgotten during Hitler's reign, he represented the new European who no longer agreed with brutal colonialism, violence, and oppression. When he was awarded the 1952 Nobel Peace Prize it was for the ideal "reverence for life" that defined his life. This ideal began to form during his childhood. He explained:

It struck me as inconceivable that I should be allowed to
lead such a happy life while I saw so many people around me
struggling with sorrow and suffering. Even at school I had felt
stirred whenever I caught a glimpse of the miserable home
surroundings of some of my classmates and compared them
with the ideal conditions in which we children of the parson-
age at Günsbach had lived . . . I could not help but think continually of others who were denied that good fortune by their
material circumstances or their health. . . . . As I awoke, the
thought came to me that I must not accept this good fortune
as a matter of course, but must give something in return.[16]

In my earlier books I explained how Gandhi, who was a soldier in the
British army and served in the Boer and Second Zulu Wars, embraced the
warrior ideals to always place the mission first, never accept defeat, never
quit, and never leave a fallen comrade. These ideals can be used for good or
evil, and as a soldier of peace they gave Gandhi the strength to accomplish
his peaceful mission. Although Schweitzer did not serve in the military, he
too embodied these ideals.

Born in 1875, Schweitzer received his PhD in philosophy at the age of
twenty-four. Over the next nine years he published several books, including
The Quest of the Historical Jesus, Johann Sebastian Bach, and *The Art of Organ
Building and Organ Playing in Germany and France.* Then, after a successful
career as an organist and theologian, he decided to dedicate his life to a new
mission: serving humanity by becoming a doctor and opening a hospital in
Africa to care for the sick. Schweitzer received much criticism from friends
and family. Today if someone decided to help the sick in Africa he or she
would be applauded as a humanitarian, but Schweitzer lived during the era
of European colonialism, a time when many European rulers supported violence and oppression around the world. Many of Schweitzer's relatives crit-
icized him for pursuing a path that would waste his talents as a scholar.
Nonetheless, he was determined to pursue his dream. At age thirty he began
his medical studies and by his late thirties had raised enough money to build
a hospital in Africa.

Despite the many obstacles and setbacks that challenged him,

Schweitzer embodied the Warrior Ethos by never accepting defeat and never quitting. In 1914, a year after he opened his hospital, World War I began. He and his wife were captured by the French in 1917 and held as prisoners of war. During his imprisonment Schweitzer almost died of dysentery; his hospital was shut down and his humanitarian dream seemed ruined. Schweitzer and his wife were not released until 1918, as the war was ending. Despite being deeply in debt, he remained undeterred. Fueled by his ideals, he worked for many years to raise enough money to reopen his hospital. Many would have quit at the first hurdle, but Schweitzer's idealism allowed him to triumph against tough odds. In 1924, after years of struggle, he returned to Africa at age forty-nine.

Schweitzer detested violence, but like Gandhi, he understood that the warrior ideals can be used for good or evil. When Schweitzer felt overwhelmed he drew inspiration from warriors, in particular the Carthaginian general Hannibal Barca and his father Hamilcar: "Whenever I was tempted to feel that the years I should have to sacrifice were too long, I reminded myself that Hamilcar and Hannibal had prepared for their march on Rome by their slow and tedious conquest of Spain."[17]

Schweitzer also embraced another ideal from the Warrior Ethos: never leaving a fallen comrade. He saw people of all races and nationalities as his brothers and sisters, and treated our global family as his comrades. Journalist Norman Cousins explained that "for more than fifty years the Hospital of Albert Schweitzer in Lambéréné, in the Gabon, became something of a contemporary shrine . . . Despite the absence of modern plumbing and other conventional aspects of modern sanitation, the recovery rate at the Schweitzer Hospital compared favorably with hospitals in the Western world . . . The main point about Schweitzer is that he brought the kind of spirit to Africa that black persons hardly knew existed in the white man. Before Schweitzer, white skin meant beatings, gunpoint rule, and the imposition of slavery on human flesh. If Schweitzer had done nothing in his life other than to accept the pain of these people as his own, he would have achieved moral eminence."[18]

As we run the marathon of life, we all experience adversity. When we are emotionally dehydrated and want to collapse, realistic hope is a cup we can drink from and realistic idealism is a lake we can swim in. As I mentioned earlier, realistic idealism is hope that spills into our actions, the way we treat people, our commitment to something larger than ourselves, our determination to make a difference, every corner of our personalities, and every aspect of our lives.

In Schweitzer's case, his realistic idealism poured into so many aspects of his being that he fully embodied his ideals of compassion, service, peace, and reverence for life. When discussing death, he said that humanity's highest ideals can never die, and when we become those ideals we too will never die. He said: "No one has ever come back from the other world. I can't console you, but one thing I can tell you, as long as my ideals are alive I will be alive."[19] The army knows that realistic idealists are powerful human beings capable of overcoming unimaginable odds, and that is why it trains its soldiers to be idealistic. In addition to selflessness, service, sacrifice, and the ideals expressed in the Warrior Ethos, General Douglas MacArthur said that warriors must also embrace the ideals of duty, honor, and country. General MacArthur, who made mistakes in his life, changed as a person and grew closer to his ideals during his final years. In a speech given at West Point in 1962, two years before his death, he expressed the importance of idealism:

> Duty, Honor, Country: Those three hallowed words reverently dictate what you ought to be, what you can be, what you will be. They are your rallying points: to build courage when courage seems to fail; to regain faith when there seems to be little cause for faith; to create hope when hope becomes forlorn. Unhappily, I possess neither that eloquence of diction, that poetry of imagination, nor that brilliance of metaphor to tell you all that they mean.
>
> The unbelievers will say they are but words, but a slogan, but a flamboyant phrase. Every pedant, every demagogue, every cynic, every hypocrite, every troublemaker, and, I am sorry to say, some others of an entirely different character, will try to downgrade them even to the extent of mockery and ridicule.
>
> But these are some of the things they do. They build your basic character. They mold you for your future roles as the custodians of the nation's defense. They make you strong

enough to know when you are weak, and brave enough to face yourself when you are afraid.

They teach you to be proud and unbending in honest failure, but humble and gentle in success; not to substitute words for action; not to seek the path of comfort, but to face the stress and spur of difficulty and challenge; to learn to stand up in the storm, but to have compassion on those who fall; to master yourself before you seek to master others; to have a heart that is clean, a goal that is high; to learn to laugh, yet never forget how to weep; to reach into the future, yet never neglect the past; to be serious, yet never take yourself too seriously; to be modest so that you will remember the simplicity of true greatness; the open mind of true wisdom, the meekness of true strength . . . They teach you in this way to be an officer and a gentleman.[20]

West Point and the army not only trained me to be hopeful, they also trained me to be an idealist. West Point's motto is "Duty, Honor, Country." For me, duty means taking responsibility for my actions and the problems I can help solve, and knowing I have a duty to serve others and make a difference. Honor means having integrity, being honest with myself and others, and treating people with respect. Country means being committed to and willing to sacrifice for something larger than myself. Although I am dedicated to serving America, my country extends beyond our national borders. Thomas Paine, one of America's Founding Fathers, said "My country is the world."[21] In the twenty-first century, our global community has become so interconnected that our country truly is the planet earth.

As General MacArthur said, cynical people will quickly criticize our ideals. One reason is that they lack the experience necessary to understand what an ideal really is. The word *ideal* comes from the word *idea*, and an ideal is the fullest expression of an idea. When we internalize ideas to the point where we not only think them but live them, they become ideals. When ideas dwell not only in our mind but also our heart, they become ideals. When ideas become an inseparable part of who we are and increase our compassion, they become ideals.

Schweitzer explained: "The maturity to which we are called means becoming ever simpler, ever more truthful, ever purer, ever more peaceful, ever gentler, ever kinder, ever more compassionate. We do not have to surrender to any other limitation of our idealism. Thus the soft iron of youthful idealism hardens into the steel of adult idealism which will never be lost."[22]

Fully Human

It is confusing to be human. It is especially confusing when we live in a society that doesn't teach us how to be human. Part of being an elephant, lion, or any mammal is instinctual, but these animals must also learn to be what they are. For example, wild animals born and raised in captivity will have difficulty surviving in their natural environment. Although a wolf is born a wolf it must also learn how to be a wolf. If members of its pack do not teach it how to hunt, survive, and live cooperatively with other wolves, it will perish.

Because our large brains take over twenty years to fully mature and human infants remain helpless for a longer period of time than the offspring of any other animal, learning to be human is a challenging process that requires many years. Mythologist Joseph Campbell said: "This altogether extraordinary prematurity of the birth of the human infant, so that throughout the period of its infancy it is dependent on its parents, has led biologists and psychologists to compare our situation with that of marsupials: the kangaroo, for example, which gives birth to its young only three weeks after conception. The tiny unready creatures crawl instinctively up the mother's belly into her pouch, where they fix themselves—without instruction—to the nipples and remain until ready for life, nourished and protected in, so to say, a second womb . . . In the human species, with its great brain requiring many years to mature, on the other hand, the young are again born too soon, and instead of the pouch we have the home, which is again a sort of external second womb."[23]

In some ways we are like marsupials, because although we are born human, when we come into this world we are far from being *fully human*. Someone born with healthy leg muscles and the capacity to run must still learn how to use those muscles. In a similar way, although we are born with the muscle of hope and the capacity for realistic idealism, we must learn how to fulfill that potential. Some might say that comparing physical and mental capacities is like comparing apples and oranges, but I will show how hope and our other innate human powers are similar to muscles in many ways. If our leg muscles are weak and we are forced to jump over an obstacle, we will fall. If we do not develop the muscle of hope and are forced to overcome a significant struggle, we will also fall.

When a wolf is born and raised in captivity, its development becomes stunted and it has difficulty surviving in its natural environment. So although wolves naturally crave the freedom of the wilderness, some confined wolves may prefer captivity because they never learned how to survive in the wild. In a similar way, when people are born and raised in slavery, their psychological growth becomes stunted, making it difficult for them to think and act for themselves. This is why some freed slaves returned to their masters: they never learned how to handle the responsibility that comes with freedom.

Being a free and responsible human being requires training, and this becomes more difficult when we live in a society that does not teach us how to be human. In addition, many of our society's values lead us away from our humanity. Instead of teaching us how to achieve our full potential as human beings, our society teaches us that hoarding money is the most important thing in life. To survive as a global family we must offer people a more fulfilling vision of what it means to be human; one that makes greed look empty in comparison.

Psychologist Erich Fromm explained: "Many people have never known a person who functions optimally. They take the psychic functioning of their parents and relatives, or of the social group they have been born into, as the norm, and as long as they do not differ from these they feel normal and without interest in observing anything. There are many people, for instance, who have never seen a loving person, or a person with integrity, or courage, or concentration. It is quite obvious that in order to be sensitive to oneself, one has to have an image of complete, healthy human functioning."[24]

To be sensitive to ourselves, to truly understand ourselves, we must explore healthy human functioning and what it means to be human. Realistic hope and hopelessness are both human potentials, but hope is a feature of our humanity that gives us inexpressible joy and the strength to change our world for the better despite overwhelming obstacles. A person without an ounce of hope would be depressed and suicidal. On the other hand, someone with enormous hope that grows into participation and realistic idealism would be called a visionary, a leader, even a saint. Most of us exist somewhere between these two poles, and our everyday choices push us in one direction or the other. We can choose to be hopeful or hopeless, just as we can choose to eat fresh vegetables or dirt. Where our emotional and physical health are concerned, not all choices produce equal results.

Together we will explore the choices that can improve our health not only as individuals but as a society, country, and global family. These are some of the same choices that Gandhi made in his life; choices that transformed him from a self-admitted coward into a *mahatma*, which means "great soul." Einstein said of Gandhi: "Generations to come, it may well be, will scarce believe that such a one as this ever in flesh and blood walked upon this earth . . . Gandhi, the greatest political genius of our time . . . gave proof of what sacrifice man is capable once he has discovered the right path."[25]

Gandhi led 390 million people to freedom from colonial oppression, yet he was neither a general nor a president. Martin Luther King Jr. said this was one of the most significant things that ever happened in world history. How did Gandhi do it? How did he become perhaps the greatest leader we have ever seen? With no official power and few material possessions, how was he able to inspire countless people across many generations? Many believe Gandhi was born courageous and holy without ever having to struggle for inner peace and joy, but he was not born a mahatma. He had to overcome many obstacles to become a great soul who was fully human.

As a teenager, the young Gandhi did not yet possess the enormous courage, strength, and compassion that would later define his life. As a self-admitted coward, he hardly resembled the later mahatma who would forever change our world. In his autobiography he said: "To be at school at the stroke of the hour and to run back home as soon as the school closed, that was my daily habit. I literally ran back, because I could not bear to talk to anybody. I was even afraid lest anyone should poke fun at me . . . Moreover, I was a coward. [In high school] I used to be haunted by the fears of thieves, ghosts, and serpents. I did not dare to stir out of doors at night. Darkness was a terror to me. It was almost impossible for me to sleep in the dark, as I would imagine ghosts coming from one direction, thieves from another and serpents from a third. I could not therefore bear to sleep without a light in the room."[26]

Gandhi was not only fearful as an adolescent. He was also troubled by his moral failings. Although he showed great integrity and selflessness in his adult life, as a child he stole money from servants to buy cigarettes. During this difficult time in his life, he even attempted suicide: "It was unbearable that we should be unable to do anything without the elders' permission. At last, in sheer disgust, we decided to commit suicide! But how were we to do it? From where were we to get the poison? We heard that *Dhatura* seeds were an effective poison. Off we went to the jungle in search of these seeds, and got them . . . But our courage failed us. Supposing we were not instantly killed? And what was the good of killing ourselves? Why not rather put up with the lack of independence? But we swallowed two or three seeds nevertheless. We dared not take more. Both of us fought shy of death, and decided to go to *Ramji Mandir* to compose ourselves, and to dismiss the thought of suicide."[27]

In our society we are taught that a pill can solve all our problems. If you are lonely, take a pill. If you cannot concentrate, take a pill. If you lack joy in your life, take a pill. But no pill can give us the wealth of realistic hope that grows into participation and realistic idealism. No pill could have transformed Gandhi from a self-admitted coward into a great soul who was fully human. The ideals that give us the power to solve our national and global conflicts do not come in a plastic bottle but through strengthening our muscle of hope.

Hope is like a bicep. If we exercise our bicep, it will grow stronger; if we never use the muscle it will atrophy. Realistic idealism is not for the lazy. I am idealistic because I have put a lot of effort into it. Like Gandhi, we can all become great souls who are fully human if we live by our ideals and strengthen the muscles of our humanity. As Gandhi said: "The ideals that regulate my life are presented for the acceptance of mankind in general . . . I have not the shadow of a doubt that any man or woman can achieve what I have if he or she would make the same effort and cultivate the same hope and faith. I am but a poor struggling soul yearning to be wholly good."[28]

Realistic ideals like justice, freedom, service, duty, honor, compassion, peace, being authentic, and never quitting helped Gandhi walk the path to becoming fully human. Hope is the psychological foundation of participation and realistic idealism, and possessing a strong muscle of hope allowed Gandhi to transform himself and our world. In the following chapters we will explore the other muscles of our humanity that give us the strength to improve our lives and the world around us, and we will uncover what it means to be fully human.

The road to peace takes us deep within ourselves and into our shared humanity. We live in a fame-obsessed society, but the important question is not, do others know you? The important question is, do you know you? When we explore our humanity and understand what it means to be human, we can stop being our own worst enemy. Knowing ourselves allows us to make peace with ourselves, which removes many of the roadblocks preventing us from having a meaningful and fulfilling life. On the path to understanding himself, first-century Greek philosopher Hecato said: "What progress have I made? I am beginning to be my own friend."[29] The road to peace not only gives us the strength to solve our national and global problems, it also leads to hope, joy, becoming fully human, and being our own friend.

In *The End of War*, I asked: What is the most difficult form of art? What art form is more challenging than painting, sculpting, or playing any instrument? The answer is the art of living. Living is certainly an art form. First-century Roman philosopher Seneca explained: "There exists no more difficult art than living . . . throughout the whole of life, one must continue to learn to live and, what will amaze you even more, throughout life one must learn to die."[30]

Just as we must learn any art, we must also learn how to live. But unlike other arts, the art of living transforms us into both the sculptor and the sculpture. We are the artist and our life is the masterpiece. Living is not only the most difficult, but also the most essential art form. Unfortunately our educational system does not always teach us what is essential. Prior to attending West Point, I was never taught in school how to overcome fear, aggression, or hatred. I was never taught how to develop courage, compassion, and hope. I was never taught how to listen, be a good friend, or have a healthy relationship. I was never taught how to overcome adversity, question authority, or be an active member of our global family.

West Point taught me some, but not all of these things. In addition to what I learned at West Point and in the army, I learned about the art of living from life experience and humanity's greatest peacemakers. When people in a democracy are not educated in the art of living—to strengthen their conscience, compassion, and ability to question and think critically—they can be easily manipulated by fear and propaganda. A democracy is only as wise as its citizens, and a democracy of ignorant citizens can be as dangerous as a dictatorship.

Educator John H. Lounsbury said: "Education, particularly in a democracy, has to involve the heart as well as head, attitude as well as information, spirit as well as scholarship, and conscience as well as competence."[31] Through practicing the art of living we can all transform our lives into the masterpiece of being fully human. And by using the wisdom others share with us to light our path, we don't have to paint in the dark.

The Swan's Journey

The *Rig Veda*, a Hindu text written nearly four thousand years ago, symbolizes our soul as a swan ascending toward understanding: "Life is a perennial search for truth . . . The restless swan—the human soul—is on the journey infinite to find the truth."[32] As we listen to the secrets of our humanity in quiet contemplation, we can observe the swan's inspiring voyage beyond the clouds and toward the sun.

To experience the highest peaks of joy we must cross the majestic landscapes of our humanity. During this adventure, each of us, like the swan, endures suffering and loss. The swan contends with storms that threaten to tear it from the sky, fog that obstructs its vision, and snow that numbs its delicate wings. Antoine de Saint-Exupéry, the writer and aviator killed in action during World War II, said: "You'll be bothered from time to time by storms, fog, snow. When you are, think of those who went through it before you, and say to yourself, 'What they could do, I can do.'"[33]

History is full of inspiring people whose hope and idealism carried them through the storms of agony, fog of despair, and cold chill of fear. Gandhi's determination allowed him to soar. Our wings of hope are no different than his, but what we do with them is up to us.

Throughout my life, I have known what it feels like to have wings that no longer seem to work, to reach a point of exhaustion where I want to descend from the sky toward death, and to feel lost in a maze of struggle. I cannot fully express why I never gave up, but I can describe how a part of my humanity always urged me to stretch my wings of hope, even when life no longer seemed worth living. Just as Guthrie, Schweitzer, Gandhi, and so many others took actions that benefit us today, we can help each other and guide future generations on their journey toward the sun. None of us are flying alone, after all. Humanity is a flock of swans yearning together for a better world, each of us searching for a life lush with hope and celebration.

On this voyage toward truth and understanding, I remember not only the storms, fog, and snow that made me stronger, but also beautiful scenery, glorious landscapes, and the warmth of the sun. I have known people who suffered long flights in cold darkness, and I have met those who saw daybreak. To survive we must help each other through these dark times by spreading our wings of hope, seeing the calm beyond the storm, and always remembering that the swan is a powerful creature. We must also understand that for a swan, every day begins a new journey with so much to learn and enjoy. With each new adventure storms come and go, night turns into day, and humanity struggles steadily toward freedom, justice, and peace.

CHAPTER 2

The Muscle of Empathy

Warrior Philosophy

The storms of life visit us all, but we don't have to go through them alone. Once when I was a twenty-three-year-old lieutenant in the army, I woke up surprised in the middle of the night. I was lying in a hospital bed. Looking up I saw steel bars on the windows and a surveillance camera in the room. *Not again*, I thought, moaning in discomfort. I knew it was late 2003 but I could not recall the month. I could not remember how I had gotten here, but I knew exactly where I was. I had been in this place twice before.

Slowly I retraced my memories. When I visited my parents for the holidays in 2002, my father had suffered a major stroke on Christmas Day. Several months later, while deployed in the Middle East during Operation Iraqi Freedom, I had trouble contacting my parents by phone. By the time I returned home to visit them in June 2003, I knew something was wrong. But I was not prepared for what I saw when I walked into their house. I immediately noticed a foul stench, and I saw feces on the carpet. Sitting naked on the floor, my father was screaming, threatening to shoot himself with a pistol he kept in another room. My mother looked like a corpse. As she tried to calm him down, he punched her. I restrained him and called the police.

Both my parents ended up in the hospital for a week. My mother was close to death but gradually recovered. My father's mind had continued to deteriorate after his stroke the previous year and he had to be placed in a nursing home. When this incident occurred, I remembered many experiences that I had repressed as a child. It was a lot of pain for one person to bear.

After my parents were hospitalized, a friend convinced me to speak with a psychiatrist, who explained that my father might have suffered from un-treated schizophrenia. He said that a child born to a forty-year-old man is twice as likely to develop schizophrenia as one born to a twenty-five-year-old. A child born to a fifty-year-old is three times as likely to inherit the mental illness. My father was fifty-four when I was born. The psychiatrist urged me to take a test to diagnose my mental condition. My results exactly matched those of a person with schizophrenia.

But that had happened months ago. Why was I here now? As I searched my jumbled memories that night, other unwelcome thoughts arose. I re-called how my family had been wrecked and I was an only child who had to pick up the pieces. Having schizophrenia would certainly get me kicked out of the army. Could I ever get another job? If my condition failed to improve, would I even be alive in a year? I had contemplated suicide through much of my childhood and now I remembered why.

Before my despair could grow too large, a memory of hope emerged, disjointed and fragmented like everything else in my mind. Several weeks after I had taken the test to evaluate my mental condition, a different psy-chiatrist had said, "You might have been misdiagnosed with schizophrenia. We aren't sure yet. So we'll keep you on these medications just in case. It's possible you're suffering from something unique that our test couldn't accu-rately diagnose. Perhaps we can best describe this as psychological trauma resulting from your childhood, which was exacerbated by what you experi-enced after returning home from your deployment. We'll know soon, de-pending on whether you improve and how well your recovery progresses."

Then he said something I had never heard before: "As a doctor and of-ficer in the army, it pains me deeply to hear about everything you've been through in your life. I'll do everything in my power to help you." He em-pathized with my agony, which seemed strange to me at the time. At that moment I realized how well I had kept my past a secret from everyone around me. Since I was an only child who grew up not having a relationship with my extended family—and my father was so paranoid that in elementary school he stopped letting me visit with friends—it was easy to keep secrets.

The day the psychiatrist spoke to me with so much empathy I had been in the same place I found myself now, surrounded by the same steel bars, constant surveillance, and white walls of the army psychiatric hospital. My memory was still blurry and it was getting difficult to stay awake. My mind felt like it was swimming in mud. Had they injected me with something? I could not remember. As I lay there that night on the verge of sleep, another memory crept into my mind. The recollection was crystal clear and I welcomed it gladly.

It was like a warmly remembered fairy tale: I was three years old and playing in my parents' backyard. Sitting alone as my mother was gardening nearby, I was building houses for insects out of small rocks. Don't all creatures deserve a home, a place where they can feel safe and protected? I often wondered about this as a child, but now I was no longer sure. I was still searching for the home and sense of peace I had lost as a child; I had begun to wonder if it existed only in my imagination. I might not have a chance to find out, I realized, because our society often abandons the mentally ill. And in a matter of weeks I had become the kind of person society gives up on.

The next morning after I woke up, took some medication, and ate breakfast, I saw one of the friends I had met during my first stay several months ago. He was a young soldier, only twenty-one, who had returned from Iraq and tried to commit suicide. We used to joke that he would set the record for the longest stay at the hospital and I would set the record for the most number of visits. Here I was again for a third time. And here he was, still hospitalized after his attempted suicide. How long had he been here? A month? Two months? Three?

He smiled when he first saw me. "Sir, you're back again? You just like this place that much?"

"I wanted to see how you're doing, and I also needed a vacation. I thought it would be easiest to do both at once."

He stood up to shake my hand. "Did you get here last night?"

"I think an ambulance brought me." Sometimes I experienced so much rage that I would go unconscious. It was my body's way of preventing me from hurting someone. "I was in my apartment lying on the floor, and then I was in an ambulance, and then I ended up here. But they tricked me." I laughed softly. "They said they weren't going to bring me back here, and that's why I agreed to go in the ambulance. When I realized where I was, I tried to run away. I think they injected me with something, so I was very confused. A big captain stood in front of me. That's all I remember."

We sat and talked for a while. I noticed that his leg still shook uncontrollably, and I saw new faces in the hospital. As the morning ended and noon approached, I realized the number of patients had increased since my last visit. Another soldier, a sergeant in his thirties, had also been hospitalized after returning from Iraq. His convoy had been attacked and in order to escape the gunfire and save the people in his vehicle, he had been forced to run over a little boy used by the attackers to prevent his escape.

Although our society often treats people suffering from deep trauma and mental illness like outcasts, the military doctors and nurses working in the hospital had not abandoned their comrades. I had never witnessed so much empathy from so many people. If my father and other soldiers from past generations had received this kind of medical treatment, so much suffering could have been prevented. In the hospital I saw how the muscle of empathy forges the bonds that make humanity strong. Two thousand years ago, Jesus of Nazareth helped lepers, thieves, prostitutes, and other outcasts. He never gave up on those who seemed worthless to so many others. His life reminded me of a line from the Warrior Ethos: "I will never leave a fallen comrade."

Because soldiers must rely on cooperation and solidarity to survive, we are taught to never leave anyone behind. Not the wounded, dying, or even the mentally ill. This ideal makes an army unit strong. Humanity's greatest peacemakers have also embodied this warrior ideal. Embracing all people as one global human family, Jesus would not leave behind the outcasts of Galilee, and Albert Schweitzer and Mother Teresa would not leave behind their fallen comrades in Africa and India.

In my struggle to heal my suffering and become fully human, I spent years studying Schweitzer and Mother Teresa as well as our greatest philosophers and religions. Whether I was deployed overseas or sleeping under the stars during an army training exercise in the United States, I always brought a book that would help me explore my humanity. I owe a great debt to the wisdom I found in Buddhism, Christianity, Hinduism, Judaism, Taoism, Stoicism, Confucianism, Sufism, and many other spiritual traditions. However, the U.S. Army, West Point, and martial arts training have also given me a mountain of wisdom, which I call *warrior philosophy.*

Schweitzer was very critical of how philosophy was being taught in his day: "[During the nineteenth and twentieth centuries, philosophy] became more and more absorbed in the study of her own past. Philosophy came to mean practically the history of philosophy. The creative spirit had left her . . . The value of any philosophy is in the last resort to be measured by its capacity, or incapacity, to transform itself into a living philosophy of the people. Whatever is deep is also simple."[1] Today students may be able to quote German philosopher Immanuel Kant, but can they offer solutions for solving our national and global problems? They may be able to quote French philosopher René Descartes, but have they developed the muscles of our humanity that give us the power to change the world?

According to Schweitzer, philosophy's original purpose was to help people achieve their full potential as human beings and live in harmony with each other. Ancient philosophers like Socrates, Lao Tzu, Confucius, Buddha, Jesus, and Seneca helped others walk the many paths toward becoming fully human. The teachings of these past philosophers provide us with a foundation. Every generation is responsible for building a house on that foundation—a house with stones made of practical solutions to our societal problems. Our participation puts those stones in place. Gandhi and Martin Luther King Jr., who transformed their ideas into constructive action, are the true modern philosophers. Like the best philosophers, they were builders.

Warrior philosophy gives us many ideals and skills to help us become builders of communities and civilization. It teaches us how to overcome adversity, survive the struggles of life, and provide security to those around us. In Japan's *Code of the Samurai*, written in the seventeenth century, we find the following guidance: "Bring security to the members of [society]. Therefore . . . as a warrior you should not abuse or mistreat [your countrymen]. To tax the farmers unreasonably . . . or to have artisans make things but not pay them for it, or to buy from merchants on credit and fail to settle accounts, or to borrow money and default on the loan—these are great injustices. Understanding this, you should be sure to treat the farmers in your domain with compassion; see to it that the artisans are not ruined; and pay off loans to merchants, in small installments if lump-sum payment is impossible, so as not to cause them to suffer loss. For a warrior whose duty it is to restrain brigandry, it will not do to act like a brigand yourself."[2]

One of our earliest archetypal warriors is found in the ancient Greek epic poem the *Iliad*. Hector, a Trojan soldier, was a loving family man who led by example and sacrificed to protect his people; he did not like war and fought as a last resort. But few samurai were like Hector. Contrary to the highest ideals of warrior philosophy, most samurai behaved like brigands, many pillaging their own people. What went wrong? Throughout history, why have soldiers more often behaved like murderers and thieves instead of warriors who serve, protect, and fight only as a last resort? Military historian Martin van Creveld notes: "As has been well said, during most of its history war consisted mainly of an extended walking tour combined with large-scale robbery."[3]

There are four reasons why soldiers have caused so much suffering around the world despite the highest ideals of warrior philosophy.

1. The powerful muscle of empathy I witnessed in the army psychiatric hospital is capable of far more than making the military strong. It is also vital for ending war. But if it is not extended to all people it can produce the worst atrocities imaginable. In this chapter I will discuss how empathy, when reserved for only a few, furthers our self-destruction. I will also explain how empathy, when it embraces all people as one global human family, gives us the power to solve our national and global problems.

2. Soldiers with the best intentions can be manipulated. I will discuss this in chapter 4, The Muscle of Conscience.

3. Not every soldier is educated about the warrior ideals, and our understanding of these ideals is still evolving. Today we must not only express the importance of these ideals but also bring our understanding of them to a new level.

4. To live according to any high ideals, we must journey toward becoming fully human. This is not easy. For example, the noble ideals expressed by Jesus include loving one's enemies, forgiveness, not judging, and being a peacemaker, but how many Christians live up to those ideals? Just as many Christians do not represent the ideals of

Jesus, many soldiers do not live up to the warrior ideals, because embracing our highest ideals requires determined effort. However, every step we take toward unlocking our full potential is more than worth the effort. As I will explain throughout the rest of this book, warrior philosophy gave me the strength to discover my humanity and survive the hardships that followed my stay in the army psychiatric hospital.

Empathy in War

What do Buddha, Jesus, Sun Tzu, Henry David Thoreau, Albert Schweitzer, West Point, Mahatma Gandhi, martial arts philosophy, Martin Luther King Jr., the U.S. Army, and Mother Teresa have in common? They all taught me that empathy is the most powerful force in the world. Anyone who thinks empathy is weak or naive hasn't studied Sun Tzu and doesn't understand the army. In *The Art of War*, written in the sixth century BC, Sun Tzu says: "Regard your soldiers as your children, and they will follow you into the deepest valleys; look upon them as your own beloved sons, and they will stand by you even unto death."[4]

In *Will War Ever End?* I explained why armies cannot survive without empathy. Although war is common throughout history, the greatest problem of every army has been this: when a battle begins, how do you stop soldiers from running away? Where our fight-or-flight response is concerned, the vast majority of people prefer to run when a sword is wielded against them, a spear is thrust in their direction, a bullet flies over their head, or a bomb explodes in their vicinity. In the U.S. Army, a complex system of conditioning trains soldiers to stay and fight, but the Greeks discovered a more effective method still used today.

The Greeks understood it is not easy to make soldiers stay and fight during a battle. Human beings are not naturally violent after all, because if we were, the majority of people would not be terrified of violence when they experience it up close and personal. General George Patton said: "Every man is scared in his first battle. If he says he's not, he's a liar."[5] If human beings were naturally violent, our fight response would be far more powerful than our flight response, but in fact the opposite is true. Getting soldiers to run away and retreat during a battle is easy. Getting them to stand their ground, fight, and kill other human beings is the challenge.

The Greeks realized, however, that one simple thing could give soldiers endless courage when their lives were threatened; it could inspire them to not only stay and fight, but to sacrifice their lives. At first glance the Greeks' solution might seem like a contradiction, because the most powerful motivator that convinces people to stay and fight is not a natural propensity for violence or killing, but their capacity for love and compassion. Halfway around the world, Lao Tzu, a Chinese philosopher who lived during the sixth century BC, also acknowledged this fundamental truth about human nature when he said: "By being loving, we are capable of being brave."[6]

When the U.S. Army uses words such as *brotherhood, camaraderie,* and *cohesion,* it is really talking about love. In this chapter we are defining what empathy and love truly mean; the military tends not to use these words because in our society there are so many misconceptions associated with them. Jonathan Shay, the 2009 Omar Bradley Chair of Strategic Leadership at the U.S. Army War College and a MacArthur Fellow, is a clinical psychiatrist who has dedicated his life to helping traumatized veterans and improving the military. The author of *Achilles in Vietnam* and *Odysseus in America,* from 1999 to 2000 he also performed the Commandant of the Marine Corps Trust Study.[7] In it he says:

> When you talk to active American military officers and NCOs [non-commissioned officers] about love—they squirm. They are embarrassed. On the one hand, their organizational culture highly values rationality, which has been packaged to them as emotion-free—and love is clearly emotional. On the other hand, they instantly start worrying about sex, which in modern forces is *always* prohibited within a [deployed] unit, whether heterosexual or homosexual. In present-day America, the ideas of love and sex have gotten mashed together . . .
>
> *Of all groups in America today, military people have the greatest right to, and will benefit most, if they reclaim the word "love" as a part of what they are and what they do . . .*

Bluntly put: The result of creating well-trained, well-led, cohesive units is—love. These Marines are "tight." They regard each other—as explained in Aristotle's discussion of *philía*, love—as "another myself" . . . The importance of mutual love in military units is no sentimental claptrap—it goes to the heart of the indispensable military virtue, courage . . . As von Clausewitz pointed out almost two centuries ago, fear is the main viscous medium that the Marine must struggle through . . . the urge to protect comrades directly reduces psychological and physiological fear, which frees the Marine's cognitive and motivational resources to perform military tasks . . . The fictional Spartan NCO named Dienikes, in the acclaimed novel *Gates of Fire*, puts it very compactly: "The opposite of fear . . . is love."[8]

Imagine how you would react if you were walking in the woods and saw a mountain lion running toward you. You would probably be terrified and your instinct would be to run. Now imagine if you saw a mountain lion attacking your spouse, child, or friend. Even with no military training, you would probably grab a stick or rock and rush to protect your loved one. The Greeks and Lao Tzu realized that our instinct to protect those we love is more powerful than our instinct for self-preservation; all of military history attests to this fact. The U.S. Army knows that soldiers fighting only for money are unreliable, but soldiers fighting to protect their comrades or family members are not easily defeated. That is why an army must create brotherhood and camaraderie among its soldiers, and why politicians must say war is necessary for the protection of family and country. Otherwise, retreating from the battlefield would be too tempting.

When men are alone and violence threatens their lives, they are usually cowards. Military strategist Charles Ardant du Picq said four men who do not know each other will be afraid to confront a lion, but if they know each other their courage cannot be overcome.[9] To build the courage that results from caring about others, the army taught me to treat my military unit like my family and to fight in order to "protect the person to my left and to my right." At West Point I learned a famous passage from Shakespeare's

Henry V: "We few, we happy few, we band of brothers; for he today that sheds his blood with me shall be my brother."[10]

Gandhi, serving as a medic for the British during the Boer War, witnessed the power of brotherhood in the military: "It was a sultry day. Water was very scarce. There was only one well. An officer was doling out tinfuls to the thirsty. Some of the [Indian stretcher] bearers were returning after leaving their charge. The soldiers, who were helping themselves to the water, at once cheerfully shared their portion with our bearers. There was, shall I say, a spirit of brotherhood, irrespective of colour or creed . . . As a Hindu, I do not believe in war, but if anything can even partially reconcile me to it, it was the rich experience we gained at the front. It was certainly not the thirst for blood that took thousands of men to the battlefield . . . they went to the battlefield because it was their duty."[11]

Just as the U.S. Army takes soldiers from every racial and religious background and trains them to unite as family, Gandhi witnessed how the bonds of brotherhood within the military transcend race and religion. Like Gandhi, my father also saw how the power of brotherhood can transcend our differences. When I was growing up, my father always told me, "The only place in America where black men are treated fairly is in the military. People will be nice to you, but when they find out you're part black they'll turn on you. The military is the only place that gives black men a chance. You'll never be able to get a decent job unless you're in the army."

Half white and half black, my father was born in 1925 and grew up in Virginia during segregation and the Great Depression. The U.S. Army was desegregated in the early 1950s, many years before segregation ended in the South. This made a strong impression on my father. During the 1940s and 1950s, his belief that he only had opportunity in the military was largely true. A hard worker who began picking fruit when he was six years old to earn extra income for his family, he excelled as a soldier and retired as the highest enlisted rank, a command sergeant major.

In *Will War Ever End?* I discussed how the American soldiers who left their jobs behind to fight in World War I were paid little more than a dollar a day for their service to our country. After the war ended, the government promised that these veterans would receive adjusted compensation to pay for their lost wages while fighting overseas. When the promise was not fulfilled, the veterans built a community where white and black people lived, protested, and fought for justice together. By applying the camaraderie they learned in the military, the Bonus Marchers lived in a desegregated community decades before the end of segregation in America.

The army is certainly not free of racism today, but when camaraderie in the army is high, racial tension among soldiers is lower than in other parts of society. The army doesn't create camaraderie through brainwashing, Gandhi realized, but by instilling genuine bonds of empathy and solidarity among soldiers.

Gandhi scholar Peter Brock explains how Gandhi's respect and admiration for the military shaped his life: "Gandhi showed here another trait that appears constantly in his later writings: his respect for the positive qualities war can bring out in men alongside the evil ones, for the heroism, comradeship and sense of duty it engenders among ordinary men . . . he would seek to create a technique that could preserve the virtues of the warrior while eliminating the negative aspects of warfare . . ."[12] [Gandhi believed people] must regain the martial qualities of the Kshatriyas [warriors] of old before qualifying to become true disciples of nonviolence."[13]

Gandhi realized if he could channel the warrior spirit toward waging peace, his movement to free India of British colonialism would have people with the discipline, strength, and courage necessary to overcome any challenge. He knew what military commanders throughout history have understood: when soldiers become a band of brothers they will perform incredible acts of heroism to protect their friends.

This is the Medal of Honor citation for Private First Class Ross McGinnis. On December 4, 2006, in Baghdad, he chose to sacrifice his life to save his friends.

> That afternoon his platoon was conducting combat control operations in an effort to reduce and control sectarian violence in the area. While Private McGinnis was manning the M2 .50-caliber Machine Gun, a fragmentation grenade thrown by an insurgent fell through the gunner's hatch into the vehicle. Reacting quickly, he yelled "grenade," allowing all four members of his crew to prepare for the grenade's blast.

Then, rather than leaping from the gunner's hatch to safety, Private McGinnis made the courageous decision to protect his crew. In a selfless act of bravery, in which he was mortally wounded, Private McGinnis covered the live grenade, pinning it between his body and the vehicle and absorbing most of the explosion.

Private McGinnis' gallant action directly saved four men from certain serious injury or death. Private First Class McGinnis' extraordinary heroism and selflessness at the cost of his own life, above and beyond the call of duty, are in keeping with the highest traditions of the military service and reflect great credit upon himself, his unit, and the United States Army.[14]

Empathy exists in war and peace; and sources as diverse as Buddha and Sun Tzu, Gandhi and the U.S. Army, and Mother Teresa and West Point agree on its importance. But what are the differences between how empathy is used in war and peace? And how does it give us the power to end war and solve our national and global problems? Before we can answer these questions we must first understand empathy. Empathy is our ability to identify with and relate to others. It allows us to recognize ourselves in them, sympathize with their problems, and share their joy and pain. Jack Tueller, an American who served as a captain during World War II, experienced the power of empathy when he saw his own humanity reflected in a German soldier.

This is two weeks after D-Day. It's dark, raining, muddy, and I'm stressed so I get my trumpet out and the commander says, "Jack don't play tonight, because there's one sniper left." I thought to myself, that German sniper is as scared and lonely as I am. So I thought, I'll play his love song [a German song called "Lili Marleen"]. The next morning here came a jeep up from the beach about a mile and a half away. And the military police said, "Hey Captain, there are some German prisoners getting ready to go to England." One of [the prisoners said] in broken English, "Who played that trumpet last night?"

And he burst into sobs. "When I heard that number that you played I thought about my fiancée in Germany, I thought about my mother and dad and about my brothers and sisters, and I couldn't fire." And he stuck out his hand and I shook the hand of the enemy. He was no enemy. He was scared and lonely like me.[15]

Every act of kindness, compassion, generosity, and forgiveness is built on the foundation of empathy; every act of hatred and cruelty results from its absence. A characteristic of psychopaths is their lack of empathy. Someone with absolutely no empathy is insane, while a person with enormous empathy is considered a saint. Furthermore, empathy is as vital for our survival as food and water. If every bit of empathy were removed from the world we would all become psychopaths; all traces of civilization would be destroyed virtually overnight.

Without the glue of empathy, the bonds of friendship and family that allow us to cooperate and sacrifice for each other cannot exist. By cultivating empathy in its soldiers, the army is able to take people from different racial, social, religious, political, and economic backgrounds and forge bonds of friendship and family between them. How does the army do this?

At West Point I learned empathy during the beginning of freshman year through an ideal called *cooperate and graduate.* West Point is unlike most other colleges, because cadets must live together in military units and cooperate to succeed. They are responsible for many duties that cannot be accomplished alone; this sense of teamwork is also emphasized in the academic program. In addition to the classes necessary to complete their major, cadets take a wide variety of mandatory courses such as calculus, physics, chemistry, philosophy, psychology, statistics, international relations, poetry, leadership, political science, engineering, world and military history, environmental science, computer science, economics, a foreign language, law, exercise physiology, swimming, gymnastics, wrestling, boxing for men, and self-defense for women.

West Point has its cadets take these diverse courses not only to make them well rounded but to also bring them out of their comfort zone. During my freshman year I was told that some people are experts at math, others excel at writing, some are best at history, and others have an advantage in athletics. Since cadets have a heavy academic workload of around twenty-one credit hours each semester, most students require at least some help. By working together and learning from each other's strengths, cadets have the best chance of overcoming adversity and graduating together.

Cooperate and graduate means thinking not only of one's personal well-being but also caring about others and helping them get through their courses. In a society where people often feel isolated and work only for their self-interest, at West Point I never felt alone. If I was struggling with a class I could ask my classmates for help and they would spend hours aiding a comrade.

In addition, classes at West Point usually consist of fifteen people or less, so professors can give each cadet a lot of attention. When I was there the professors had to give us their home phone number so we could call them if we needed help with schoolwork; their daily schedule also had a couple of hours allotted for those who wanted additional tutoring. If you were willing to help yourself you found an impressive support network willing to help you.

At West Point my empathy grew from the understanding that my classmates were experiencing the same hardships as I was. We all missed our families. We were all trying to pass our classes and graduate. We were all in this together. Empathy exists when you can see yourself in others, and when you can relate to their worries, fears, agony, and joy. There was plenty of worry, fear, agony, and joy to empathize with at West Point.

The training in empathy and cooperation I received at West Point still influences my actions today. West Point taught me that life is not about making the most money, but serving others. A community is stronger than a single person, and if we care about and serve those around us we can create a community powerful enough to overcome any obstacle. Rudyard Kipling expressed it this way:

Now this is the Law of the Jungle—as old and as true as the
  sky;
And the Wolf that shall keep it may prosper, but the Wolf that
  shall break it must die.
As the creeper that girdles the tree-trunk the Law runneth
  forward and back.
For the strength of the Pack is the Wolf, and the strength of
  the Wolf is the Pack.[16]

To build the empathy that makes strong community possible, we must develop our ability to see our humanity in others, recognizing the deep similarities that far outweigh our minor differences. I learned how to do this in the army, which has soldiers from every racial, religious, and social background. Despite these differences, we shared experiences, suffering, ideals, and a mission. But we shared something even deeper than that. We were all born human. We all felt pain and fear. And we all wanted hope, joy, and a life with meaning and purpose.

These similarities are the starting point for empathy, because not only do all American soldiers share them. So do all human beings. Jack Tueller realized this when he decided to play his trumpet for a German soldier after D-Day, and Erich Fromm described the process we must go through to increase our empathy: "If I perceive in another person mainly the surface, I perceive mainly the differences, that which separates us. If I penetrate to the core, I perceive our identity, the fact of our brotherhood."[17]

Gene Hoffman, founder of the Compassionate Listening Project, said: "An enemy is a person whose story we have not heard."[18] The key to developing our empathy is increasing our understanding and knowing people's stories. Only then can we penetrate to the core of our humanity and recognize ourselves in others.

Sun Tzu taught that we cannot effectively confront our enemies unless we know them. Because empathy allows us to recognize ourselves in others, we need it to wage peace. Like Sun Tzu, Gandhi also believed we must know our enemies, but where waging peace is concerned the only way to truly know our enemies is by understanding and empathizing with them. When we do this they cease being our enemies and we can see them for who they truly are: fellow human beings held hostage by fear, hatred, or misunderstanding.

Empathy teaches us to attack fear with compassion, hatred with love, and misunderstanding with dialogue. By knowing his enemies through understanding and empathy, Gandhi developed a strategy that sought to transform them not into corpses, but friends. He knew winning people over to his cause was more effective than killing countless people in war. Empathy is as vital for waging peace as weapons are for waging war. In *Will War Ever End?* and *The End of War* I discuss waging peace in greater detail.

A strong muscle of empathy also benefits us in many other ways. It is a form of education: by empathizing with others and being interested in their well-being we increase our knowledge of life, joy, and suffering. It also puts our suffering and personal problems into perspective. For example, if I am completely absorbed in my own interests, living in a tiny bubble where the troubles affecting other people do not concern me, a minor personal problem can seem like the end of the world. But if I have empathy for the billions of people on the planet who earn less than two dollars a day, I can see my minor problems from a wider perspective and they become less overwhelming.

Not only does empathy reduce our suffering by putting our personal problems into perspective, but our suffering can also increase our empathy. Losing a loved one can increase our empathy for those who lose loved ones, because shared experiences help us relate to and understand people's pain. In my own life, experiencing racism as a child has increased my empathy for those affected by racism, suffering from war has increased my empathy for the victims of war, and facing the challenges of being human has increased my empathy for everyone born into our confusing world.

By exploring what empathy is we can better understand why an army unit cannot function without this powerful bond among its soldiers. Empathy is so vital in the military that in addition to the motto "I will never leave a fallen comrade" from the Warrior Ethos, the U.S. Army's Non-Commissioned Officer Creed states: "All soldiers are entitled to outstanding leadership; I will provide that leadership. *I know my soldiers and I will always place their needs above my own* [emphasis added]. I will communicate consistently with my soldiers and never leave them uninformed."[19]

Because the army trains its soldiers to empathize with their comrades, it is not uncommon for them to empathize with the enemy. In his ground-breaking book, *On Killing: The Psychological Cost of Learning to Kill in War and Society*, Lt. Col. Dave Grossman shares a story in which a soldier was unable to kill an enemy:

> Then I cautiously raised the upper half of my body into the tunnel until I was lying flat on my stomach. When I felt comfortable, I placed my Smith Wesson .38-caliber snub-nose (sent to me by my father for tunnel work) beside the flashlight and switched on the light, illuminating the tunnel.
>
> There, not more than 15 feet away, sat a Viet Cong eating a handful of rice from a pouch on his lap. We looked at each other for what seemed to be an eternity, but in fact was probably only a few seconds.
>
> Maybe it was the surprise of actually finding someone else there, or maybe it was just the absolute innocence of the situation, but neither one of us reacted.
>
> After a moment, he put his pouch of rice on the floor of the tunnel beside him, turned his back to me and slowly started crawling away. I, in turn, switched off my flashlight, before slipping back into the lower tunnel and making my way back to the entrance. About 20 minutes later, we received word that another squad had killed a VC emerging from a tunnel 500 meters away.
>
> I never doubted who that VC was. To this day, I firmly believe that grunt and I could have ended the war sooner over a beer in Saigon than Henry Kissinger ever could by attending the peace talks.[20]

In another book, *On Combat: The Psychology and Physiology of Deadly Conflict in War and in Peace*, Lt. Col. Grossman shares a story of an American soldier who empathized with a Vietnamese soldier he killed after finding a family picture while searching the dead man's body.

For 22 years I have carried your picture in my wallet. I
was only 18 years old that day that we faced one another on
that trail in Chu Loi, Vietnam. Why you didn't take my life
I'll never know. You stared at me for so long, armed with your
AK-47, and yet you did not fire. Forgive me for taking your
life, I was reacting the way I was trained to kill V.C. . . . . So
many times over the years I stared at your picture, and your
daughter, I suspect. Each time my heart and guts would burn
with the pain and guilt. I have two daughters myself now . . .
I perceive you as a brave soldier defending his homeland.
Above all else, I can now respect the importance that life held
for you. I suppose that is why I am able to be here today . . .
It is time for me to continue the life process and release my
pain and guilt. Forgive me, Sir.[21]

Empathy is vital for armies to function well, but these examples show
that when empathy excludes no one, there can be no more war. Although
empathy is a necessary component in organized warfare, in the next section
I will explain how war also requires the absence of empathy. Empathy for
the other side is removed through dehumanization, and the dehumanization
process that makes war possible is a science that our society has perfected.

The Many Faces of Dehumanization

Dehumanization is a monster with many faces, and it plays a significant
role in almost all our human problems. This section will explain how the
many forms of dehumanization make war, genocide, injustice, racism, and
oppression possible.

In *On Killing* Lt. Col. Dave Grossman says that human beings have a
natural aversion to killing other human beings, just as many other animal
species have an aversion to killing their own kind. A rattlesnake will inflict
a lethal bite on another animal but wrestle another rattlesnake. Bulls, buffalo,
and other horned animals defend themselves by goring a predator's side and
belly, but when they fight their own species they ram horns, which is the

least lethal form of combat. Many predators deliver strangulation and abdominal bites when hunting but avoid them when fighting their own species.[22]

Not all animals have a natural aversion to killing members of their own species, but many do. In the documentary series *Life in Cold Blood*, naturalist Richard Attenborough explains how this aversion can promote the animal's survival: "The King Cobra [is] highly venomous . . . Disputes between rival male King Cobras are potentially very dangerous indeed, for this species specializes in eating other kinds of snakes. So they observe strict rules in their fights, which prohibit the use of their lethal bite . . . each contestant strives not to kill his opponent, but simply to slam him to the ground."[23]

Since buffalo spend most of their time around other buffalo, if they did not have a natural aversion to killing their own kind they would go extinct. Although ramming horns is the least lethal form of combat for buffalo, this can certainly lead to injury and even death on rare occasions. However, entire buffalo herds would perish if they attacked each other's sides and bellies the way they fight predators. Just as buffalo spend most of their time around other buffalo and therefore have an aversion to killing their own species, we also spend most of our time around other human beings. What evidence do we have that human beings have an aversion to killing other human beings? The evidence is all of military history.

Lt. Col. Dave Grossman says that every war in history has required dehumanization of the enemy, and in *On Killing* he outlines three kinds of dehumanization that take place in war. The first form is *psychological distance*, which occurs when people are portrayed as subhuman. One example of psychological distance is derogatory name-calling, and *On Killing* offers examples of how Americans used racial slurs in past wars to create psychological distance between themselves and the people they were fighting. During World War II, our name for the Germans was "Krauts" and we referred to the Japanese as "Japs." During the Vietnam War, we knew the Vietnamese not as human beings but as "Gooks." Over two thousand years ago, the Greeks also used psychological distance by calling all non-Greeks barbarians.

The word *barbarian*, a racial slur, was a way of making fun of how people talked. Many Greeks believed that people who spoke a different language were uncivilized subhumans, and the word *barbarian* came from the Greek view that foreign languages were nothing more than unintelligent chatter, which to them sounded like "barbarbarbarbar." Making fun of how foreigners talk is a subtle way to dehumanize people, but a more overt form of psychological distance could be seen during the Rwandan genocide when the people being massacred were called "cockroaches."

The second form of dehumanization is *moral distance*. While psychological distance portrays people as subhumans and cockroaches, moral distance depicts human beings as evil monsters. Moral distance occurs when someone has the attitude, "I represent everything that is good, my enemy is pure evil, and God is on my side." Moral distance is one reason why civil wars are so bloody. Civil wars are conflicts where both sides often share the same language, customs, and appearance. Since psychological distance is less effective when people have the same culture, moral distance is used during civil wars to convince people that killing the enemy is not a violent act that hurts human beings, but a holy activity that expels evil from the world.

Historian Alfred Vagts describes the mentality of moral distance: "Enemies are to be deemed criminals in advance, guilty of starting the war; the business of locating the aggressor is to begin before or shortly after the outbreak of the war; the methods of conducting the war are to be branded as criminal; and victory is not to be a triumph of honour and bravery over honour and bravery but the climax of a police hunt for bloodthirsty wretches who have violated law, order, and everything else esteemed good and holy."[24]

The third form of distance is *mechanical distance*, which means the farther away you are from someone the easier it is to kill him. Dropping a bomb from ten thousand feet is easier than shooting a person with a rifle at three hundred yards; killing with a rifle is easier than stabbing a person with a knife at close range.[25]

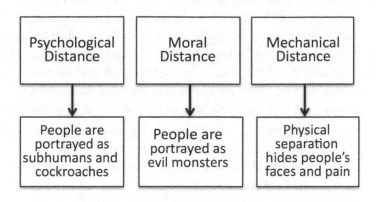

Figure 2.1: Three Forms of Dehumanization in War

The Nazis used the gas chambers as a form of mechanical distance. They initially relied on firing squads to execute their prisoners, but they switched to gas chambers because too many of their soldiers were becoming traumatized from shooting women and children. Many believe the Nazis used the gas chamber for its efficiency, but a firing squad is one of the most efficient ways to kill people. What is more efficient than making people dig a ditch that will become their grave, forcing them to stand in their grave, shooting them with inexpensive bullets, and throwing dirt on top of them? Unlike firing squads, the gas chamber allowed the Nazis to kill people without having to watch them die, and it allowed a few people to do most of the killing. Historian Klaus Fischer explains:

> The culmination of mass shootings came at Babi-Yar on the outskirts of Kiev where thirty-three thousand Jews were killed. The first wave of mass killings came to an end by the winter of 1941. By that time seven hundred thousand Jews had been murdered. The men of the *Einsatzgruppen*, however, were physically and psychologically drained. Some sought refuge in alcohol, some became physically ill, a few committed suicide. Under these circumstances, the question arose of how to maintain the pace of murder and even to expand the

killings that were being planned in order to eradicate the remaining Jews of Europe. So far, the killings had been random
and personal; they were messy and nerves were frayed. It became necessary to find a more efficient and less personal
method of murdering the remaining Jews . . . Himmler then
spelled out that "every Jew that we can lay our hands on is to
be destroyed now during the war, without exception." He also
explained that such a task could only be done "by gassing,
since it would have been impossible by shooting to dispose of
the large number of people that were expected, and it would
have placed too heavy a burden on the SS men who had to
carry it out, especially because of the women and children
among its victims."[26]

To protect their executioners from the trauma of killing women and
children, the Nazis began to use the gas chamber on a massive scale. Concern
for the executioner is the same reason why people's faces are usually covered
when they are executed by electric chair and hanging. This is not done for
the well-being of the person being executed, but to protect the executioner
and people watching the execution from being traumatized. Even gangsters,
when they execute people at close range, usually shoot them in the back of
the head. It is difficult to watch someone's face as they die; it reminds us of
their humanity.

Shooting thousands of women and children at close range and watching
their writhing bodies as they lie dying in a ditch; being continually surrounded by screams, blood, and rotting corpses, will cause many to become
traumatized. The Nazi soldiers had mothers. Many of them had sisters. And
some of them had daughters. In *The Architect of Genocide,* historian Richard
Breitman explains:

> [Bach-Zelewski asked] Himmler to spare not the victims
> but the policemen. Pointing out how shaken the executioners
> were, he complained that these men were now finished for
> the rest of their lives: they would either be neurotics or savages
> . . . Höss and Eichmann also discussed methods of killing.

> Because of the large numbers of Jews involved, shooting was out of the question: it would have placed too heavy a burden on the executioners, Höss said. Eichmann told Höss about the gas vans used in the East for euthanasia killings. Their capacity, however, was too limited. The euthanasia killing centers in Germany dealt with larger numbers, but employing this model meant constructing many buildings, and it was questionable whether there was a sufficient supply of bottled carbon monoxide. So there was no easy answer. Eichmann said he would try to find a gas available in large quantities that would not require special installations . . . Himmler had wanted a neater, cleaner, less upsetting way of killing large numbers of people, and poison gas was the obvious solution.[27]

In addition to the mechanical distance of the gas chamber, the Nazis also used psychological distance by calling people subhuman and moral distance by calling people evil. A massacre as big as the Holocaust requires all three forms of dehumanization: psychological, moral, and mechanical distance.

Lt. Col. Dave Grossman states in *On Killing* that approximately 2 percent of the population are psychopaths, a minority that can kill in the most gruesome ways without becoming traumatized or going insane. Why are psychopaths able to kill without going insane? Because according to Lt. Col. Grossman, they are already insane. Klaus Fischer explains how some psychotic executioners are able to kill in ways that most people cannot:

> Only the most sadistic or hardened executioners could stomach such barbaric horrors indefinitely . . . Major Rösler, commanding the 528th Infantry Regiment, came upon a mass execution near Zhitomir and was horrified by the picture of an execution pit in which bodies were still twitching; he ordered a policeman to kill an old man with a white beard clutching a cane in his left hand who was still writhing in agony. The policeman laughed and said: "I have already shot him seven times in the stomach. He can die on his own now."

In one town the Jews had gone into hiding and when the SS
swept through the town they discovered a woman with a baby
in her arms. When the woman refused to tell them where the
Jews were hiding, one SS man grabbed the baby by its legs
and smashed its head against a door. Another SS man recalled:
"It went off with a bang like a bursting motor tire. I shall never
forget that sound as long as I live."[28]

Mechanical distance is not always necessary for genocide to occur. As I
explained earlier, psychological distance convinces people that they are not
killing human beings, but subhumans and cockroaches, and moral distance
convinces people that they are not killing human beings, but evil monsters.
Psychological and moral distance are gears that turn the machine of death,
and mechanical distance is a lubricant that greases the gears and makes genocide easier. The gears of psychological and moral distance are capable of creating a level of rage and hysteria that can grind life away even at close range.
Psychological and moral distance produce hatred, and a large amount of hatred can decrease the need for mechanical distance.

For example, during the Rwandan genocide the Hutus used machetes
to hack thousands of Tutsis to death. Daniel Johan Goldhagen, who has
spent his life studying genocide, says genocide is always political. Prior to
the Rwandan genocide the Tutsis had oppressed the Hutus; Hutu political
leaders used these past injustices to create hysteria that the oppression would
happen again if the Tutsis were not destroyed. A Hutu extremist radio broad-
cast asserted: "The Tutsis have always been evil. They may smile and wink,
but they will take your children away. While we, the Hutus, are innocent."[29]
The attitude that "they are determined to kill us so we have to kill them
first" led to mass slaughter.

Unlike the bitter history between the Hutus and Tutsis, the Nazis
needed the gas chamber because they were murdering groups of people who
had never hurt the Germans. The Holocaust is the only genocide in history
where a country tried to exterminate an entire race of people, including all
of its women and children, across vast continents. To dehumanize entire
groups of people and see them as monsters, we must silence our humanity.
This often causes us to behave as monsters. As philosopher Friedrich

Nietzsche said: "Whoever fights monsters should see to it that in the process he does not become a monster. And when you look long into an abyss, the abyss also looks into you."[30]

Dehumanization—a type of manipulation that blocks empathy and hides the truth that we are all human beings—is not only a root cause of war but also a major source of injustice and oppression. Just as a country cannot wage war without dehumanizing the enemy, a group cannot exploit its own people without dehumanizing them. And just as three forms of distance make killing easier in war, three forms of distance make exploitation easier in modern societies, corporations, and organizations.

The first form of distance used in exploitation is *industrial distance*, which I will contrast with the psychological distance used in war. When psychological distance is concerned, the enemy are viewed as cockroaches that must be exterminated. But in corporations, workers cannot be treated like pests needing extermination because they are necessary for the organization to function. Instead of portraying people as cockroaches, industrial distance depicts people as machines.

Unlike cockroaches, machines have utility, and corporations cannot function without them. However, machines are expendable. Industrial distance values human life as much as it values any other machine in the assembly line. The purpose of a machine is to serve a corporation, and a corporation has no moral responsibility to the machine. When workers are treated like machines, corporations will use and abuse them as long as it serves their interests. And when it serves their interests to throw them away, they don't give it a second thought.

Not all companies view their employees through the distorted lens of industrial distance; I have seen workplaces where employees are treated well. But when employees are treated like machines the results can be devastating. Where industrial distance is concerned, firing ten thousand American employees to exploit cheaper workers overseas is no different from throwing out old equipment to buy faster, cheaper machines. A machine that works eighty hours a week for two dollars a day is preferable to one that works only forty hours a week for ten dollars an hour.

I use the term industrial distance because this form of distance increased significantly during the industrial revolution when the use of machines became widespread. During the era of state-sanctioned slavery, slaves were dehumanized and treated like domesticated animals. But sheep and horses, unlike machines, are living creatures capable of feeling pain. Many who approved of slavery believed the slave owner had a moral responsibility to treat his slaves well, just as a shepherd had an obligation to protect his flock and a knight to care for his horse.

But machines are not living creatures to which we owe moral responsibility. Despite the flawed moral argument that a slave owner could be benevolent to his slaves, state-sanctioned slavery was a cruel system that caused immense suffering—and most slave owners were far from benevolent. However, industrial distance is completely devoid of morality, which led to many atrocities during the industrial revolution. There were no national child labor laws or worker's rights legislation in the United States until the early twentieth century. Large numbers of employees, laboring for pennies an hour in unsafe conditions, died in factory accidents.

Industrial distance differs from state-sanctioned slavery in another way. Replacing a strong slave, like replacing a valuable horse, was expensive. But performing simple repetitive tasks on an assembly line requires little training, and new workers recruited from a starving population can be hired for almost nothing. Industrial distance views people not only as machines, but cheap machines. People are treated not like expensive jets, but as expendable cogs and gears. Industrial distance is so dangerous not only because it views human beings as machines, but as the cheapest and most disposable of all machines.

The second form of distance that makes exploitation easier in societies, corporations, and organizations is *numerical distance*, which transforms people into numbers. A famous example of a person who dehumanized through numerical distance is Adolf Eichmann, who organized the massacre of civilians in Germany and the territories conquered by the Nazis. According to Erich Fromm:

> Adolf Eichmann does not give the impression of being particularly evil; rather, he is entirely alienated. He is a bureaucrat for whom it makes no particular difference whether he kills, or whether he takes care of, small children. For him,

life has completely stopped being something alive. He "organizes." Organization becomes an end in itself, whether it has to do with the gold teeth or the hair of murdered humans or whether it is railroad trains or tons of coal. Anything else is indifferent for him. When Eichmann defends himself and states that he is only a bureaucrat and has, in reality, only regulated trains and worked out schedules, then he is not altogether off the mark . . . Eichmann's arguments are not all that different from the considerations advanced by today's atomic strategists. I cite as an example Herman Kahn, one of the most important American atomic researchers. Kahn says that it is acceptable if 60 million Americans die during the first three days of an atomic war; if 90 million die, then it is too many. The issue here has to do with the *same* calculating, the *same* balance of life and death as in Eichmann's leading people to their murder.[31]

When I was deployed to Iraq in 2006, I heard an American news commentator say that only a couple of thousand American soldiers had been killed in Iraq, a small number compared to the 58,000 American soldiers who died during the Vietnam War. Using the same logic, one could say that the number of American soldiers killed in Vietnam is small compared to the more than 600,000 Americans who died during the Civil War. A couple of thousand dead soldiers is not a small number, not when you are the friend or relative of a soldier that has died.

Unlike psychological and moral distance, which depict human beings as subhumans and evil monsters, numerical distance dehumanizes people by turning them into numbers without faces. Firing ten thousand employees does not mean putting people with families out of work; it means removing a number from your payroll. Many corporations have fired thousands of people even during profitable quarters to further increase profits.

Industrial and numerical distance are represented metaphorically by the Borg in the television series *Star Trek,* created by Gene Roddenberry. Star Fleet, the organization in which the main characters are members, embodies the best potentials of human society such as freedom, compassion, tolerance, individuality, solidarity, justice, and respect for other cultures. Star Fleet's archenemy is the Borg, an alien race whose purpose is to conquer and assimilate all intelligent forms of life. Just as industrial and numerical distance turn human beings into machines and numbers, the Borg literally transform everyone they conquer into machines with numbers instead of names. When people are assimilated into the Borg collective, they are robbed of their humanity. They become mindless drones, incapable of thinking for themselves, whose only purpose is to serve the organization.

The Borg symbolize the darkest aspects of corporations, societies, and organizations. The Borg are plunderers who tell everyone standing in their way "resistance is futile." Their mission is to conquer with no regard for life, and during their conquest for endless expansion they ravage cultures and entire civilizations. The Borg collective in *Star Trek* is a useful metaphor that allows us to explore the dangers of industrial and numerical distance, along with *collectivism*, an attitude that results when industrial and numerical distance cause us to see human beings as part of a collective machine. David Henderson, a professor at the Naval Postgraduate School, explains the danger of collectivism:

> The great tragedy of collectivism . . . is that it makes people heartless—they become incapable of seeing the real losses and hurts inflicted on innocent people because they stop seeing them as individuals . . . While reading a draft of one of my students' thesis chapters a few years ago, I came across the statement, "Fewer than 150 people were killed in the 1991 Gulf War." I wrote in the margin that the number killed was likely in excess of 100,000 people, three orders of magnitude higher than the number he mentioned. When we went over his chapter together, he said that when he wrote "people," he had meant "Americans." His mistake was an innocent one, but it was an innocent consequence of a selective collectivism: seeing Americans as individuals, but people of other societies—particularly ones living in countries on which the U.S. government had made war—as part of an organism . . .
>
> Kevin S., a Navy officer and former colleague of mine at

the Naval Postgraduate School, was burned by fuel from the airplane that flew into the Pentagon on Sept. 11. It looked as if he wouldn't live, but he did. It was a heroic story that was written up in his local Virginia newspaper. The article talked about his recovery and had me cheering for him and his spirit. But then the article stated that Kevin had contacted some of his buddies in the Air Force and asked them to write on one of the bombs to be dropped on people in Afghanistan, "Kevin sends." As much as I sympathized with Kevin, I was equally sympathetic toward some of the people whom "Kevin's" bomb would injure or kill, who were at least as innocent as he was. Unfortunately, Kevin's collectivist thinking prevented him from distinguishing between those who had hurt him and those who had not.

Collectivism is the ugliest ideology in the world. It has been directly responsible for well over 100 million deaths in the twentieth century. Let's do our part by not participating in it, even—maybe especially—in our language. The only hope we have for a peaceful world is to hold guilty people responsible for their actions and to treat the innocent people in all countries as innocent.[32]

The third form of distance is *bureaucratic distance.* Just as long-range weapons give us mechanisms that make killing easier from afar, bureaucracy creates mechanisms that make exploitation more likely. Long-range weapons transform human beings into specks that look like ants on the ground, while bureaucracy turns people into pieces of paper. If a soldier's only experience with killing is dropping bombs on specks from ten thousand feet, this method of killing is easier on the human conscience than shooting people at close range and seeing their faces when they die. Similarly, if a corporate executive's only experience with his or her lowest-ranking employees is shuffling pieces of paper that contain their personal information, it is much easier to make decisions that disregard their well-being than if the executive knew these people and their families.

Just as psychological, moral, and mechanical distance exist in degrees, the same is true of industrial, numerical, and bureaucratic distance. Distance can be used in small and extreme amounts, and if humanity is going to survive in the twenty-first century and beyond, we must dramatically reduce the forms of distance that lead to war and exploitation around the world.

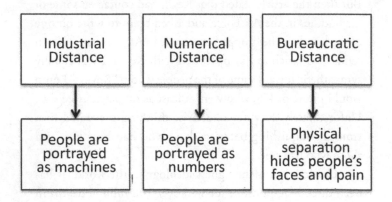

Figure 2.2: Three Forms of Dehumanization for Exploitation

Where does dehumanization come from? George Orwell said: "One of the most horrible features of war is that all the war-propaganda, all the screaming and lies and hatred, comes invariably from people who are not fighting."[33] By taking a closer look at war propaganda we can learn a lot about human nature.

To learn whether love or hate is the more powerful instinct in human beings, we can examine the way war propaganda has functioned throughout history. According to political leaders, wars are always about self-defense, protecting our families, fighting for freedom, defending our way of life, and liberating oppressed people. During the Roman Empire's attempt to conquer the known world, many Romans believed they were liberating barbarians from darkness by giving them Roman civilization and wisdom. During the time of European colonialism, many Europeans believed they were liberating barbaric natives by civilizing them and giving them Christianity. There has never been a war where the war propaganda told a population, "We are fighting for money, gold, or oil. We are fighting so the rich can get richer."

War propaganda makes people believe they are fighting for a noble cause in defense of their family, country, or an ideal. It also hides the enemy's humanity by portraying them as inhuman. Most people will risk their lives for their family. Wouldn't you? And if you truly believed that evil monsters in another country were determined to kill your family and oppress your country, wouldn't you be much more likely to support a war?

Just as our ancestors protected their families from predators on the dangerous African plains, politicians portray the enemy as monstrous predators trying to kill our family. War propaganda is like a magic trick. Once we understand how the illusion works, it is much harder to be fooled. (See Appendix A for visual illustrations of psychological and moral distance.)

Unconditional Love: A Higher Expression of Empathy

True love begins when nothing is looked for in return.
—Antoine de Saint-Exupéry

Empathy is our ability to identify with and relate to others. It allows us to recognize ourselves in them, sympathize with their problems, and share their joy and pain. When empathy consists not only of caring about others but also taking action to make a positive difference in their lives, the muscle of empathy grows into unconditional love. Like the downpour of rain that transforms a trickling stream into a nourishing river, unconditional love is a natural result of increased empathy. When our muscle of empathy is strong the river of unconditional love flows forcefully in many directions.

Unconditional love occurs when empathy motivates us to act selflessly on someone's behalf, and it can be summarized in three simple words: *no strings attached*. This means helping others because we care about them, not because we want them to do something for us in return. The fourteenth-century Persian poet Hafiz saw the nature of unconditional love as follows:

Even after all this time
The sun never says to the Earth,
"You owe me."
Look what happens with a love like that—
It lights the whole sky.[34]

When the river of unconditional love nourishes those around us, it not only lights up our lives but the whole world. I have often heard the criticism that love spoils people, but this myth comes from misunderstanding what love truly is. Unconditional love can brighten the lives of those around us without spoiling them, because being a good friend is far different from being a doormat for someone's every indulgence. Unconditional love says yes to being a good friend and no to letting people walk all over us.

Spoiling people makes them worse off because it encourages them to have an irresponsible sense of entitlement, and if we care about someone's well-being the last thing we should do is spoil them. The idea that we can love people without spoiling them is common sense to most parents. Unconditional love motivates parents to help their children become healthy and happy adults, but truly loving parents do not spoil their children by buying them a toy every time they ask for one or letting them eat chocolate for breakfast, lunch, and dinner. The army teaches that if you care about the soldiers in your unit, one of the best gifts you can give them is discipline. I have learned that discipline is necessary not only in the army but it is also vital to accomplishing any challenging goal. Without discipline I would not be able to dedicate the thousands of hours of hard work required to write this book. The most capable musicians, painters, writers, soldiers, athletes, and peacemakers all have one thing in common: discipline.

Selflessness is the water in the river of unconditional love. Without selflessness an army cannot function effectively. U.S. Army doctrine has an ideal called *selfless service* that every soldier is supposed to aspire toward. The army describes selfless service as follows: "Put the welfare of the Nation, the Army and your subordinates before your own. Selfless service is larger than just one person. In serving your country, you are doing your duty loyally without thought of recognition or gain. The basic building block of selfless service is the commitment of each team member to go a little further, endure a little longer, and look a little closer to see how he or she can add to the effort."[35]

According to the army, selfless service means taking an action to serve a person, cause, or mission because we are committed to something larger than ourselves, not because we want something in return. When we genuinely care enough to help, the act of serving others gives us a reward too profound to measure. Gandhi said that expressing unconditional love allows us to achieve the greatest heights of meaning, purpose, and joy. But in an interesting paradox, we cannot fully reap the reward of a meaningful life if we are shackled by the desire for a reward.

Like a falcon that must let go of the branch it clings to before soaring freely in the sky, we cannot ascend the highest peaks of meaning, purpose, and joy while clinging to a desire for a reward. Gandhi, the person I consider most deserving of the Nobel Peace Prize in the twentieth century, never received it. But he was the person who cared least about winning it; his focus was on helping others, living fully, and building a better world.

The army and Gandhi agree that selfless service, which causes us to care about something larger than ourselves and perceive our existence as part of a bigger whole, is necessary to achieve our full potential as human beings. In the words attributed to World War I veteran General Peyton Conway March: "There is a wonderful, mystical law of nature that the three things we crave most in life—happiness, freedom, and peace of mind—are always attained by giving them to someone else."

But selfless service does not require us to completely ignore our personal well-being; if we did not take care of our health and happiness we would be of little benefit to our community. Instead, selfless service shifts our attitude from self-interest to *community-interest*. When we are self-interested we think only of ourselves. But when we are community-interested we think of other people along with ourselves, and we are willing to sacrifice to help the group. Self-interest is a lonely feeling, while community-interest creates the bonds of friendship and family that make life worth living.

When we strengthen our unconditional love by exercising the muscle of empathy, we can become a better friend and family member to those around us. We can also increase the meaning, purpose, and joy in our lives. Unconditional love is an attitude, a way of looking at the world, a power of the soul that grows weaker if we neglect it and stronger if we are committed to becoming fully human. Erich Fromm describes it this way:

> Love is not primarily a relationship to a specific person; it is an *attitude*, an *orientation* of *character* which determines the relatedness of a person to the world as a whole, not toward one "object" of love. If a person loves only one other person and is indifferent to the rest of his fellow men, his love is not love but a symbiotic attachment, or an enlarged egotism. Yet, most people believe that love is constituted by the object, not by the faculty. In fact, they even believe that it is a proof of the intensity of their love when they do not love anybody except the "loved" person. This is the same fallacy which we have already mentioned above. Because one does not see that love is an activity, a power of the soul, one believes that all that is necessary to find is the right object—and that everything goes by itself afterward. This attitude can be compared to that of a man who wants to paint but who, instead of learning the art, claims that he has just to wait for the right object, and that he will paint beautifully when he finds it. If I truly love one person I love all persons, I love the world, I love life. If I can say to somebody else, "I love you," I must be able to say, "I love in you everybody, I love through you the world, I love in you also myself."[36]

Just as people must learn to paint, sculpt, or play music, we must learn how to love. Love is a skill and an art, and our canvas is the world. As a child the messages I received from television and society taught me how to be competitive and selfish, but not how to love. Although Western countries are rich in many ways, they are sometimes poor in the ways that matter most. Mother Teresa said: "In the developed countries there is a poverty of intimacy, a poverty of spirit, of loneliness, of lack of love. There is no greater sickness in the world today than that one."[37]

Soldiers in combat must harness the power of their muscles to overcome physical struggle, and as soldiers of peace we must harness the power of unconditional love to end war and create a brighter future. Humanity has not come close to fully unlocking the enormous potential that unconditional love has to offer. Henry David Thoreau explains: "Suppose we could compare the moral with the physical, and say how many horse-power the force of love, for instance, blowing on every square foot of a man's soul, would equal . . . [Love's] power is incalculable; it is many horse-power. It never ceases; it never slacks; it can move the globe without a resting-place; it can warm without fire; it can feed without meat; it can clothe without garments; it can shelter without roof; it can make a paradise within which will dispense with a paradise without. But though the wisest men in all ages have labored to publish this force, and every human heart is, sooner or later, more or less, made to feel it, yet how little is actually applied to social ends . . . Shall we not contribute our shares to this enterprise, then?"[38]

When we do not understand the power of unconditional love, we will not understand what it means to be human and the road to peace will remain hidden from sight. But exploring the nature of unconditional love reveals new and hopeful possibilities for our future. Understanding unconditional love not only allows us to imagine the kind of world that could exist, it also gives us the strength to transform that bright future into reality.

Solidarity: The Highest Expression of Empathy

Two are better than one . . . If one falls down, his friend can help him up. But pity the man who falls and has no one to help him up! . . . Though one may be overpowered, two can defend themselves. A cord of three strands is not quickly broken.
—Ecclesiastes 4: 9–12[39]

What is the ultimate sin in the military? Is it turning against your comrades? During my junior year at West Point, my classmates and I were fortunate to attend a lecture by Hugh Thompson. He is the American helicopter pilot awarded the Soldier's Medal for his heroism at the My Lai Massacre, where several hundred unarmed Vietnamese children, women, and elderly were systematically executed by U.S. soldiers. Witnessing the carnage from above, Thompson landed his helicopter and went into the village to save the remaining Vietnamese civilians. He told his door gunner Larry Colburn and crew chief Glenn Andreotta that if the Americans killed any more civilians during his rescue attempt they must turn their guns on the Americans. Fortunately, Colburn and Andreotta were not forced to shoot at the American soldiers as Thompson risked his life to save as many civilians as he could.

Even though Thompson turned against his comrades, West Point honored him as a hero. West Point taught me that if your comrades violate the Geneva Conventions by massacring civilians, turning against them is not a sin; it is an act of loyalty to the army values.

What then is the ultimate sin in the military? Is it treason against your government? When Claus Schenk Graf von Stauffenberg and a group of German soldiers tried to assassinate Hitler in 1944, were they guilty of the ultimate sin? Although caught before completing their mission and executed for treason, they were later honored for their heroism. *The Memorial to the German Resistance* was created by the German government at the site of the execution. A plaque there reads: YOU DID NOT BEAR THE SHAME. YOU RESISTED. YOU BESTOWED AN ETERNALLY VIGILANT SYMBOL OF CHANGE BY SACRIFICING YOUR IMPASSIONED LIVES FOR FREEDOM, JUSTICE, AND HONOR.

Thompson demonstrated that turning against his murderous comrades was not an act of betrayal but the highest act of loyalty to human dignity and the army values; and von Stauffenberg showed that trying to bring down Hitler was not an act of treason but the highest act of loyalty to Germany and humanity. Nevertheless, there is an ultimate sin in the military, an act universally despised.

Seven Samurai, created by the brilliant Japanese filmmaker Akira Kurosawa, illustrates the ultimate sin in the military. It tells the story of seven samurai hired to defend a village against bandits. The seven noble samurai defend the villagers not for money but out of compassion. The Jedi warriors in George Lucas' *Star Wars* are based on Kurosawa's heroes. In *Star Wars* most of the Jedi are good and only a few are bad, but in *Seven Samurai* most of the samurai are bad and only a few are good. In Japan this is historically true, because more samurai behaved as brigands who exploited the poor than warrior protectors who defended the helpless. Kurosawa was aware that throughout history many warriors did more harm than good.

Just as many Christians do not embrace the highest ideals of Jesus such as loving one's enemies, forgiveness, not judging, and being a peacemaker, many warriors do not embrace the highest ideals of warrior philosophy such as courage, discipline, humility, professionalism, resilience, a willingness to challenge injustice even at personal risk, a duty to protect the helpless, and struggling not for personal glory but for the common good. Kurosawa believed these warrior ideals are among the highest ideals of humanity; *Seven Samurai* is about the samurai who behave as all warriors should.[40]

The leader of the seven noble samurai is Kambei, who embodies the highest ideals of warrior philosophy. As Kambei is developing a strategy to protect the village, he tells the villagers that a few houses across a stream cannot be defended due to their location and must be abandoned to protect the community. Kambei asks the people living in the indefensible outlying houses to join the defense of the village. At first they agree, but then one of them throws down his spear and says he doesn't care about the village; he is going to focus on protecting his house.

This is the only time Kambei becomes angry, because the villager has committed the ultimate sin in the military: he has behaved selfishly with no regard for the well-being of those around him. Realizing that selfishness is destructive within a military unit or any community, Kambei says to the villagers, "This is the nature of war—by protecting others, you save yourself. If you only think of yourself, you'll only destroy yourself."

Jonathan Shay says, "Military organizations function most effectively when they are about love. They function badly when they are about fear. And they don't function at all when they are about selfishness."[41] Selfishness is destructive to a military unit or any community because it makes solidarity impossible. But what is solidarity, and why is it vital to human survival?

In an ant colony, worker ants will risk their lives to protect the group. However, the group will not risk itself to save the lowliest worker ant, but only the highest-ranking ant: the queen. The same is true in a beehive, where worker bees sacrifice for the group, but the group treats worker bees as expendable. The most effective military units are much different from ant colonies and beehives, because not only will soldiers risk their lives for the group, but the group will also risk itself for every member, even the lowest in rank. When human solidarity exists in a community, one person will sacrifice for all, and all will sacrifice for one person.

The strongest military units resemble families, and solidarity is expressed in the line "I will never leave a fallen comrade" from the army's Warrior Ethos. This means the group will come back for its lowest-ranking people, even if it puts the group at risk. *Star Trek* is a television show about the military where solidarity is often displayed. Star Fleet, the name of the military in *Star Trek*, uses military rank and protocol; and Star Fleet Academy is based on West Point and even has the same rank insignia and honor code. But in Gene Roddenberry's vision of the future there is no war, poverty, or hunger on earth, so the military's mission has changed from war to peace, humanitarian aid, and exploration.

In the series spin-off *Star Trek: Voyager*, the crew of the starship *Voyager* rescue a woman who was assimilated into the Borg collective as a young child. Brainwashed by the Borg, she prefers her identification number, Seven of Nine, to her birth name, and throughout the series she must relearn what it means to be human. In the episode "Day of Honor" an alien species ravaged by the Borg demands that Captain Katherine Janeway turn over Seven of Nine to them, or they will destroy her ship.

Because life is expendable in the Borg collective, Seven of Nine immediately agrees to turn herself over. But Janeway refuses, putting her entire crew at risk to protect one member. In that moment Seven of Nine learns a crucial lesson about what it means to be human. When solidarity exists in a community, people will not only risk their lives to protect the group, but the group will also risk itself to protect one person.

The warrior motto in Alexander Dumas' *The Three Musketeers* is "One for all, all for one," which expresses how solidarity creates individual loyalty to the group and group loyalty to the individual. If people believe this makes a community weak, it is because they don't understand that the strongest army units have enormous solidarity. The army does not teach its soldiers to never leave a fallen comrade purely as a moral matter; it is also a practical one. If people trust their community to not leave them behind, their willingness to serve their community increases significantly. On the dangerous

African plains, the trust created by solidarity allowed our ancestors to survive in the harshest conditions.

The military has learned that solidarity is stronger than blood ties, and the military demonstrates this every time it takes people from diverse demographics and transforms them into a cohesive unit that resembles a family. A strong muscle of empathy makes a family unbreakable, but if empathy is missing from a family, its members can betray each other even if they are related by blood.

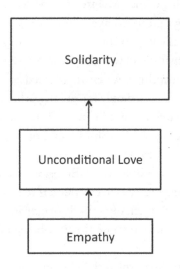

Figure 2.3: The Muscle of Empathy

Empathy occurs when we care about the well-being of others. When the muscle of empathy grows strong, it becomes unconditional love, a higher expression of empathy that causes us to serve the well-being of others. When the muscle of empathy reaches its highest expression, the experience of solidarity causes us to become deeply united with others, even if it means putting ourselves at risk.

Solidarity can be seen not only in military units but also in relationships everywhere. Wouldn't you risk your life to protect your family, and wouldn't your family risk itself to save you? Like the sturdy foundation required for any building to stand, whether it is a house, hospital, school, or store,

solidarity is the sturdy foundation necessary for any powerful human relationship, whether it exists in the military, community, family, or friendship.

The Roman philosopher Seneca tells us how solidarity creates the
foundation for all true friendships: "[A wise person has friends] not for the
purpose of having someone to come and sit beside his bed when he is ill or
come to his rescue when he is hard up or thrown into chains, but so that on
the contrary he may have someone by whose sickbed he himself may sit or
whom he may himself release when that person is held prisoner by hostile
hands. Anyone thinking of his own interests and seeking out friendship with
this in view is making a great mistake. Things will end as they began; he has
secured a friend who is going to come to his aid if captivity threatens; at the
first clank of a chain that friend will disappear. These are what are commonly
called fair-weather friendships. A person adopted as a friend for the sake of
his usefulness will be cultivated only for so long as he is useful . . . To procure
friendship only for better and not for worse is to rob it of all its dignity."[42]

Would you rather have friendships based on solidarity, or friends who
will stab you in the back to benefit themselves? To create powerful friendships based on solidarity, Ralph Waldo Emerson offered some useful advice
when he said: "The only way to have a friend is to be one."[43] Today we must
all make an effort to strengthen our muscle of empathy to create more meaningful human relationships, because the well-being of our society, country,
and planet depend on it.

Psychologist Carl Jung explains: "The question of human relationship
and of the inner cohesion of our society is an urgent one in view of the at-
omization of the pent-up mass man, whose personal relationships are un-
dermined by general mistrust. Wherever justice is uncertain and police
spying and terror are at work, human beings fall into isolation, which, of
course, is the aim and purpose of the dictator State . . . To counter this danger, the free society needs a bond of an affective nature, a principle of a kind
like 'caritas,' the Christian love of your neighbor . . . It would therefore be
very much in the interest of the free society to give some thought to the
question of human relationship from the psychological point of view, for in
this resides its real cohesion and consequently its strength. Where love stops,
power begins, and violence, and terror."[44]

Free societies that lack the sturdy foundation of empathy, unconditional love, and true solidarity fall apart. Although in the 1930s Germany had many complex problems, its lack of empathy contributed to its decline into fascism. To prevent this from happening in our own society, we must move beyond the false solidarity that unites people around hatred and fear, and we must move toward real solidarity, which unites people around empathy and unconditional love. During times of turmoil, real solidarity brings us together and gives us the strength to overcome significant challenges.

If humanity is to survive in the twenty-first century and beyond, we must strengthen our muscle of empathy to achieve not only national solidarity but also global solidarity. Our world is so interconnected that we are truly one global family, in which the fate of America is tied to the well-being of other countries and our planet. When other countries in an interconnected world are not safe and secure, it endangers the safety and security of us all.

Two hundred years ago in America, people saw themselves as Virginians or Georgians first and Americans second. But today most of us in the United States have broadened our perspective to see ourselves as Americans first and Virginians or Georgians second. If we take one more step we can go from identifying with our country to feeling connected to the world. This shift will occur when more of us perceive the reality becoming more and more apparent each day: our similarities as human beings outweigh our differences—and we all want hope, opportunity, friends we can trust, and a meaningful life.

Being loyal to our global human family and planet does not mean being disloyal to our country, just as being loyal to our country does not mean being disloyal to our family. The army taught me that loyalty never goes in one direction. In the army I learned that loyalty to one's subordinates through the willingness to sacrifice for them is just as important as loyalty to the Geneva Conventions.

Global solidarity means recognizing our shared humanity in others and working with people around the world to overcome the problems that threaten us all. According to Schweitzer: "The awareness that we are all human beings together has become lost in war and politics. We have reached the point of regarding each other only as members of a people either allied with us or against us and our approach: prejudice, sympathy, or antipathy are all conditioned by that. Now we must rediscover the fact that we—all together—are human beings, and that we must strive to concede to each other what moral capacity we have."[45]

The army has a saying, "One team, one fight." This motto reminds soldiers they are one team involved in a shared struggle to accomplish a mission and what they have in common transcends their differences. The motto "One team, one fight" also applies to soldiers of peace. Whether we realize it or not, humanity is one team, and together we are involved in a shared struggle to ensure our survival and create a brighter future.

The Jewel Within

I believe in that great love, that comes, or should come from our heart, should start at home: with my family, my neighbors across the street, those right next door. And this love should then reach everyone.

—Mother Teresa[46]

As a young child living in Alabama, I did not yet have the intellectual capacity necessary to answer life's difficult questions, but as I grew older I began to read and learn with a growing appetite for understanding. Obsessed with ending the wars between people and the war within my heart, I read hundreds of books on philosophy, religion, history, psychology, and many other subjects. In the military I read Nietzsche, Thoreau, the major religious texts, Hafiz, and ancient Greek philosophy during spare minutes underneath an army tent. While deployed I read many other pioneers of thought as the desert sands shifted around me. What did I learn during those years of intensive study and contemplation?

The greatest gift I received was the kind of wisdom that not only offers guidance but also leads to deeper questioning. Reading the wisdom of our ancestors pointed me in new directions. As I studied our timeless philosophies and religions, I detected the recurring themes of empathy, unconditional love, and solidarity. But these are merely words until we transform them into action. These words are only clichés until we realize how we can apply their strength to our lives. An ancient Buddhist tale, rewritten and expanded to suit our modern times, illustrates a treasure buried within us all:

On the journey of life, a man was walking with a priceless jewel in his hand. Stumbling over one of the many obstacles that challenge us on this journey, he lost his balance. Closing his eyes in fear as he fell to the ground, he dropped the gem and landed facefirst in the mud with a splash. Unbeknown to him, his head struck the fallen gem, lodging it into his forehead. His entire face, including the jewel, was covered in mud. Frantically he searched for the jewel, not realizing that it rested comfortably in his forehead, concealed by a layer of sludge. He looked under rocks and behind trees, but as he searched far and wide he did not think to look within himself.

The jewel of joy and meaning cannot be found under rocks or behind trees. Its full radiance does not exist in mansions or expensive cars. During times of struggle we may believe we have lost the joy and meaning that make life worth living, but although the jewel can be hidden by adversity, we can always find it within us if we know where to look.

Like the person who does not realize he carries a priceless jewel wherever he goes, the jewel of joy and meaning exists in our mind, heart, and shared human spirit. When we look for joy and meaning outside ourselves, the happiness we find is often fleeting and fragile, but the bliss that shines in the depths of our humanity is always there, always strong, always smiling. The Roman philosopher Boethius explains:

> The man who enjoys great wealth may be scorned for his low birth; the man who is honored for his noble family may be oppressed by such poverty that he would rather be unknown. Someone else may enjoy both wealth and social position, but be miserable because he is not married. Still another may be happily married but have no children to inherit his fortune. Others have children, only to be saddened by their vices. Therefore, no one is entirely satisfied with his lot; each finds something lacking, or something which gives pain. Besides, those most blessed are often the most sensitive; unless everything works out perfectly, they are impatient at disappointment and shattered by quite trivial things . . . You see, then, how shoddy is the enjoyment provided by mortal things.

They forsake those who are content with them, and they do
not satisfy those who are discontented. Why then do men
look outside themselves for happiness which is within?[47]

We may lose money and material objects against our will, but we cannot
lose our humanity unless we voluntarily give it away. People can betray us,
but as long as we do not betray our hope and empathy, those human muscles
will never betray us. The highest form of happiness comes from our capacity
to hope, love, appreciate the many gifts of life, and exercise the other muscles
of our humanity. Leo Tolstoy said: "The best way to be happy is, without
any rules, to throw out from oneself on all sides, like a spider, an adhesive
web of love to catch in it all that comes."[48]

Alice Paul and Nelson Mandela demonstrated that the power of hope
and empathy can help us withstand any storm. Alice Paul, an activist who
helped create the constitutional amendment giving American women the
right to vote, was imprisoned and tortured because she struggled for women's
rights; but a solid foundation of hope and empathy gave her the strength to
endure, overcome, and win.

Although Nelson Mandela spent twenty-seven years in prison, his attitude toward his oppressors reminds me of Booker T. Washington's words: "I
will permit no man to narrow and degrade my soul by making me hate
him."[49] During his imprisonment Mandela's respectful and compassionate
attitude toward the prison guards showed his oppressors he could not be
broken. No matter how harshly they treated him, they could not make him
abandon his humanity. Mandela's strength of character earned him respect
among his oppressors and caused a number of them to sympathize with his
cause. Like Alice Paul, the power of Mandela's hope and empathy allowed
him to overcome significant obstacles.

When James Lawson, a civil rights leader whom Martin Luther King
Jr. called "the leading theorist and strategist of nonviolence in the world,"
was asked what made King so effective, Lawson replied: "Love. His ability
to love those who opposed him."[50] King and countless other peaceful warriors showed that Jesus' advice to love our enemies is a mighty weapon in
the struggle to defeat oppression and injustice.

Without the foundation of empathy that leads to unconditional love and solidarity, the understanding and dialogue necessary for peace cannot begin. Loving those who are like us is easy, but the true test of our love's power is the amount of empathy we have for those unlike us. Just as warriors must strengthen the muscles in their bodies, strengthening the muscle of empathy is a rite of passage that all peace warriors must take, and it begins when we strive to see our shared existence with others. Albert Einstein explains: "A human being is part of the whole called by us 'universe,' a part limited in time and space. We experience ourselves, our thoughts, and feelings as something separate from the rest. A kind of optical delusion of consciousness. This delusion is a kind of prison for us, restricting us to our personal desires and to affection for a few persons nearest to us. Our task must be to free ourselves from the prison by widening our circle of compassion to embrace all living creatures and the whole of nature in its beauty . . . We shall require a substantially new manner of thinking if mankind is to survive."[51]

Whether we realize it or not, we all carry the jewel of joy and meaning. For some it is concealed by the mud of ignorance, which makes it possible to dehumanize others. We must clean off the mud that prevents the jewel from surrounding humanity and our planet in its light. The jewel within us shines when we exercise the muscles of our humanity. As our empathy grows and the layers of mud hiding the truth of who we are fall away, we will go beyond an isolated existence. We will become part of something larger than ourselves by experiencing unity with humanity and even all life. We yearn for connection with others just as plants crave sunlight, and the deepest forms of connection result from empathy, unconditional love, and solidarity.

As our empathy grows, our kindness, generosity, and ability to forgive will also increase. Kindness, generosity, and forgiveness are veins in the muscle of empathy. Like the veins in an athlete's arm, which become more visible when the athlete's biceps flex and grow, the stronger the muscle of empathy becomes, the more prominent its veins will be.

The vein of kindness that flows through the muscle of empathy is one of the strongest forces in the world. Schweitzer tells us: "All ordinary force limits itself, for it calls forth a counterforce which sooner or later becomes equal or superior to it. Kindness, however, works simply and steadily. It produces no tensions which impair it. It relaxes existing tensions; it makes mistrust and misunderstandings vanish; it grows stronger, calling forth more kindness. That is why it is the most practical and intensive force. The kindness that a person radiates into the world works on the hearts and thoughts of men. It is our foolish failure that we do not dare practice kindness in earnest. We want to move a great load without availing ourselves of the lever that increases our power a hundredfold."[52]

In future books I will share many exercises for strengthening our empathy and the other muscles of our humanity, but first we must explore what these muscles are and show how they allow us to create greater security, prosperity, and justice for our country and the world. Like all beautifully cut jewels, the jewel of joy and meaning has many facets of which empathy is only one. The following chapters will continue to remove the mud that conceals the light within us.

CHAPTER 3

The Muscle of Appreciation

The Long Journey Home

"Thanks," I said, after tasting the baked potato my friend had cooked for me. "It's very good." He and I were sitting at a table during our evening break. Two soldiers in uniform, we were on another deployment. He was a sergeant in his late thirties; I was a captain in my midtwenties. After working with him during the past several months, I had learned a lot about the person sitting across from me. He possessed the kind of gentleness that arises from struggle. Born in a poor community and educated by hardship, he had developed enormous appreciation for the many joys most people take for granted. I was a better person for knowing him.

"Where did you learn to cook so well?" I asked him.

"Practice." He smiled. "And I'm really not a good cook."

My taste buds disagreed with him. After taking a few more bites, I said, "I'll have to take you up on your offer to visit your family once we leave here."

He looked up from his food and nodded agreeably. I noticed how peaceful everything was in that moment. The nights when schizophrenia loomed over my future seemed so long ago. It had been a misdiagnosis after all. I was well again, and my mother was recovering. My father had died, and so much had changed within me since then.

After my father's stroke on Christmas Day in 2002, his brain had continued to deteriorate. As the months passed he lost his ability to walk and speak, and he rarely recognized me. On one occasion shortly before he died I helped a nurse change his clothes. When we rolled him onto his back, he began screaming and writhing in agony as if he were being beaten. Witnessing this trauma from his childhood, I better understood the pain we both shared, and I became more committed to breaking the cycle of violence.

Those abused during childhood often become adults who repeat the violence toward their own children. Child abuse is a cycle of violence hidden behind closed doors, but it is not the only tragedy concealed from public view. Before medical treatment was available to soldiers with post-traumatic stress disorder, how many veterans throughout the centuries brought their war trauma home to their families? How many tried to drown their suffering in alcohol or took their agony out on those around them?

"Were you always like this?" I asked my sergeant friend. "Were you always so calm and relaxed?"

"Not always," he replied, taking a moment to think quietly. "When I was younger, about your age, I went up to a mountain with the intention of killing myself. I even put a pistol in my mouth, but then I thought about my son and decided this wasn't the right answer."

I stopped eating for a moment.

"Besides you, I've told only one other person that story in my whole life." I understood, because I also rarely spoke about my past.

His words reminded me I was fortunate to be alive and that my journey toward inner healing was far from over. For those of us who have experienced childhood trauma, it is difficult to make peace with the injured parts of ourselves. A dog constantly beaten becomes vicious; the same is true of human beings. The rage we learn is not easily healed, but there is a road leading away from rage that offers hope for each of us. By walking that road the cycle of violence can be put to rest and a new cycle of peace can begin.

"I guess we never know how much someone has suffered, or where they've come from," I said. "Even Gandhi once attempted suicide when he was younger. Most people don't know this about him, but it's in his autobiography." I began eating again.

"And he became Gandhi," my friend said with a laugh. "So maybe there's hope for us all."

The night filled us with its calm, and there was much reason to rejoice. How did I ever forget what was most important in life? How do any of us forget what is so obvious?

"We should probably get back to work," I said.

"Still hungry?" he asked me. "I have some chips left."

"No, I feel pretty good," I said, stretching.

It had been a fulfilling evening. Two friends had shared good food and conversation, and enjoyed the miracle of simply being alive. Forgiveness is like medicine that heals the wounds within us, but forgiveness is a path, not a destination. I savored this moment, remembering that a long journey still awaited me, and I was far away from home.

The Joy of Perspective

When I was fifteen I wrote a short story for an English assignment. A few days later my teacher Mrs. Vaughn said, "I really liked your story. You should think about being a writer." Sometimes a few simple words can radically change our lives. If she had not put the idea of being a writer into my head, I would probably not be alive today.

I had never thought about being a writer before, because I had never liked reading books. But I pondered what she said and realized I had enjoyed writing that story. So I wrote another, and another, and another. I began writing every day and soon realized this was a tool for discovering who I was. It allowed me to explore the festering psychological wounds that had never been tended; it helped me to heal. When I felt powerless in the midst of turmoil, writing helped me maintain my sanity.

My upbringing conditioned me in violent and destructive ways. Writing was the lifeboat that saved me from drowning, but I have met others who pursued music, sports, activism, martial arts, and many other endeavors as vehicles for personal growth and healing. Writing and philosophy soothed my inner wounds in ways alcohol or drugs never could.

When I was not reading books about philosophy in my spare time at West Point, I was usually writing. Sometimes I would write late into the night and barely be able to stay awake in class the next day. I rarely did my homework, and most of my professors saw me as a bad student who didn't pay attention in class and did just enough to get by. But if they could have seen what was underneath my distant stare, they would have known I was preoccupied with an obsession. I was obsessed with finding a solution to the war that raged within me, as well as society's outer wars. Years of research, introspection, and life experience helped me understand how inner and outer conflicts are interconnected; writing allowed me to deepen my search for answers.

One of my roommates at the time mentioned to his girlfriend that I spent every evening writing or reading books that had nothing to do with my classes, and that I had confided in him my secret obsession with solving our human problems. Years later after they were married, she told me about their conversation and how she had responded by saying, "He's either on to something, or he's insane. I think he's insane."

My obsession increased while I was in the army, but as an army officer I was responsible for people's lives, so I had to take my military duties seriously. However, I always took a book with me to work, and I wrote and did research nearly every evening, including Friday and Saturday nights.

Without those countless hours of hard work this book would not exist, yet I owe more to others than I owe to myself. In 2006 Jo Ann Deck, a publishing vice president, called me to discuss her interest in helping me get published. I had sent her an unpublished book, *Nature's Intent*. By that point I had received hundreds of rejection letters for my previous books and stories. But I did not give up, and Jo Ann began working with me daily to further develop my writing.

Although I had started writing at fifteen, I had never taken a writing class and never met a published writer or anyone who worked in the field. After working with Jo Ann for three years to improve my writing, *Will War Ever End?* (the fifth book I had written) was published in 2009.

A few words uttered by Mrs. Vaughn and Jo Ann's dedicated help changed my life in more ways than I can count. Their kindness also changed my perspective on life. I remember the way I bottled up my anger before discovering the healing power of writing. I remember the frustration of not being able to express my thoughts because my writing skills were not properly developed. I remember what it was like to be without a lifeboat, and these recollections make me grateful. When you know what it is to be without, you can experience more joy and appreciation for life's many gifts.

In *The End of War*, my second published book, I asked a question that caused me to see appreciation, joy, and life in a new way. *What always feels good, every single time, with no exceptions?*

The answer is not eating or sleeping, because consuming too much food and spending too much time in bed can make us feel ill. Since most pleasures hurt when we experience them in excess, is it possible for anything to always feel good, every single time, with no exceptions? When I was in the army, I realized this riddle does have an answer.

A few years ago, during the winter, I came home to my apartment after spending two weeks on an army field exercise. After sleeping in a cold desert during that time, I ended up coming home to a different apartment. Physically it was the same, but my attitude toward it made it seem entirely different. My hot shower felt like absolute bliss and my warm bed felt like paradise on earth. Simple things such as having food in my refrigerator, a nice shave, and indoor plumbing were gifts to savor and appreciate every day.

This encouraged me to ask and answer some life-changing questions. Why did my apartment, and its warmth, feel like paradise after returning from two weeks in the cold desert? And why did I, like so many other people, often take these gifts for granted?

When I asked myself these questions, I had an epiphany. Appreciation always feels good, every single time, with no exceptions. When I appreciate something it is always a joyful experience. Although it is not easy, I have even learned to appreciate the strife and struggle in my life because these challenges have taught me valuable lessons, making me into who I am today.

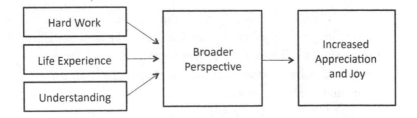

Figure 3.1: Perspective

When you have to work hard for something, the sweat and toil broaden your perspective, giving you more appreciation for your achievement. Writing and military life widened my perspective not only through hard work, they also changed how I saw the world by increasing my life experience and understanding. Owen Morris, a sergeant in the Marine Corps who deployed twice to Afghanistan, explains how his military service broadened his perspective and appreciation:

> On an unusually warm summer night I find myself walking down the streets of San Francisco with a group of friends. I am recently returned from Afghanistan on my second tour with the Marines, and the city scene is a stark contrast to the places I've recently been. In my head, as we walk, I realize the overwhelming pleasantness of my situation. The weather is a perfect summer night. The restaurants are teeming with activity that spills out of the open doors and windows then down on the street. Our pace is slowed by a person in an electric wheelchair, but there's no reason for this to frustrate us. It's like she's there as the universe's way of forcing us to slow down and appreciate our surroundings. Several blocks down, an ambulance drives through the intersection, sirens wailing. A man passes us going the other direction wearing what can only be described as a onesie, dreadlocks, elton john glasses, and a man purse. I suddenly feel connected to all of it all at once.
>
> How great of a place do we live in that we have medics just waiting to help us? How great that you can be born handicapped, but still have the freedom in your life to enjoy the night walk with us? How great that people can dress how they want and live how they want?
>
> It's like the night is proof that the world isn't quite the shitbox everyone keeps saying it is. And if that's true, then maybe we aren't such horrible life forms after all.[1]

When we broaden our perspective as Sergeant Morris did, we can embrace the many joys of life most of us take for granted. However, we don't have to serve in the military or experience a war zone to increase our perspective and appreciation. Many paths allow us to work hard and gain more life experience and understanding. Also, we don't have to be shot at on a daily basis to appreciate being alive, because contemplation, meditation, and other techniques can help us savor the gift of life.

Albert Schweitzer said: "We must all become familiar with the thought of death if we want to grow into really good people. We need not think of it every day or every hour. But when the path of life leads us to some vantage point where the scene around us fades away and we contemplate the distant view right to the end, let us not close our eyes. Let us pause for a moment, look at the distant view, and then carry on. Thinking about death in this way produces true love for life. When we are familiar with death, we accept each week, each day, as a gift. Only if we are able thus to accept life—bit by bit—does it become precious."[2]

Savoring: A Higher Expression of Appreciation

The *American Heritage Dictionary* defines *savor* as "to appreciate fully; enjoy or relish." Although savoring and joy are synonymous with appreciation, a strong muscle of appreciation gives us far more than just a pleasant feeling. In the last section I discussed how hard work, life experience, and understanding can broaden our perspective in a way that increases our appreciation. In this section I will explain how an increase in appreciation can also broaden our perspective on life.

As our muscle of appreciation grows stronger, it changes how we relate to the world, allowing us to savor the present moment. When we savor the moment as we would our favorite food, we become more fully alive, more aware. Like a powerful microscope, the muscle of appreciation brings the present moment into focus. Just as a microscope allows us to see deeper, appreciation helps us observe our thoughts, actions, and humanity with greater clarity. The Buddhist monk Thich Nhat Hanh explains how savoring the moment changes our perspective and brings life into focus:

To my mind, the idea that doing dishes is unpleasant can occur only when you aren't doing them. Once you are standing in front of the sink with your sleeves rolled up and your hands in the warm water, it is really quite pleasant. I enjoy taking my time with each dish, being fully aware of the dish, the water, and each movement of my hands. I know that if I hurry in order to eat dessert sooner, the time of washing dishes will be unpleasant and not worth living. That would be a pity, for each minute, each second of life is a miracle. The dishes themselves and the fact that I am here washing them are miracles!

If I am incapable of washing dishes joyfully, if I want to finish them quickly so I can go and have dessert, I will be equally incapable of enjoying my dessert. With the fork in my hand, I will be thinking about what to do next, and the texture and the flavor of the dessert, together with the pleasure of eating it, will be lost. I will always be dragged into the future, never able to live in the present moment . . .

I must confess it takes me a bit longer to do the dishes, but I live fully in every moment, and I am happy. Washing the dishes is at the same time a means and an end—that is, not only do we do the dishes in order to have clean dishes, we also do the dishes just to do the dishes, to live fully in each moment while washing them.[3]

Our attitude toward washing dishes depends on our perspective. There were many times in Iraq when I wished I were home in America washing dishes. How many starving people around the world wish they could be washing dishes in their own home with a belly full of food? Just as appreciation allows Thich Nhat Hanh to see washing dishes not as a chore but as a pleasure, the muscle of appreciation helps me perceive my living situation from a joyous perspective. Appreciation allows me to perceive my apartment as a paradise on earth, where I have luxuries unimaginable a few hundred years ago. The philosopher Francis Bacon said "knowledge is power," and one of the luxuries I enjoy every day is access to knowledge.

Books are some of the most powerful things in the world. If you doubt this, consider why it was illegal to teach slaves how to read.[4] Also think about why the Nazis burned books and why throughout history dictators have banned books. One of the biggest threats to slavery, the Nazis, dictators, or any unjust system is books. Slave owners knew this. The Nazis knew this. Dictators know this today. Yet so many people take books for granted, just as I did when I was a teenager.

What makes books so dangerous is that they are filled with ideas, and once ideas are unleashed into the world they cannot be destroyed by violence. Ideas such as liberty, justice, and peace spread like viruses. But unlike the viruses that make us physically ill, the ideas spread by Socrates, Susan B. Anthony, Gandhi, and Martin Luther King Jr. heal the human spirit and are lethal to hatred, greed, oppression, and injustice.

Unlike people, not all books are created equal. Some books increase our fear and hatred. Others contain great wisdom and serve as teachers and guides. In our quest to create a brighter future, they give us a solid foundation of ideas and history to stand on. On this foundation we can build a future with a degree of peace and justice unthinkable to many of us living today, just as my ancestors who were slaves could not imagine the luxury of my modern daily existence.

Although my income is modest, in many ways I am wealthy beyond measure. A thousand years ago books were extremely expensive. Only a handful of people could afford them and very few knew how to read. But today in my apartment I have hundreds of books. I also have hundreds of films and documentaries filled with knowledge, wisdom, and inspiring stories. Since humanity has existed, we have marveled at stories. Our earliest ancestors told them around campfires, and in my apartment technology gives me access to a vast wealth of human stories.

I also have Internet access, which still seems miraculous to me. The Internet puts the world at my fingertips. Not only does it allow me to explore any subject with a few clicks of my keyboard, it also lets me communicate with people all over the world. A few hundred years ago, it would have taken months for a message to travel halfway across the world. Today email lets me send a message around the globe at virtually the speed of light. Time spent on the Internet can be a waste of time, or it can be a priceless investment of our time.

With the flick of a switch, the miracle of electricity allows me to summon light into any room in my apartment. If I want food I simply have to open my refrigerator door. If I want heat I just have to turn a dial. If I am hurt I only have to tap a few buttons on my cell phone and medical workers will rescue me. If I am in danger a few taps on my cell phone will also summon the police to help me—men and women who will risk their lives to save mine. And perhaps the greatest luxury of all is access to clean water, the stuff of life. To get it I only have to turn a handle, and I can make it hot, warm, or cold.

As the moments pass in the paradise on earth that is my apartment, I savor these luxuries as I explore the great mysteries of the universe. And there is so much to savor, because although I live in a small one-bedroom apartment, I have a higher quality of life than kings and queens who lived hundreds of years ago. Yet despite these luxuries, the gifts I appreciate most are the treasures I cannot buy with a credit card or ever truly own. Friendship. Family. Good health. A beautiful day. The joy of savoring the moment. The happiness that flows from strengthening my hope, empathy, appreciation, and the other muscles of our humanity. Love.

But because appreciation is an attitude, a way of looking at the world, occasionally old psychological wounds reopen that prevent me from seeing how fortunate I am. Sometimes the trauma from my childhood blocks appreciation and turns my apartment into a frightening place. On days like this my heart hardens to protect itself. Because I am afraid, my empathy retreats from the world like a turtle withdrawing into its shell. We all have good days and bad, and by working to strengthen our muscles of hope, empathy, and appreciation, we can experience more moments of heightened appreciation and awakened perspective.

On a good day, my apartment feels like a paradise on earth. When I am at war with myself, it is hell on earth. There are also varying degrees of appreciation where I live somewhere between heaven and hell. By exploring appreciation's ability to shape our perspective, I realize that John Milton was correct when he wrote in *Paradise Lost*: "The mind is its own place, and in itself can make a Heaven of Hell, a Hell of Heaven."[5]

Stewardship: The Highest Expression of Appreciation

Appreciation allows me to savor the luxuries and joys most of us take for granted, and it helps me put my life in perspective. From the viewpoint of my ancestors who were slaves and the billions of people on the planet who lack food and clean water, my apartment is indeed a paradise. But as I explained in *The End of War*, appreciation is not only an inherently joyful experience that allows us to savor the moment. It also profoundly changes our behavior.

After spending two weeks in the cold desert on an army field exercise, as I mentioned earlier, I pondered why appreciation always feels good. This caused me to ask several questions that changed my life.

What happens if I appreciate my apartment? I wondered. If I appreciate my apartment, I will tend to it and cherish it. I will not trash the things I own; I will take good care of them. I will take nothing for granted, no matter how small or insignificant it might seem to other people, and I will be grateful for everything I have.

What happens if I appreciate my friends? I wondered. If I appreciate my friends, I will care about them and treat them well. I will not take our time together upon this earth for granted, and I will show my appreciation by trying to be a good friend.

What happens if I appreciate my freedom? I wondered. If I appreciate my freedom, I will never take it for granted. I will be an active and responsible citizen who understands that I must safeguard the liberties my ancestors fought so hard for. I will make the most of my freedom by using this gift to make my country and planet a better place to live.

What happens if I appreciate my health? I wondered. If I appreciate my health, I will never take it for granted, and every day I wake up healthy will be a day to celebrate. Because I do not take my health for granted I will try to exercise, eat well, and take care of my body.

What happens if I appreciate writing? I wondered. If I appreciate writing, I will remember all of the people and countless hours of hard work that were necessary for me to grow as a writer. I will realize how fortunate I am to not only have the ability to write, but to live in a country where I have freedom of expression. I will make the most of this gift by continuing to work hard and never taking writing for granted.

What happens if I appreciate our planet? I wondered. If I appreciate our planet, I will never take clean air and green trees for granted. I will be grateful for the simple joys of nature and I will do everything in my power to take care of these gifts.

What happens if I appreciate being alive? I wondered. If I appreciate being alive, I will never take life for granted and I will live every day to its fullest. The Roman poet Horace encouraged us to "Carpe diem!" Appreciation allows me to "Seize the day!" and to remember that life is a gift we must never squander.

Wow, I thought.

Not only does appreciation always feel good, it also dramatically improves our behavior. It urges us to behave as stewards: as responsible people. It causes us to take nothing for granted, to make the most of every opportunity, and to see everything in life as a gift. Why? Because in reality everything in life is a gift.

Appreciation allows us to relate to the world without a sense of entitlement. In this way, appreciation allows us to perceive reality because this is how the world really works. I am not owed tomorrow and being alive today truly is a gift. Since I might die tomorrow it makes sense to live life to its fullest, to never take my life for granted, and to "Seize the day!"

In reality I am also not entitled to a warm apartment, friends, freedom, a healthy body, or a clean planet. Because these gifts are fragile and easily lost through my carelessness or irresponsibility, I should never take them for granted; I should always nurture and protect them.

By encouraging us to take care of our friends, family, freedom, and planet, appreciation helps us behave responsibly. Appreciation is the psychological foundation of stewardship, and stewardship is the highest expression of appreciation.

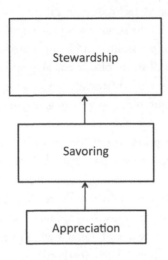

Figure 3.2: The Muscle of Appreciation

Here is an example of how appreciation leads to stewardship. If you want to teach children to take care of their health, they will be most receptive to hearing this message right after recovering from the flu. Many of us take our health for granted and only appreciate the bliss of being healthy when we become ill. Right after recovering from the flu, the illness is recent enough in our memory to remind us that being healthy is a gift we should never take for granted.

If we do not make an effort to strengthen our muscle of appreciation, we will take our health for granted soon after regaining our health. A strong muscle of appreciation protects us from the amnesia of ingratitude that quickly makes us forget how fortunate we are.

Hard work is one way to strengthen our appreciation. Those who work hard to buy their first car and appreciate what they have take better care of their vehicle than spoiled people who never have to work for anything and take everything for granted. Working hard increases our appreciation by helping us realize we are not entitled to something; if we were entitled we wouldn't have to work so hard for it. Hard work is one of many paths toward increasing our appreciation. There are also many mental exercises for transforming a weak sense of appreciation into a large muscle of stewardship. I present a simple meditative technique for this in *The End of War*.

Stewardship is one of the surest signs of strength in a human being, because it means taking responsibility and being a protector. If we do not take responsibility for the well-being of our country and planet, humanity will not survive. We must develop an attitude of stewardship to create the future needed for humanity's survival, and we can gain guidance from our ancient traditions.

A Native American proverb says: "Before eating, always take a little time to thank the food."[6] Expressing appreciation before a meal is also a tradition practiced in many religions. Although appreciation is an essential part of being human, we live in a world where expressing it has become a form of lip service. Strengthening our muscle of appreciation allows us to transform gratitude from words into a way of life, allowing us to *live in gratitude*.

Joseph Campbell tells us: "These [early tribal] societies had such respect for nature that they would not kill more animals than they could eat . . . So they killed only as many as they actually needed, and they thanked the animals, performing a ritual so there would be food again. You don't have people strip-mining the earth when they respect it in that way. Then comes our Western tradition, where man is made to use the animals and use the earth and all that kind of thing with complete disregard . . . That's a ruthless attitude."[7]

Campbell is describing the ruthless attitude of ingratitude that takes and takes and takes without ever contributing. Or if it does contribute, it gives with one hand and takes with both. Greed has made people behave like plunderers, but our survival depends on stewards, not plunderers.

Citizenship is a form of stewardship, and as active citizens who practice democracy we can become stewards who protect our country and planet. When we take the responsibility of citizenship seriously we become stewards of justice, liberty, and peace. The theme of citizenship as a form of stewardship is embodied in John F. Kennedy's famous saying: "And so, my fellow Americans: ask not what your country can do for you—ask what you can do for your country."[8]

When we do not appreciate our country, we lean toward selfishness rather than service. When we do not appreciate our planet, we become plunderers instead of protectors. When we do not appreciate people's kindness, we may try to take advantage of their kindness. But beware when you take advantage of someone's kindness. When we do not appreciate something, we will behave in a way that makes us more likely to lose it.

Remembering Prometheus

Developing a true sense of gratitude involves taking absolutely nothing for granted, wherever it be, whatever its source.[9]
—Albert Schweitzer

In Greek mythology, Prometheus was the wisest of the Titans. Descended from Gaia, ancient goddess of the earth, and brother of Atlas, who held the sky on his shoulders, Prometheus' compassion for humanity led to an incident that not only defined him, but condemned him.

Against the wishes of Zeus, king of the gods, Prometheus stole the gift of fire from the gods and gave it to humanity. As punishment, Zeus had him chained to a rock where he remained helpless while a giant eagle ate his liver. Every night his liver grew back so that the eagle could consume it again the next day.

Prometheus is the first Christ figure—a person who sacrifices himself for the well-being of humanity—to appear in the annals of literature, history, or mythology.[10] Although he is a mythological hero, Prometheus represents something very real.

The discovery of how to create and control fire has been as vital to the growth of human civilization as the inventions of writing and the wheel, yet fire is something we often take for granted. To me, the gift of fire symbolizes the endless gifts we take for granted every day: gifts such as liberty, freedom of speech, clean water, education, food, access to information, the opportunity to practice democracy, and so much more. Prometheus represents the countless people who sacrificed so we could have better lives today. Because of them I have benefitted in more ways than I can fathom.

Socrates, Jesus, Lao Tzu, Confucius, Buddha, Henry David Thoreau, Leo Tolstoy, Susan B. Anthony, Albert Schweitzer, Mahatma Gandhi, Martin

Luther King Jr., and countless others have increased the peace in our world. They have also changed my life with their words and actions. Their words reached me at a critical time when my hope and sanity were fading, and their actions helped create the liberties and human rights we have today. But for every person whose name is known and celebrated, so many remain unknown.

Martin Luther King Jr. said: "Help me to realize that I'm where I am because of the forces of history and because of the fifty thousand Negroes of Alabama who will never get their names in the papers and in the headlines."[11] King succeeded because many people waged peace with him. They built the foundation that makes positive change on a large scale possible. And Schweitzer remarked: "The sum of these [actions from people who aren't famous], however, is a thousand times stronger than the acts of those who receive wide public recognition. The latter, compared to the former, are like the foam on the waves of a deep ocean."[12]

For every person we know of who worked so future generations could have a better life, there are countless others whose names are hidden. Yet they live on through us. Their service is part of us, and every time we appreciate the liberties so many of us take for granted, we honor the people who made those liberties possible.

A simple act of kindness can make as much difference in a person's life as a social movement. Receiving a few encouraging words from my English teacher Mrs. Vaughn was one of the most life-changing things that ever happened to me. An act of kindness, like pebbles creating ripples in a pond, can affect people in ways we cannot imagine. David Krieger, president of the Nuclear Age Peace Foundation, spoke at a high school graduation in 2000. Ten years later, a woman who graduated that day came up and talked to him. Now a third-year medical student, she said that she heard him speak during a very difficult time in her life, and that his words inspired and helped her immensely.

When you perform an act of kindness or speak for the change our world needs, you are creating a ripple and planting a seed. You never know what effect the ripple may have and you never know what the seed might become. In our educational system the ripples of peace, which have dramatically improved our lives for the better, are rarely taught.

America's Founding Fathers rebelled against Great Britain because they felt unfairly treated. They believed it was unjust to be taxed or controlled without the opportunity to participate in the political process. The motto "No taxation without representation" echoed their outrage and became a call to arms, leading to the American Revolution. But until the 1820s, fifty years later, less than 10 percent of the American population could vote. Women could not vote. African Americans could not vote. And most white people could not vote unless they owned land. During the early nineteenth century "No taxation without representation" only seemed to apply to the rich.

How did so many Americans increase their liberties during the past two hundred years? Did nonlandowners fight a war to obtain the right to vote? Did women fight a war to get the right to vote? Did African Americans fight a war to attain their civil rights? Did American workers fight a war to gain their rights? Was a war fought for child labor laws? These victories for liberty and justice were achieved because people waged peace, but this is a part of our history that many people do not remember.

Waging peace is more than opposing problems that personally affect us. German citizen Albert Schweitzer healed the sick in Africa and advocated for the humane treatment of animals. Martin Luther King Jr. tried to improve the lives of poor white people, and Thoreau—a white man—spoke against slavery. I, along with every other African American, owe a great debt to women such as Susan B. Anthony, Elizabeth Cady Stanton, Lucretia Mott, and Lucy Stone, because these female activists struggled for the abolition of slavery during a time when women were forbidden from voting and owning property.

Frederick Douglass said, "When I ran away from slavery, it was for myself. When I advocated emancipation, it was for my people; but when I stood up for the rights of woman, self was out of the question, and I found a little nobility in the act."[13] Today white women are allowed to vote and own property because of black men like Frederick Douglass, and black men have benefitted from the sacrifices of many white female activists. That is the beauty of waging peace.

Take a moment to ponder the millions of people who struggled and were beaten, imprisoned, tortured, and even killed so civil, women's, children's, and human rights could spread. And think of how much work still has to be done for justice to achieve its full potential in the United States and the world. Consider all the people today who still lack the gifts of liberty, opportunity, freedom of speech, clean water, education, food, access to information, and the chance to practice democracy. Do we have a responsibility to do something about it?

In the movie *Saving Private Ryan*, Captain John Miller leads a group of soldiers on a mission to save Private James Ryan. Captain Miller and his men save Private Ryan but are all killed during the mission. As Captain Miller is dying from his wounds, his last words to Private Ryan are "Earn this. Earn it."

Just as a group of people struggle and die to save Private Ryan, countless people throughout history struggled and died to give us a better quality of life. I could spend a hundred lifetimes working for peace and not come close to earning the sacrifices that made me who I am. But as long as I try to earn the life I have been given, I will be honoring those who came before me, serving those who are alive today, and contributing to the well-being of future generations.

Every day, I am grateful to Mrs. Vaughn, Jo Ann, and so many others who made my writing possible. Every day, I appreciate the multitudes who struggled and are still struggling for liberty, justice, human rights, and peace. Because my appreciation gives me a sense of stewardship, I try to make myself worthy of the sacrifices that allowed me to be here today by taking action. The writer Alice Walker said: "Activism is my rent for living on the planet."[14] We must all try our best to pay the rent.

In the last chapter I discussed how kindness, generosity, and forgiveness are veins in the muscle of empathy. In a similar way, humility is a vein in the muscle of appreciation. Like the veins in an athlete's arm, which become more visible when the athlete's biceps flex and grow, the stronger the muscle of appreciation becomes, the more prominent the vein of humility will be. Increasing our perspective through appreciation helps us realize how much we owe to others, which enlarges our humility. Albert Einstein explained:

> When we survey our lives and endeavors, we soon observe
> that almost the whole of our actions and desires is bound up
> with the existence of other human beings. We notice that our

whole nature resembles that of the social animals. We eat food that others have produced, wear clothes that others have made, live in houses that others have built. The greater part of our knowledge and beliefs has been communicated to us by other people through the medium of a language which others have created. Without language, our mental capacities would be poor indeed . . . The individual is what he is and has the significance that he has not so much in virtue of his individuality, but rather as a member of a great human community, which directs his material and spiritual existence from the cradle to the grave.[15]

Astronomer Carl Sagan said: "If we see far, it is because we stand on the shoulders of giants."[16] If you find my ideas hopeful, uplifting, and useful for creating positive change, it is because I stand on the shoulders of giants. My ideas are built on a foundation of ideas that came before me. I am simply a link in a chain that grows stronger with every generation—a chain that is working to bind war and injustice.

Everyone who works for peace is a link in the chain that will someday imprison war and injustice, but to know where we are going we first have to remember where we came from. To solve our national and global problems we must appreciate the people who, like Prometheus, sacrificed for liberty, justice, and peace. We must savor the endless gifts of life and transform our appreciation into stewardship. Other words for stewardship are *citizenship*, *responsibility*, and *action*.

Motivated by his compassion for human beings, Prometheus took action by giving the gift of fire to humanity. He symbolizes our capacity to also take action. He is a metaphor that lives in all of us, but what we do now is up to us. What gifts will we continue to take for granted? What gifts will we give to future generations? And where would our world be without Prometheus?

CHAPTER 4

The Muscle of Conscience

The Hunter That Never Sleeps

It was a dusty afternoon in Iraq. I was standing on a roof overlooking the concrete wall and barbed wire that separated our forward operating base from the rest of Baghdad. Less than a hundred meters away, Iraqi civilians went about their daily routines. Adults did not look at us, and children gathered in a group to mock us and make obscene gestures. I stood guard with two soldiers, looking at the houses and roads for any signs of danger while several soldiers behind us assembled a small radar.

We had already assembled several radars across the perimeter. When this last one was ready, incoming mortars and rockets could be detected, and an alarm would warn people on the base when a deadly impact was imminent, giving them time to take cover. The radars could also be linked with an automatic machine gun capable of intercepting mortars and rockets. If we performed our job properly, fewer U.S. soldiers and Iraqi civilians working on the base would be injured or killed.

Although I believed my actions would lead to fewer casualties, my mind was deeply troubled for reasons I was trying to understand. A year ago a soldier on this mission had been shot by a sniper while repairing a radar near the perimeter. On this dry October day in 2006, none of us knew that before the deployment was over another sniper would kill a soldier on the radar team. At this height we were an easy target, but something else was troubling me.

Because I was in the air and missile defense branch, I had been deployed with the Patriot air defense system during Operation Iraqi Freedom in 2003. The Patriot units, whose primary purpose was to intercept Iraqi missiles launched at Kuwait, had successfully destroyed nine missiles. After the defense of Kuwait my branch's mission was focused on defending South Korea from a North Korean missile attack, so we were rarely sent to Iraq.

I had deep concerns about the Iraq War, but as hostilities escalated during 2006 and U.S. casualties grew, I became increasingly frustrated by many things. Soldiers had been deployed without proper body armor and many vehicles lacked sufficient armor plating. As my frustration grew, I decided to volunteer for a deployment helping to install the counter-rocket, artillery, and mortar (C-RAM) system in bases across Iraq.

I had seen the C-RAM system grow from its experimental stages and had spent more time with it than most soldiers. Since I could contribute to the success of this life-saving system in Iraq, didn't I have a responsibility to act? But if I had deep concerns about the Iraq War, was it right for me to volunteer for the deployment? Although it would have been easier for me not to question and just do what I was told, West Point had taught me to think, and my humanity urged me to question. As I searched for answers I wondered, *What would Gandhi do?*

Gandhi was possibly the most famous army recruiter in history. He served as a recruiter for the British Empire during the Boer War in 1899, Second Zulu War in 1906, and World War I in 1914. He was also a medic during the Boer and Zulu Wars, and his aim was to save lives.[1] The British awarded him the War Medal for his courage during the Boer War, and he intended to serve as a medic during World War I, but an illness prevented him.[2] If Gandhi believed it was ethical for someone to serve in war as a medic, couldn't I volunteer for a mission that would save lives by destroying mortars and rockets?

Although Gandhi recruited medics in 1899, 1906, and 1914, he went even further in 1918 by recruiting Indians to fight in the infantry during World War I. He said:

> I have been travelling all over India these days and I tell you, from what I have seen for myself, that India has altogether lost the capacity to fight. It has not a particle of the courage it should have. If even a tiger should make its appearance in a village, the people would not have the strength to

go and kill it and so they petition the Collector to have it
killed. Nor do they have the strength to fight back dacoits
[robbers], should any descend on the village. Can a nation,
whose citizens are incapable of self-defense, enjoy swaraj [in-
dependence]? Swaraj is not for lawyers and doctors but only
for those who possess strength of arms. How can a people who
are incapable of defending their lives, their women and children, their cattle and their lands, ever enjoy swaraj? . . . When
the people become physically fit and strong enough to wield
the sword, swaraj will be theirs for the asking . . . From my
experience during the last three months, I know that we are
utterly timid.[3]

Like many of us, Gandhi was conflicted over his views and tried to reconcile his love of peace with his participation in war. He dedicated his life
to peace but disliked cowardice and timidity. Although he saw people refuse
to participate in war because of their moral courage and inner strength, he
also saw many refuse because they were afraid of putting themselves at risk.
Gandhi was concerned that his fellow Indians were avoiding military service
not out of high moral principles but because they were surrendering to fear.

Anything worthwhile requires risk. This is true not only in waging peace
but also in life. Martin Luther King Jr. said: "A man who won't die for something is not fit to live."[4] Most of us are willing to die for something, such as
our family, country, freedom, or ideals. This fact of human nature makes
war propaganda extremely effective, yet war propaganda has had to evolve
in the twenty-first century because dehumanization is more difficult today
than ever before.

During World War II, the United States was openly at war not only
with the German and Japanese governments, but also with their civilians.
American bombing campaigns targeted heavily populated civilian areas, and
countless women, children, and elderly were killed by bombs dropped on
Dresden, Tokyo, Hiroshima, Nagasaki, and other cities. Posters were used
to dehumanize the German and Japanese people; one official government
poster read STAY ON THE JOB UNTIL EVERY MURDERING JAP IS WIPED OUT![5]

However, prior to the invasion of Iraq in 2003 the American government portrayed the Iraqi people as human beings very similar to us. Instead of trying to dehumanize the entire Iraqi population, American politicians said that most Iraqis crave freedom and democracy just like we did, and it was our responsibility to liberate them from Saddam Hussein's brutal reign. On October 7, 2002, President Bush said:

> America believes that all people are entitled to hope and human rights, to the nonnegotiable demands of human dignity. People everywhere prefer freedom to slavery, prosperity to squalor, self-government to the rule of terror and torture. America is a friend to the people of Iraq. Our demands are directed only at the regime that enslaves them and threatens us. When these demands are met, the first and greatest benefit will come to Iraqi men, women and children. The oppression of Kurds, Assyrians, Turkomen, Shia, Sunnis and others will be lifted, the long captivity of Iraq will end, and an era of new hope will begin.
>
> Iraq is a land rich in culture and resources and talent. Freed from the weight of oppression, Iraq's people will be able to share in the progress and prosperity of our time. If military action is necessary, the United States and our allies will help the Iraqi people rebuild their economy and create the institutions of liberty in a unified Iraq, at peace with its neighbors.[6]

What makes war propaganda so dangerous is not its lies but its half-truths. President Bush's speech is effective because it is not an outright lie. There is truth when he says, "People everywhere prefer freedom to slavery, prosperity to squalor, self-government to the rule of terror and torture . . . Iraq is a land rich in culture and resources and talent. Freed from the weight of oppression, Iraq's people will be able to share in the progress and prosperity of our time." But when we look deeper at the real motivations behind the U.S. invasion of Iraq, we begin to see that only half the truth was being told.

A lie is similar to an enemy intent on hurting you. Like attackers who hide in the darkness, lies are most dangerous when they are hidden, when we don't realize they are there. A half-truth, on the other hand, can be compared to a trusted friend who betrays you. President Bush's speech contains elements of truth that honor our highest ideals and lift our human spirit, which leads to trust. A speech that is merely an outright lie is dangerous, but a speech composed of half-truths is far more dangerous.

As our world becomes more interconnected and information flows more freely around the globe, it is becoming more difficult to dehumanize people. Director Akira Kurosawa believed films have the power to bring humanity together, because they can put us in the shoes of people from different times and cultures. In *Seven Samurai* he shows us life from the perspective of peasant farmers and samurai living in sixteenth-century Japan. What makes this film so powerful is the way Kurosawa created so many characters we can identify with.

Some movies certainly perpetuate division and hatred, but many broaden our perspective by helping us see the world from a different point of view. Popular films such as *Rocky*, *Forrest Gump*, and *The Shawshank Redemption* urge us to feel compassion for characters in situations much different from our own. The ability of a film to summon our empathy is perhaps best demonstrated in Pixar's *WALL-E*, which led me to feel immense compassion for the main character—a robot. If a movie can humanize a machine, imagine the potential to humanize actual human beings.

Films, books, songs, and other forms of art can summon our empathy. This makes dehumanization much more difficult, but war propaganda is a clever and adaptive foe. Dehumanization still happens in America, but it is subtler and more sophisticated than it was fifty or a hundred years ago.

Being in Baghdad gave me a lot of time to think and be alone with my thoughts. I realized the important question is not "What would Gandhi do?" but "What should each of us do to be a force for good in the circumstances that surround us?" During the days and nights in Iraq, in my waking thoughts and in my dreams, something within me hunted for justification. Could I justify volunteering for a deployment to Iraq? Could I justify my participation in a war that broke the Charter of the United Nations and thereby violated the U.S. Constitution, which states treaties are the "supreme law of the land"?

When our conscience does not find adequate justification for our actions, we become its prey. Its arrows are made of guilt and their maddening sting can drive us to suicide. However, there are three ways to escape the wrath of a guilty conscience. The first is to hide in ignorance, because when we are unaware of our wrongdoing or how our actions hurt others, guilt loses its sting. Second, we can decrease our empathy to a point where our heart turns to stone. A hardened heart deflects the arrows of guilt, because a person who lacks empathy for people has little reason to feel guilty. Third, we can give the hunter what it wants.

Ignorance is a fragile hiding place continually threatened by new information, and only the most ruthless psychopaths can completely shut off their empathy. But if we choose the third way and give our conscience what it wants—justification that arises not from deceiving ourselves but from being honest with ourselves—it becomes one of our greatest allies in the quest for a more humane and peaceful world. When we stop running from our conscience, it guides us on the road to inner and outer peace. When we cooperate with rather than fight our conscience, it becomes a moral compass pointing us toward ethical decisions that help rather than harm.

After seeing Iraqi civilians suffer immensely from the consequences of war, I realized that rationalizing my decision to deploy based on Gandhi's participation in war and my determination to help my comrades did not give my conscience the justification it craved. When I tried to sleep, my conscience kept me up at night. When I slept, it haunted my dreams. As I stood on that rooftop in Baghdad, my conscience was not content with the path I had chosen. And as long as my conscience was not at peace, I would never be at peace.

The Ultimate Survival Guide

While waiting at an airport on a quiet afternoon, I began to understand why our conscience is vital to human survival. It was 2006 and I was an army captain traveling with an air force captain and army major. The three of us were returning home from a work-related trip. As we waited to board the airplane, the airline told us the flight only had two open seats available, so one of us would have to stay behind. The next flight would not depart until the following morning. Who should stay behind? Me, the air force captain, or the army major who outranked us both and also had the flu?

The air force captain and I both offered to stay behind, but the army major would not let either of us give up our seat. We tried to persuade him, pointing out he had the flu and should return home immediately to rest, but he refused to put his well-being above ours. In a society that conditions people to be selfish and greedy, his attitude might seem strange. But when I pondered his decision I was able to peer into the secrets of the human conscience and comprehend its power.

To understand the situation at the airport, we must journey back thousands of years to the African plains where our ancestors struggled for many generations. In nature it is common for the largest lion, wolf, or chimpanzee to assert its authority and control the members of its group by relying on superior size and strength. But human beings are different from other mammals because we cannot effectively control each other with size and strength.

For example, in a pride of lions or pack of wolves the highest-ranking male usually eats first. But in the U.S. military the highest-ranking soldiers are supposed to eat last, putting the well-being of others above their own. Why does the U.S. military seem backward from lion prides, wolf packs, chimpanzee troops, and other mammal groups where the dominant males serve themselves before others? The reason is simple, and it begins with our large brains.

Imagine an early human tribe where a physically small male is trying to feed his children but a much larger and stronger male is unfairly hoarding all the food. The larger male who puts his personal welfare above the well-being of his community will not be able to maintain his dominance with physical size and strength, no matter how big he is. Why not?

Lions, wolves, and chimpanzees can dominate each other with superior size and strength, but human beings are different because we can do something these mammals cannot. If I am living in the wilderness and a much larger male is bullying me and the other members of our tribe, I can crush his skull with a rock while he sleeps. Intelligence is the great equalizer. It not only allows us to recognize fundamental differences in fairness, but our large brains also give us the ability to kill people while they sleep. No other mammal has the ability to commit premeditated murder in this way.

Studies show other animals are also capable of recognizing some differences in fairness. In an article written for National Public Radio, Nell Greenfieldboyce says:

Dogs have an intuitive understanding of fair play and become resentful if they feel that another dog is getting a better deal, a new study has found. The study, in the Proceedings of the National Academy of Sciences, looked at how dogs react when a buddy is rewarded for the same trick in an unequal way. Friederike Range, a researcher at the University of Vienna in Austria, and her colleagues did a series of experiments with dogs who knew how to respond to the command "give the paw," or shake. The dogs were normally happy to repeatedly give the paw, whether they got a reward or not. But that changed if they saw another dog was being rewarded with a piece of food, while they received nothing.

"We found that the dogs hesitated significantly longer when obeying the command to give the paw," the researchers write. The unrewarded dogs eventually stopped cooperating. Scientists have long known that humans pay close attention to inequity. Even little children are quick to yell "Not fair!" But researchers always assumed that animals didn't share this trait. . . .

That changed in 2003 when [Frans de Waal, a professor of psychology at Emory University in Atlanta] and a colleague named Sarah Bronson did a study on monkeys. Monkeys had to hand a small rock to researchers to get a piece of food in return. Monkeys were happy to do this to get a piece of cucumber. But the monkeys would suddenly act insulted to be offered cucumber if they saw another monkey was getting a more delicious reward, a grape, for doing the same job.

"The one who got cucumber became very agitated, threw out the food, threw out the rock that we exchanged with them, and at some point just stopped performing," says de Waal.

In that experiment, the monkeys considered the fairness

of two different types of payment. But when Range and her
colleagues did a similar study with their trained dogs, testing
to see if dogs would become upset if they only got dark bread
when other dogs received sausage, they found that dogs did
not make that kind of subtle distinction. As long as the dogs
got some kind of food payment, even if it wasn't the yummiest
kind, the animals would play along.[7]

Just as monkeys have a greater cognitive ability to recognize differences
in fairness than dogs, human beings have a heightened capacity to recognize
differences in fairness that exceeds that of all other mammals. Dogs and
monkeys can feel outrage over food, but human beings can feel outrage over
the use of physical force many animal species rely on to maintain social order
in their groups. Although intimidation through superior size and strength
maintains stability in a pride of lions, for example, it leads to instability in
a human tribe for several reasons.

Because our large brains give us a heightened capacity to recognize differences in fairness, it causes us to resent being bullied, abused, and pushed
around. Also, our ability to commit premeditated murder allows the smallest
adult to kill the largest. Since the ability to commit premeditated murder is
an inevitable consequence of having a large brain capable of imagining
countless solutions to every problem and planning days and even years in
advance, what is to stop a tribe from descending into murder and chaos?
The answer is much simpler than we realize.

In nearly all human tribes, physical size and strength do not determine
who leads. How do I know this? Throughout history, tribal leaders were
often elders who possessed experience, knowledge, and wisdom, traits more
vital to the survival of the tribe than having superior size and strength. Stability, especially in small nomadic tribes similar to the communities of our
earliest ancestors, is more effectively maintained if leaders have an attitude
of service rather than intimidation. Tecumseh, Native American warrior and
leader of the Shawnee tribe during the late eighteenth and early nineteenth
centuries, echoes the wisdom of many tribal leaders throughout the world:

Seek to make your life long and its purpose in the service of your people. Always give a word or a sign of salute when meeting or passing a friend, even a stranger, when in a lonely place. Show respect to all people and grovel to none. When you arise in the morning give thanks for the food and for the joy of living. If you see no reason for giving thanks, the fault lies only in yourself. Abuse no one and no thing, for abuse turns the wise ones to fools and robs the spirit of its vision. When it comes your time to die, be not like those whose hearts are filled with the fear of death, so that when their time comes they weep and pray for a little more time to live their lives over again in a different way. Sing your death song and die like a hero going home.[8]

For thousands of years our ancestors lived as families in small tribes, but as our numbers grew the tribes became cities and nations. When human communities went from a few dozen to many thousands and then millions, it became easier for leaders to exploit their people and protect themselves from the oppressed by building palace walls and hiring guards. In the next section we will discuss three techniques, often used by leaders of countries, that cause people to *willingly* agree to be exploited and oppressed, but before we can comprehend humanity on a large scale we must first explore ourselves on a smaller scale.

To understand why an attitude of service is more effective at creating stability in a small group of human beings than fear and intimidation, we need to understand the military. Alexander the Great led his men to the ends of the known world, but how did he inspire his soldiers to follow him into uncertainty and danger? Military historian J. F. C. Fuller states:

What appealed to his men probably more than anything else, were his unexpected kindnesses toward them; such as when, after the capture of Halicarnassus, he sent his newly married men home to spend the winter with their families . . . and when after the great reconciliation at Opis he not only rewarded his departing veterans in a princely way, but "also ordained that the orphan children of those who had lost their lives in his service should receive their father's pay."

He never asked his men to do what he would not do himself. When, before he set out on his march to India, he found that the army train was cumbered with booty, he first ordered the contents of the wagons which belonged to him and his companions to be burnt. Also, he always placed the needs of his men before his own. When he led his men on foot to set an example to them during the march through Gedrosia, he was distressed by thirst and some of the light-armed troops found a little water in a water-hole and carried it in a helmet to [Alexander].

He received it, and thanked those who had brought it; and taking it poured it out in the sight of all his troops; and at this action the whole army was so much heartened that you would have said that each and every man had drunk that water which Alexander had poured out . . . Incidents such as these bound his men to him with invisible and unbreakable moral ties. They endowed them with particles of his invincible will, and, under his leadership, they obliterated dangers, smoothed away adversities, and enabled him to lead them to what for them appeared to be the ends of the world.[9]

By pouring the water on the ground, Alexander showed he would not drink until his soldiers also had water. Leading by example is one of the most important traits an effective military leader can have. Stability in a military unit does not result when leaders behave in a tyrannical way, but when they sacrifice for their subordinates, treat the least among them well, don't ask others to do what they are unwilling to do, and promote fairness.

At West Point every freshman has to memorize a passage from a speech Major General John M. Schofield gave there in 1879. A section of it reads: "The discipline which makes the soldiers of a free country reliable in battle is not to be gained by harsh or tyrannical treatment. On the contrary, such treatment is far more likely to destroy than to make an army . . . He who feels the respect which is due to others cannot fail to inspire in them regard for himself, while he who feels, and hence manifests, disrespect toward others, especially his inferiors, cannot fail to inspire hatred against himself."[10]

If a leader's skull is crushed with a rock while he is sleeping, but he is a selfish bully who hoards at the expense of others, many in the tribe will feel relieved and even thrilled. But if someone murders a leader who sacrifices for his people and "feels the respect which is due to others," the members of the tribe will more likely want to punish the murderer.

Not every military unit has leaders who put the well-being of others above their own, but the strongest do, and so do the most powerful tribes. When our nomadic ancestors left Africa millennia ago, they took their families into unexplored lands that must have seemed like the ends of the world. With only a few simple tools and their meager possessions, they walked for thousands of miles into Asia, Europe, and the other continents. Facing adversity and danger at every turn, they could not have made such an incredible journey if tribal members were constantly trying to undermine or kill each other.

A tribe has the best chance of surviving adversity and danger if its members are fed and healthy. When there are drastic differences in fairness between members of a human community, the imbalance weakens it. Our conscience is a powerful ally in the struggle for survival, because when our intellect notices differences in fairness, our conscience adjusts our behavior to correct the unfairness. For example, our conscience encourages us to correct our behavior when we take more than we need at the expense of others, put our community at risk for our own selfish gain, and treat people badly. When fairness between people is severely imbalanced, our conscience functions as a counterbalance that puts fairness back into alignment. When we don't obey our conscience it attacks us with arrows of guilt.

But if what I am saying about the human conscience is correct, why do so many people act in ways that perpetuate unfairness, oppression, and exploitation? There are several reasons.

1. The human conscience relies on our intellect's ability to notice differences in fairness. But to function properly, our conscience must also rely on empathy's ability to experience the emotions of others. Lacking empathy, we will have a difficult time understanding when

we are behaving unfairly because we become detached from the suffering of others. Lacking empathy, we can even take pleasure in their pain.

If we want to treat others well, empathy and conscience are two muscles that must work together, just as a person cannot perform a bench press exercise unless their triceps and pectoral muscles cooperate. Empathy flows more naturally when we are living in small tribes where we know and live with everyone around us. When we are part of a massive society where we can walk in a city for hours and never see anyone we know, empathy does not flow as naturally and more effort is required on our behalf to feel empathy for the millions of people around us.

2. Like any muscle, our conscience must be strengthened and developed, yet many societies do not emphasize the importance of developing it. In school I was never taught how to strengthen my muscle of conscience. Were you?

3. Even a developed conscience can be deceived through the process of rationalizing and justifying our actions. Although I believed the Iraq War was wrong, I was able to momentarily deceive my conscience by rationalizing that my participation in the war would save lives. Later in the chapter I discuss the process of rationalizing and justifying our actions in more detail.

Not every single person in an early human tribe was a bastion of conscience, but the more members of a small community who treated each other fairly, the stronger the bonds between them and the greater the tribe's chances of surviving hardship. A small tribe led by people with highly developed consciences had the best chance of survival; the same is true of our world today.

If you doubt conscience has an important role to play in our survival, please consider this. Who is more capable of leading our global human family toward a brighter future? Would our world be better off if there were more people with less developed consciences, like Hitler and Stalin, or more people with stronger consciences, like Gandhi and Albert Schweitzer? Where the survival of a community is concerned, be it a small tribe or our global human family, our conscience is the ultimate survival guide.

One of my friends at West Point was an exchange cadet from Croatia. One day he told me a story about a young general from his country who escorted several high-ranking foreign generals on a military base tour. When it was time for lunch he and the other generals went to the dining facility, where they saw a long line of low-ranking Croatian soldiers. The foreign generals cut to the front, grabbed trays and silverware, and filled their plates with food, expecting their host to do the same. When they were ready to sit down and eat, they found him at the back of the line. Realizing it would be bad diplomacy to start eating without him, they decided to wait. The young Croatian general made them wait in line with him, even though they stood impatiently watching their food get cold. The Croatian soldiers were inspired by their leader, who would not cut in front of them even to please officers from the most powerful military in history. The foreign generals were of course Americans.

Although the military taught me to eat with or after lower-ranking soldiers but not before, this story demonstrates that certainly not all U.S. officers live up to this ideal. It might seem like I am constantly applauding the U.S. military, but what I am really praising are the timeless warrior ideals soldiers are supposed to live up to. I have seen many soldiers betray the ideals of serving others, living with integrity, leading by example, and defending the helpless; and I have witnessed the flaws of the U.S. military up close. I know its flaws well, just as I know mine, which reminds me of the greatest benefit conscience gives us: its ability to act as a mirror.

The conscience is a mirror that enables me to see my behavior objectively. Looking into it, I can gaze deeply into my heart and recognize when I acted selfishly, when I was cruel, when I was dishonest, and when I behaved unjustly. Although it is not always easy to look in the mirror of conscience, it can become our best friend, by helping us learn from our mistakes and grow as human beings.

The mirror of conscience also allows us to observe our society's behavior objectively. When Thoreau looked at his culture in the mirror of conscience, he realized slavery was wrong, even though it was a legal tradition to buy and sell "men, women, and children, like cattle at the door of its senate-house."[11] Because he felt personally responsible for the society he was a part of, he decided to use his power as an American citizen to oppose this injustice. In 1849 he said: "But, to speak practically and as a citizen, unlike those who call themselves no-government men, I ask for, not at once no government, but *at once* a better government. Let every man make known what kind of government would command his respect, and that will be one step toward obtaining it."[12]

Our global human family, and every smaller community within it, needs people willing to look in the mirror of conscience. We live in a critical era in history. We have the ability to destroy ourselves and most life on the planet, yet it seems so few are looking in the mirror of conscience. What are some of the reasons preventing us from looking at ourselves and our society in this mirror? And what are we afraid to see?

How to Sell Oppression to the Masses

Twenty-five hundred years ago, the Chinese philosopher Confucius realized ordinary people have a natural capacity to recognize fairness, justice, and oppression. Wandering through the countryside with his disciples, he saw a peasant woman weeping by a grave. Concerned by her sorrow, Confucius approached the woman and asked, "What's wrong?"

She replied, "My father-in-law, husband, and son were all killed by a man-eating tiger. I'm worried the tiger might also kill me."

Confucius asked, "If this man-eating tiger killed your family and now threatens your life, why don't you move to another village?"

"Because the government here is very good, and I don't want to move to a region with a more oppressive government," the woman responded.

Confucius looked at his disciples and said, "Indeed this is true. An oppressive government is much worse than a man-eating tiger."

This story illustrates a basic truth about human nature. Most people do not want to live under an oppressive government, and many would rather die than be oppressed. In fact, the American Revolution was inspired by this truth. John Stark, one of New Hampshire's most highly regarded soldiers during the Revolutionary War, said: "Live free or die. Death is not the worst of evils." And Founding Father Patrick Henry said: "Give me liberty or give me death!" Yet despite our natural yearning for fairness and freedom, three methods cause people to *willingly* agree to be oppressed, exploited, and enslaved. These three methods have been used to sell oppression to the masses throughout history.

Conditioned Inequality

As I explained in the last section, our large brains give us a heightened capacity to recognize differences in fairness. If you and I are living in a tribe and I am hoarding food while everyone else is hungry, this creates a kind of tension I refer to as *resentment*. When people are mistreated, resentment is the discontent that results. A person filled with resentment yearns for fairness.

In a small community, it is natural for people to resent someone who hoards food at the expense of everyone else. But what happens when fairness is not restored and resentment increases? The buildup of resentment is similar to pressure building up in a pipe. If resentment continues to increase and the pressure is not relieved through peaceful means the pipe can explode. Sometimes an explosion of resentment results in a bully's skull getting crushed with a rock; sometimes it leads to violent revolt.

One of the biggest explosions of resentment in history occurred during the first century BC, when Spartacus led a slave revolt against Rome. A slave and a gladiator, Spartacus helped plot an escape from the gladiator school where he was imprisoned. During the escape he and around seventy others fought for freedom using kitchen utensils as weapons. Within a few years after the successful prison break, Spartacus gathered enough slaves and people oppressed by the Romans to form an army of nearly 100,000 soldiers. His rebellion, known as the Third Servile War, ended when he was killed and his army was destroyed in a climactic battle with the Romans.

A similar explosion of resentment almost occurred in the United States during the twentieth century. By the 1950s African Americans had been oppressed by white society for over three hundred years, and resentment had been building for centuries. Martin Luther King Jr. helped prevent the race war that nearly exploded as tensions mounted during the civil rights era. Imprisoned in a Birmingham, Alabama, jail for conducting a peaceful protest in 1963, he wrote: "If this [peaceful] philosophy had not emerged, by now many streets of the South would, I am convinced, be flowing with blood . . . If [African Americans'] repressed emotions are not released in nonviolent ways, they will seek expression through violence; this is not a threat but a fact of history. So I have not said to my people: 'Get rid of your discontent.' Rather, I have tried to say that this normal and healthy discontent can be channeled into the creative outlet of nonviolent direct action."[13]

Although some African Americans rebelled against slavery, why did so many agree to be oppressed for so long? Why did it take over three hundred years to spark a massive revolt, in this case a peaceful one? The first method I will discuss that causes people to accept being oppressed is something I call *conditioned inequality*. This involves the use of brainwashing, intimidation tactics, and violence to condition people to believe they are unequal, less than human, and not worthy of fair treatment. Conditioned inequality trains them to have low self-worth and a weak sense of their own dignity. During King's first television interview, *The Open Mind* in 1957, host Richard Heffner said:

> The attitude of the Negro toward the white, of the white toward the Negro, and of the Negro toward himself has been conditioned and tempered and molded in very large part by the fact of a long history of slavery . . . Slavery as an institution put a premium not upon self-assertiveness and the understanding of one's own human dignity, but upon acquiescence by the Negro slave. And I think that one can fairly say that the acquiescent, submissive, Negro slave was generally, well to put it very bluntly, generally safer than the self-assertive Negro who was conscious of his own human dignity and of the democratic philosophy that is the American heritage.
>
> As a matter of fact I think we can admit that the whole myth that we have built up about the old South in which slavery existed has been a myth in which we see the picture of the happy, acquiescent slave. The Negro is a slave. The Negro who

is acquiescent is happy. The Negro who is happy is by definition acquiescent. Negroes are happy because they accept their
lot. And think of the movies and the books and the plays and
the novels that we read and see about slavery in the old South,
we see the Negro who is acquiescent as happy. The Negro slave
who is self-assertive and looks for his own rights is considered
a troublemaker.

Even when slavery was brought to an end by the Civil
War it was said that acquiescence and acceptance by the Negro
of his lot were the greater part of wisdom. It was said that the
Negro could gain more by submerging his own sense of dignity than by asserting it, that the Negro would so antagonize
others by demanding his own rights that it was better for him
to bide his time at each step along the way, wait for something
to be given to him rather than demand it as of his own right.[14]

King responded in the interview by describing the "new Negro":

The new Negro is a person with a new sense of dignity
and destiny, with a new self-respect. Along with that, is this
lack of fear which once characterized the Negro . . . I think
also I would like to mention this growing honesty which char-
acterizes the Negro today. There was a time that the Negro
used duplicity and deception as a survival technique. Although he didn't particularly like conditions, he said he liked
them because he felt that the boss wanted to hear that. But
now from the housetops from the kitchen from the classrooms
and from the pulpits, the Negro says in no uncertain terms
that he doesn't like the way he's being treated.[15]

Gavin de Becker, widely regarded as one of the world's leading experts
on violence and violence prevention, has described how women can also be
conditioned to believe they are unequal and unworthy of respect. If a young
girl spends her childhood watching her father abuse her mother, it can
severely damage the child's self-respect, sense of worth, and understanding

of her own dignity, increasing her chances of entering into an abusive relationship as an adult.

There are many techniques for creating conditioned inequality in human beings, but the end result of all conditioned inequality is decreasing people's self-respect, sense of worth, and understanding of their own dignity. As I explained in the first chapter, we have to learn how to be human. Just as our physical growth can be stunted if we are not given proper nutrition, our psychological growth can also be stunted if we are not given proper psychological nutrition that allows our humanity to develop.

Superhumanization

Conditioned inequality is one method that causes people to willingly agree to be exploited and oppressed. Now I will discuss an equally dangerous method that I refer to as *superhumanization*.

If you and I live together in a community, it becomes obvious that my hoarding more than I need while you suffer is unfair. But what if I tell you I deserve more than you because I am not like you. In fact, I am not really a human being. I am a god. To understand how superhumanizing a person into someone more than human can cause us to accept oppression, please consider this. Have you ever wondered why Egyptian pharaohs, Roman emperors, and countless rulers throughout history were considered divine? Have you ever wondered why so many cult leaders tell their followers they are God?

In societies where people willingly accept oppression, we often see rulers who either portray themselves as gods or as chosen by God to lead. We can see this not only in countless cults, but also in the concept of *divine right of kings*, the belief that monarchs derive their right to rule from God. Consequently a king can do no wrong and any attempt to overthrow him contradicts God's will.

The divine right of kings lost much of its influence during the seventeenth through nineteenth centuries for various reasons, but mainly due to a shift in ideology. During the Enlightenment of the eighteenth century, European philosophers convinced people that governments must derive their right to rule from the consent of the people rather than God's, and it is human nature to yearn for freedom and fairness. These ideas had a strong influence on America's Founding Fathers as well as Henry David Thoreau, Martin Luther King Jr., and many others who realized that rulers are not chosen by God but must be elected by the people. Prior to the Enlightenment, playwright William Shakespeare also helped shatter the myth that monarchs in Europe were divine. His plays depicted monarchs behaving in ways anything but divine. *Macbeth*, *King Lear*, and other plays showed rulers who weren't holy and infallible, but motivated by greed, selfishness, and other vices.[16]

The concept of divine right of kings has lost much of its influence today, yet beliefs grounded in a similar viewpoint persist. The *prosperity gospel* is one example, which suggests that God rewards those he favors with material wealth. In other words, the wealthy are chosen by God to be rich. Martin Luther King Jr. saw severe economic disparity in a society as a sign of injustice, but according to the prosperity gospel it is actually the will of God.

China has a concept called the *mandate of heaven* that is similar to the divine right of kings. But it differs in a very interesting way. They both claim that leaders have a divine mandate to rule, but the mandate of heaven, unlike the divine right of kings, claims that if a ruler does not behave in a just and fair way the people have a divine mandate to overthrow their ruler. Although the mandate of heaven is over two thousand years old, it sounds very similar to the American Declaration of Independence: "That whenever any Form of Government becomes destructive to these ends, it is the Right of the People to alter or to abolish it, and to institute new Government, laying its foundation on such principles and organizing its power in such form, as to them shall seem most likely to effect their Safety and Happiness."

In the second chapter, I discussed the many faces of dehumanization. Just as there are many ways to depict people as subhuman, there are also many ways to portray them as superhuman. In addition to the divine right of kings and the prosperity gospel, the belief in reincarnation has also maintained systems of oppression in various parts of the world.

How can the belief in reincarnation cause people to willingly accept being oppressed? If I believe I am poor and starving because I behaved badly in my past life and you are in charge because you were good in your past life, I will be more likely to consent to your rule. And if you oppress and exploit me, who am I to question you? To be so rich and powerful you must surely have been a saint in your past life, and being poor and starving is my punishment for being bad in my past life. This attitude helped support the oppressive caste system in India for centuries. Today many believe in a different concept of reincarnation that encourages them to struggle against rather than blindly accept injustice.

Just as it is easier to kill people when you dehumanize them, it is easier to exploit and oppress people when you superhumanize yourself. Unlike those who abuse their power, Gandhi had an impressive ability to look at himself objectively in the mirror of conscience. He also took active steps to portray himself as a human rather than superhuman. Martin Luther King Jr. explains:

> Gandhi had the amazing capacity for self-criticism. This was true in individual life, in his family life, and was true in his people's life. Gandhi criticized himself when he needed it. And whenever he made a mistake, he confessed it publicly. Here was a man who would say to his people: I'm not perfect, I'm not infallible, I don't want you to start a religion around me, I'm not a god. And I'm convinced today that there would be a religion around Gandhi, if Gandhi had not insisted, all through his life: I don't want a religion around me because I'm too human, I'm too fallible, never think I'm infallible. And any time he made a mistake, even in his personal life, or even a decision that he made in the independence struggle, he came out in the public and said, "I made a mistake."[17]

Misinformation

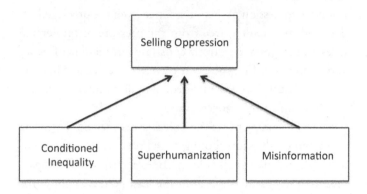

Figure 4.1: Three Methods of Selling Oppression to the Masses

For many years composer Ludwig van Beethoven pretended to be descended from nobility; when the truth came out he was humiliated. In most of Europe during his time, only members of the aristocracy enjoyed high social standing. This is one reason American ideals inspire so many people around the world.

The American dream originally meant that people would not be judged by who their parents were and could achieve success based on their own merits. Royal titles were not used in America, and immigrants from around the world flocked to a country where opportunity was not determined by bloodline but rather by talent and work ethic. Beethoven lost credibility for not being part of the nobility, but in the United States we gain credibility when we achieve success after coming from humble beginnings. There is nothing Americans love more than a good rags-to-riches story or an underdog who overcomes seemingly impossible hurdles. Films like *Rocky*, which tells the story of a poor Italian American boxer who achieves success through determination, hard work, and talent, reflect these American ideals. In 1851 F. W. Bogen, a German pastor and immigrant, explained why he wanted to live in the United States:

A great blessing meets the German emigrant the moment
he steps upon these shores: He comes into a free country; free
from the oppression of despotism, free from the privileged orders and monopolies, free from the pressure of intolerable
taxes and imposts, free from constraint in matters of belief
and conscience. Everyone can travel... and settle where he
pleases. No passport is demanded, no police mingles in his af-
fairs and hinders his movements . . .

Fidelity and merit are the only sources of honor here. The
rich stand on the same footing as the poor; the scholar is not
above the humblest mechanic . . . [In America] wealth and pos-
session of real estate confers not the least political right on its
owner above what the poorest citizen has, where there exists no
nobility, no privileged orders and no sinecures, where no standing armies weaken the physical and moral power of the people
. . . and above all, where no princes and their corrupt courts
represent the so-called "divine right of birth" . . . in such a
country the *talents*, *energy*, and perseverance of a person must
have a far greater opportunity for display, than in monarchies.[18]

It is obvious this man's description was not entirely accurate. How much
opportunity really exists in America, and is our system truly fair? These were
some of the questions King asked when he saw that the American dream
was more fantasy than reality for millions of people in our country.

Is the American dream a truth or half-truth? It is certainly true for some
but is it true for all Americans? Do all children have access to opportunity,
quality education, nutritious food, health care, and the other ingredients
necessary for a fulfilling life? Do we live in a fair system where talent and
work ethic are more important than the status and wealth of our parents?

I have seen the unfairness of our system up close. After my father retired from the army, he worked nights as a security guard until I was five.
Having grown up during the Great Depression, he wanted to give me the
opportunities he never had, so every year he got a bank loan to send me
to a private school in Alabama. Most of the other kids there were wealthy;
I was one of the poorest. I was also one of the few who wasn't white.

In sixth grade I was kicked out of school. The school faculty said it was due to my behavioral problems, but even a child can recognize the hypocrisy of a double standard. I had noticed that when I misbehaved I would get in trouble, but when a rich white student did the same some teachers didn't seem to care. I am grateful not to have been born a slave as some of my ancestors were. Every day I give thanks for the opportunities I was given. But I can never forget the game was rigged. The wealthy white kids at that school were given a head start. I've had to work much harder to get where I am today.

This experience fueled my work ethic as a writer. When I was trying to get published and read about the background of other authors, I noticed many of them had parents who were writers, professors, academics, or respected professionals. Neither of my parents graduated from college. I wrote seriously for fourteen years and received hundreds of rejection letters before being published, but my childhood had prepared me for an uphill struggle. During my lowest lows, when the struggle to write and remain sane seemed too great and life seemed unfair, appreciation helped me keep everything in perspective. After all, I considered myself fortunate to live in a country where I received rejection letters instead of prison time or a death sentence for expressing my thoughts.

In the United States everyone gets to play the game of life. But when we truly make the American dream a reality in our country, the playing field will be a lot more level and everyone will have a fair chance at winning a decent quality of life.

Misinformation is most dangerous when built on half-truths. Believing our society is fair for everyone, when it is really only fair for some, can lead us to accept oppressive conditions. Misinformation can even cause us to vote against our own interests. If we think those in power are working for the benefit of the American people when they are actually working for their own selfish interests, this misinformation can pacify our opposition to them. If we believe the American dream is a reality for everyone when so many are excluded, this misinformation can prevent us from transforming the American dream into a reality for all.

Misinformation comes in many shapes and sizes, but its most destructive forms tell us we cannot make a difference when there is really so much we can do to create positive change. The most destructive forms of misinformation also tell us war is inevitable and peace is impossible. As I explain in the Plato's Cave metaphor in *The End of War*, misinformation is all around us. Will we continue to listen to these harmful myths? Or will we boycott the oppression being sold to us and challenge those who sell it?

The Hand of Justice: A Higher Expression of Conscience

Oppressed people cannot remain oppressed forever. The yearning for freedom eventually manifests itself, and that is what has happened to the American Negro. Something within has reminded him of his birthright of freedom, and something without has reminded him that it can be gained . . . Was not [the Jewish prophet] Amos an extremist for justice: "Let justice roll down like waters and righteousness like an ever-flowing stream."
—Martin Luther King Jr.[19]

When we look at ourselves in the mirror of conscience, we perceive ourselves in an objective way that allows us to improve our behavior. But a powerful muscle of conscience is more than just a mirror. It is also a hand of justice working to shape our society for the better. Like the hand of a sculptor molding a lump of clay into a masterpiece, the hand of justice works to mold an increase in fairness, freedom, and opportunity in our society. And it strives to create humanity's greatest work of art: a world that respects the dignity of life and promotes our full development as human beings.

Once strengthened, conscience demands that we not only treat others well but that we also work to create a fair society and just world for all. Fairness is one of the most effective safeguards against societal violence. If we suffer from wrongdoing but believe there is a fair system for peacefully resolving our grievances, such as an unbiased legal system, we will often choose this peaceful method of conflict resolution. But if the courts are corrupt and people perceive a lack of fairness in their society, they will more likely choose violence as a way to solve their problems. With his groundbreaking JACA model, Gavin de Becker describes four factors that cause people to commit societal violence.

Justification: Does a person feel justified in committing a violent act? As I discussed earlier, unfairness creates resentment, similar to pressure building in a pipe. When people are treated unfairly and their basic human needs are not met, they will more likely feel justified in committing violence. For example, if a bully hoards food while others in the community are starving, a man trying to feed his children will more likely feel that smashing the bully's head with a rock is justified.

Alternatives: Does a person have alternatives to violence? Violent acts often arise out of desperation. If you wanted to correct a wrong done to you, what road would you prefer to take? Would you choose a fair court system or would you choose a violent act that was not only illegal but also put you in harm's way? When people lack peaceful alternatives to resolve their grievances, they often feel that others have forced them to commit violence. Those who commit violence due to a lack of alternatives commonly say things like "I was left with no other choice."

Consequences: Does a person care about the consequences? If we are oppressed and impoverished, living in a society where basic human needs like freedom and opportunity are not met, the consequences of committing violence become less significant. A society filled with immense unfairness increases the likelihood of violence, because if we are drowning in injustice we are more likely to think, *I have nothing to lose. Death can't be any worse than what I'm already going through.*

Ability: Does a person believe he or she has the ability to successfully commit violence? To resort to violence we must first believe our action is likely to succeed.

The JACA model shows that for many people violence is a last resort. This is why a peaceful society requires fairness, freedom, opportunity, and a court system that is not corrupt.

The justification component of de Becker's model is especially important to understand, because to make our world more peaceful we must realize how people justify their actions through *rationalizing*. When someone refers to "people without conscience" a more accurate description would be "people able to deceive their conscience." No matter how evil an act might seem, the perpetrator almost always has to rationalize the act. Even Hitler had to rationalize his actions in order to convince himself that his actions were good. In his autobiography *Mein Kampf*, he says: "Today I believe that I am acting in accordance with the will of the Almighty Creator: by defending myself against the Jew, I am fighting for the work of the Lord."[20]

Just as Hitler believed massacring people was an act of self-defense, virtually every war in history has been waged under the guise of self-defense. When we study Hitler's motivations as well as those of other tyrants, we see that human beings have a nearly universal need to justify their actions, which allows them to convince their conscience their actions are good even when they are not. This involves a kind of mental gymnastics. When our conscience puts a hurdle in front of us to prevent us from acting unjustly, rationalization allows us to jump over it.

One of Sigmund Freud's greatest insights was his realization that human beings can lie and not realize they are lying. According to Freud, we have the ability to deceive not just others but also ourselves. For example, a political leader seeks power, claiming his only desire is to serve his people, when his real motivations are greed and domination. After gaining power he censors the press, claiming he has to protect his society from troublemakers, when his real motivation is to protect himself from criticism.

Countless rulers throughout history have served their selfish interests while claiming to serve others. But Freud's insights reveal that our capacity for self-deception is so powerful that some leaders, especially when they lack the self-awareness that allows them to peer into their deepest motivations, might actually believe their own propaganda.

If we do not make an effort to be self-aware, our conscious mind will not know what our unconscious mind is doing. A person who lacks self-awareness is similar to someone driving a car while blindfolded, because being unaware of our innermost thoughts puts us and those around us at risk. When we have the skills to look deeply into our unconscious mind, like an explorer with the skills to unlock the secrets of a mysterious cavern, we can grow into stronger and more authentic human beings. Unfortunately, we live in a society where people are not trained to develop self-awareness.

If children were given the same training in hope, empathy, appreciation, and conscience as they are in other subjects, our society would produce more people with the capacity to create positive change in their communities, our country, and the world. Without that kind of education the results can be devastating. Did Hitler, Stalin, or any other tyrant in history believe they were bad people? Did slave owners wake up every morning and see themselves as horrible human beings? One thing we know from studying dictators, mass murderers, and those who commit injustice is nearly all of them believed they were on the right side of history.

Moral Fury: The Highest Expression of Conscience

In 2002, I heard a radio interview with a seventy-three-year-old woman that changed my perception of the warrior spirit. She described how she had been walking in her neighborhood when she saw a pit bull running toward her. What would you do in this situation? As I explain in *Will War Ever End?* when we are threatened by violence our flight response is more powerful than our fight response. Most people would rather run to a safe place than fight a pit bull. If a tree was a few feet away, most people would rather climb the tree than risk getting torn apart.

But the seventy-three-year-old woman was not alone. She was walking her small terrier. Reaching them, the pit bull latched its jaws onto her tiny dog. The woman, driven by concern for her loved one, bent down and bit the pit bull on the neck until it let go. How would you react if you saw a pit bull attacking your dog, child, spouse, parent, or friend? Would you not feel compelled to protect your loved one? Although our flight response is often more powerful than our fight response when violence threatens us, our instinct to protect our loved ones is often stronger than our flight response. Protecting those we love can even be more powerful than self-preservation.

During an appearance on *The Oprah Winfrey Show*, Gavin de Becker told a story about a woman who was attacked by a man while she was getting into her car. He grabbed her legs and she started kicking. When he would not let go she gouged out both of his eyes with her car keys. He had made the mistake of attacking her when she had her four-year-old daughter in the back seat. Gavin de Becker said: "The reason I tell you this story, not to scare you at all, but to know that there's a reason men do not attack women who have their kids with them. Too damn dangerous. I asked her afterwards, 'Are you sorry about what happened to that man?' She said, 'You know what? He got into something really dangerous. He attacked me when I was with my little girl.'"[21]

The spirit of the warrior protector resides in women as well as men, and one of the most dangerous creatures on the planet is a woman defending her loved ones. To protect the survival of our community, an emotion I call *fury* arises when we see our loved ones in danger, our unconditional love fuses with adrenaline, and we rush to their aid. The women in these stories demonstrated fury when they took action to defend their loved ones.

Fury is an emotion that motivates us to "stop the fight," and when people are driven by fury they are satisfied when their loved ones are safe. Fury seeks to protect, not to take revenge, and it usually employs violence as a last resort. There are many examples of fury that don't involve the use of violence, such as the many Medal of Honor recipients who died protecting their comrades on the battlefield. During the Korean War, Private First Class Bryant Womack showed how fury can lead to acts of courage and selflessness:

Pfc. Womack distinguished himself by conspicuous gallantry above and beyond the call of duty in action against the enemy. Pfc. Womack was the only medical aid man attached to a night combat patrol when sudden contact with a numerically superior enemy produced numerous casualties. Pfc. Womack went immediately to their aid, although this necessitated exposing himself to a devastating hail of enemy fire, during which he was seriously wounded. Refusing medical aid for himself, he continued moving among his comrades to administer aid. While he was aiding one man, he was again struck by enemy mortar fire, this time suffering the loss of his right arm. Although he knew the consequences should immediate aid not be administered, he still refused aid and insisted that all efforts be made for the benefit of others that were wounded. Although unable to perform the task himself, he remained on the scene and directed others in first aid techniques. The last man to withdraw, he walked until he collapsed from loss of blood, and died a few minutes later while being carried by his comrades.[22]

Military units rely on fury to survive, a powerful emotion to which humanity owes its existence. Our ancestors were the most vulnerable mammals in Africa because early humans were tall, tempting targets for hungry predators on the African savanna. We are not very fast, and lack natural weapons such as fangs, claws, tusks, or horns. We are physically weaker than chimpanzees and gorillas, and lack the climbing agility that allows them to quickly escape to the safety of trees. And we cannot burrow underground for protection like small rodents. Because our large brains take many years to fully mature, our children also remain helpless longer than the offspring of any other organism.

When a pride of lions attacks a herd of zebra, the zebra are fast enough to flee. But running away was not an option for a small human tribe that consisted not only of young adults, but also infants, pregnant women, and elderly. To compensate for our lack of speed, size, and strength, our ancestors relied on the gift of fury.

Early tribes were basically human families, and imagine how you would react if lions threatened everyone you loved. Imagine an entire tribe of early humans experiencing the fury of the seventy-three-year-old woman who bit the pit bull and the mother who gouged out an attacker's eyes to protect her daughter. When our ancestors experienced fury and used rocks, large sticks, and spears as defensive weapons, they became an extremely dangerous prey for any predator.

Fury allowed our ancestors to protect the survival of their communities, but to understand how fury is also necessary to protect the survival of our country and global community in the twenty-first century we must distinguish between two kinds of fury. *Physical fury* is a fusion of unconditional love and adrenaline that erupts quickly like an intense burst of flame. *Moral fury* is unconditional love, fusing with our conscience, coming to a slow boil. Physical fury surges through the muscles in our body, but moral fury surges through the many ways of waging peace. Martin Luther King Jr., whose actions were fueled by moral fury, talked about how it shaped his life:

Every now and then I guess we all think realistically about that day when we will be victimized with what is life's final common denominator—that something we call death. We all think about it. And every now and then I think about my own death, and I think about my own funeral. And I don't think of it in a morbid sense. Every now and then I ask myself, "What is it that I would want said?" And I leave the word to you this morning:

I'd like somebody to mention that day, that Martin Luther King Jr., tried to give his life serving others.

I'd like for somebody to say that day, that Martin Luther King Jr., tried to love somebody.

I want you to say that day, that I tried to be right on the war question.

I want you to be able to say that day, that I did try to feed the hungry.

And I want you to be able to say that day, that I did try, in my life, to clothe those who were naked.

I want you to say, on that day, that I did try, in my life, to visit those who were in prison.

I want you to say that I tried to love and to serve humanity.

Yes, if you want to say that I was a drum major, say that I was a drum major for justice. Say that I was a drum major for peace. I was a drum major for righteousness. And all of the other shallow things will not matter. I won't have any money to leave behind. I won't have the fine and luxurious things of life to leave behind. But I just want to leave a committed life behind. And that's all I wanted to say.

If I can help somebody as I pass along, if I can cheer somebody with a word or song, if I can show somebody he's traveling wrong, then my living will not be in vain.[23]

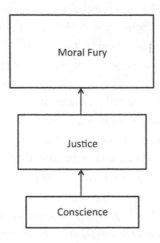

Figure 4.2: The Muscle of Conscience

Language is a faculty that must be developed, and strengthening our ability to communicate, like strengthening a muscle, requires work. In a similar way, our conscience is also a faculty that must be developed. As our muscle of conscience grows stronger it becomes a hand of justice trying to shape our society and world for the better. Moral fury arises when our conscience becomes even stronger and works with our muscle of empathy to lift the weight of injustice.

Thus far I have defined justice and moral fury as two expressions of conscience that urge us to shape our community for the better. But what is the difference between them? The hand of justice extends from our conscience to create positive change; moral fury transforms the hand into a fist intent on smashing injustice. Just as a martial artist's punch flows through the air with swiftness and strength, moral fury contains an emotional depth motivating us to act with urgency and determination.

Waging peace allows us to channel our moral fury and strike injustice in a way that leads to meaningful progress. Moral fury causes our conscience to boil, and Pablo Neruda described the fiery nature of moral fury when he said: "What did you do? Did your word ever come for your brother of the deep mines, for the grief of the betrayed, did your fiery syllable ever come to plead for your people and defend them?"[24]

In *The End of War* I devote a full chapter to explaining moral fury's many nuances. Here I want to focus on why it is crucial for solving our national and global problems. Because moral fury moves us to take constructive action, it is vital for ridding our world of injustice, oppression, and the problems that threaten our very survival, such as apocalyptic war. By training our conscience and unlocking the full power of our moral fury, we can become the kind of warrior protectors our world needs now more than ever—warrior protectors whose metaphorical weapons are the many ways of waging peace.

To create the future needed for humanity's survival, the spirit of the warrior protector flows through the hearts of women as well as men. Despite thousands of years of oppression, there have been many female peace warriors, and this is just the beginning. Women are natural protectors and nurturers, and they will play a crucial role in the struggle for global peace and prosperity. How do I know this? Women are capable of biting a pit bull to defend a loved one. They can even gouge out a man's eyes to protect a helpless child. As women and men wage peace in greater and greater numbers, the systems of injustice and oppression around our world will be torn to shreds by the full might of their fury.

Sour Grapes

Aesop, a Greek storyteller from the sixth century BC, communicated profound wisdom through simple fables. His story of the fox and the grapes can help us understand our responsibility to work for peace and the role apathy plays in preventing change. A fox was wandering through a forest when he noticed some juicy grapes hanging high on a vine. He wanted the grapes so badly his mouth started watering. Filled with excitement he said, "I'm hungry and I need a snack!" Standing on his hind legs he tried to reach the grapes, but they were still too high. So he jumped with all his might, yet the grapes were still beyond his reach. After pondering for a few moments whether to try again, the fox decided to give up. As he walked away he said to himself, "I didn't want those grapes anyway! I'm sure they were sour!"

Just as the fox rationalized his decision to quickly give up, I have met many people like the fox. They see the goal of a peaceful world hanging high above us like the grapes hanging from a vine. Aware of the hunger human beings have for peace, they think, *Our world has many problems and we need more peace!* But just as the fox quickly gave up on getting the grapes, many of us give up on solving our world's problems after expending little or even no effort. To rationalize our lack of effort we might think, *Peace isn't possible anyway! Our world is sour and cannot be fixed! Human nature is violent and beyond hope!*

I cannot count the number of times someone has told me I am wasting my time by working for peace. I am often told I should stop what I am doing because "war is inevitable" or "we cannot make a difference" or "human nature is inherently violent, so peace is impossible." If war truly is inevitable and peace really is impossible, it is easier to sleep comfortably at night as a passive bystander, when in truth the world demands our participation.

Thoreau said: "There are thousands who are *in opinion* opposed to slavery and war who yet do nothing to put an end to them. There are nine hundred and ninety-nine patrons of virtue to every virtuous man."[25] According to Thoreau, for every thousand people who think something is a good idea, only one person actually does something about it. In other words, for every thousand people who want the grapes, which to us symbolize a peaceful world, only one refuses to give up and is determined to overcome the most challenging obstacles.

This is not just Thoreau's viewpoint. It is also a fact of history. Less than one percent of Americans were actively involved in the women's rights movement, or in the civil rights movement. When opinion polls tell us a large percentage of Americans oppose a war, we must keep in mind that only a small fraction are actively involved in solving the problem. Opinion without action makes no impact.

Active involvement as a U.S. citizen means doing a lot more than voting. Misinformation tells us voting is the be-all and end-all of practicing democracy, but if we want to be active citizens we must do more than show up to the polls a couple of times every few years. Voting is certainly important, but it is only one tool in the toolbox of democracy. During the women's and civil rights movements, people with limited or no voting rights achieved some of the most important victories in American history because they used the many other tools in our democratic toolbox such as boycotts, sit-ins, protests, and so much more.

The apathy and lack of effort that cause people to have a sour grapes attitude toward peace is often a result of misinformation. As I explain in *The End of War*, studies have shown that apathy is largely caused by feelings of helplessness. Many Americans do not vote because they do not think their vote matters. Many Americans ignore our national and global problems because they do not think they can make a difference.[26] To fight the sour grapes attitude that rationalizes apathy, we must heal the feeling of helplessness that causes so much indifference in our world.

According to writer Arundhati Roy, once we are aware of the many problems in our world that include injustice, war, crime, poverty, societal violence, oppression, and environmental destruction, just to name a few, we become accountable and are no longer innocent. "The trouble is that once you see it, you can't unsee it. And once you've seen it, keeping quiet, saying nothing, becomes as political an act as speaking out. There's no innocence. Either way, you're accountable."[27] None of us have the time to confront every single issue, but so many people are unwilling to confront any issue that challenges the status quo.

I did not fully understand the power of waging peace when I deployed to Iraq in 2006, even though I had been studying war and peace for many years. Since then I have learned a great deal about waging peace, the muscles of our humanity, and how truth is the food most capable of satisfying a conscience hungry for answers. As human beings we have to rationalize our actions. The more we are able to rationalize our actions with truth instead of misinformation, excuses, and self-deception, the more at peace we will be with our conscience and the more effective we will be at creating the change our world needs most.

In the following chapters I will continue to show why human nature is not sour in a way that makes us naturally violent, and why our world is not sour in a way that makes war inevitable. By strengthening our hope, empathy, appreciation, conscience, and the other muscles of our humanity, we will gain the strength to reach the grapes of a peaceful world. No matter how high. No matter how seemingly out of reach.

CHAPTER 5

The Muscle of Reason

Summoning Death

It was a bleak November day in 2006, and I had just traveled to another forward operating base in Baghdad. As winter approached, cold gradually replaced the heat, and new questions replaced old doubts. On this chilly morning, my comrades and I explored the upper levels of a palace struck by an American Tomahawk cruise missile during the invasion in 2003. We were looking for a suitable location to place another radar. Every day mortars and rockets continued to rain from the sky. Violence in Baghdad was at a high point, and witnessing the devastation around me pushed my thinking in new directions.

Disturbing the dust in the dark corridors, I waded through rubble, squeezed through tight passages, and avoided loose stones and twisted steel—the result of a catastrophic explosion years earlier. None of the wreckage had been removed. As the sun bled through cracked walls, I felt as though I was walking through a museum where every piece of debris testified to our ability to summon death. The preserved ruins seemed like an instant frozen in time: the decisive moment when a new war began and the world would never be the same.

It was during this winter in Baghdad that the words *peaceful revolution* entered my mind and found a home. They symbolized the lifetime of searching and suffering that had lured me onto the road to peace. With increasing urgency I struggled to understand how we could solve our national and global problems without using war. The peaceful revolution within me had reached a new stage, but I would soon discover that my searching and suffering were far from over.

Several of us had been in the same section of the palace, but the next day I was the only one who became ill. I noticed something was wrong when I began to lose my sense of taste; everything tasted like metal. I saw a doctor who told me I had probably been exposed to chemicals in the palace debris. "Perhaps these toxins were part of the cruise missile," he suggested. "Or maybe they were from the destroyed palace." Several days later my sense of taste returned, but then I began to experience a constant burning sensation all over my body. My skin didn't have any appearance of redness or irritation, yet it felt like ants were eating my flesh. After two days the pain faded, but several questions remained.

If we as human beings have the ability to poison ourselves and the world we live in, can we use our intelligence to heal ourselves and the planet? If we are smart enough to build machines that summon death, can we use our brilliance to protect the gift of life? And if humanity is confronted with choices that will lead either to our survival or extinction, what will we choose?

The Psychological Oxygen for Rational Thinking

Since I was a child society taught me that reason and emotion, like oil and water, don't mix. But my army experiences taught me there are two kinds of emotion. Some, like fear and hatred, strangle reason; others, like empathy and appreciation, give reason the oxygen it needs to breathe. According to Gavin de Becker, politicians often use fear to manipulate people. "Governments throughout history like to be the way that you are spared from death. They want to tell you, 'Only we can save you from being killed.' . . . Every government in world history has used fear for political goals."[1]

Although politicians throughout history have used fear for political goals, few people used it to advance their agendas more than Adolf Hitler. By fanning the flames of fear, he was able to control people, because fear is a noose around the neck of reason. Lt. Col. Dave Grossman explains: "Have you ever tried to have an argument or a discussion with a truly frightened or angry person? It cannot be done, because the more frightened and angry the person is, the less rational he is. This is because his forebrain has shut down and his midbrain, the one like a dog's, is in control. In fact, you might as well try to argue with your dog; he might be intrigued by the experience but it will not accomplish much. Nor will you accomplish much when trying to talk to a human being in this heightened condition. To connect with him, you must first calm him down."[2]

Where politics is concerned the ability to instill fear can be a useful tool for controlling the population. The fable of Chicken Little shows how politicians can use fear to manipulate people. When an acorn falls on a chicken's head he panics and runs around telling the ducks, geese, and other chickens the sky is falling. Terrified, the animals don't know what to do to save themselves. When a fox comes by and tells them they can take shelter in his lair, they follow him in. The fox blocks the entrance to the lair and eats them.

Chicken Little shows how fear can be used to manipulate people. The animals are so afraid they cannot think clearly, which allows the fox to take advantage of them for his personal gain. If I make you sufficiently afraid, I can manipulate you into doing almost anything I want. For example, if I tell you someone is trying to kill you, then convince you the only way to stay alive is to do exactly what I say, I can make you do things you would not normally do. By convincing the German people the Jews were a mortal enemy intent on destroying them, Hitler was able to use fear to sanction genocide.

Herman Goering, a Nazi leader and military commander later executed for war crimes, explains how the Nazis used fear to manipulate people into going to war: "Why, of course, the people don't want war. Why would some poor slob on a farm want to risk his life in a war when the best that he can get out of it is to come back to his farm in one piece. Naturally, the common people don't want war; neither in Russia nor in England nor in America, nor for that matter in Germany. That is understood. But, after all, it is the leaders of the country who determine the policy and it is always a simple matter to drag the people along, whether it is a democracy or a fascist dictatorship or a parliament or a communist dictatorship.... Voice or no voice, the people can always be brought to the bidding of the leaders. That is easy. All you have to do is tell them they are being attacked and denounce the pacifists for lack of patriotism and exposing the country to danger. It works the same way in any country."[3]

As Hitler, Goering, and the fox from the Chicken Little fable demonstrated, fear can be used to advance one's self-interest at the expense of others. This is a common form of manipulation, which combines exploitation and deception. But if you asked a group of people, "Raise your hand if you like to be manipulated," how many would raise their hands? Would you raise your hand? Most people do not like to be manipulated for the self-interest of others, yet why do so many of us fall for these deceptions?

Manipulation is like a magic trick. Once we know how the illusion is performed it becomes much more difficult to fool us. Instilling fear is a cunning sleight of hand used to manipulate others, because terror causes the critical-thinking part of our brain to shut off. Therefore, when people try to make us afraid we must be skeptical of what they say and not believe them blindly.

By saying issues like war, environmental destruction, and nuclear weapons threaten human survival, am I appealing to your fear? Many people use a frightening doom-and-gloom tone when talking about our national and global problems, but I prefer an uplifting tone of hope and empowerment when I talk about these issues. When I discuss the need to end war, for example, I don't want people to be terrified and unable to think clearly. Instead, I want to call them to action by igniting their compassion, conscience, and reason. I want them to have the psychological oxygen necessary for rational thinking. Fear, hatred, and anger are metaphorical nooses around the neck of reason that shut off the critical-thinking part of our brain, but hope, empathy, appreciation, and conscience give reason the psychological oxygen it needs to breathe deeply.

Consequently, when people say reason and emotion, like oil and water, don't mix, they have not distinguished between emotions such as hatred that strangle reason and emotions such as empathy that calm our mind and improve rational thinking. Gandhi, Martin Luther King Jr., and Nelson Mandela demonstrated how empathy can help us remain calm and rational in the face of adversity. Oloajo Aiyegbayo, a researcher on leadership, explains how empathy allowed Mandela's mind to be at its best:

> Mandela went to prison a bitter, frustrated and angry
> young man fighting against a racist regime but came out a

wise, empathic old man. In his youth he hated the [white] Afrikaners and he employed violent tactics against the system but in the confined space of prison, he started to seek to understand the Afrikaners. He spent time on the inside learning the language and the history of the "enemy."

It was during his time in prison that he was able to empathize with the Afrikaners by understanding their motivations and their fears. His understanding enabled him to deal with the infamous Robben Island prison guards and helped him on his road to freedom and uniting a divided nation. Leaders need to learn how to empathize with both their supporters and critics. Daniel Goleman [in his book *Emotional Intelligence*] classified empathy as a key component of emotional intelligence . . . Empathy requires leaders to put themselves in the shoes of those they are trying to lead and those who are fighting against them. It is a required skill set for leaders who desire to lead effectively.[4]

Empathy allowed Mandela to think clearly and rationally during incredibly difficult circumstances, and empathy also allowed Schweitzer to calm his mind when he was on the verge of losing his temper. Schweitzer explained:

Mausche, a Jew from a neighboring village, who dealt in cattle and land, occasionally passed through Günsbach with his donkey cart. Since there were then no Jews living in our village, this was an event for the local boys each time. They ran after him and made fun of him. In order to advertise that I was beginning to feel grown-up, I felt compelled to join in one day, even though I did not really know what it was all about. So I followed him and his donkey with the other boys, shouting "Mausche, Mausche!" like them. The most courageous of us folded the corner of their apron or their jacket to look like a pig's ear and jumped with it to him as close as possible. In this manner we pursued him beyond the village down to the bridge. Mausche, however, with his freckles and his gray

beard, continued on his way as unperturbed as his donkey.
Only now and then did he turn around and look at us with
an embarrassed, good-natured smile. This smile overwhelmed
me . . . From that time on, I used to greet him respectfully.
Later, as a high school student, I got accustomed to shaking
hands with him and accompanying him a little way. But he
never knew what he meant to me . . . To me he remains
Mausche with the forgiving smile, who even now forces me
to be patient when I feel like fuming and raging.[5]

When Schweitzer felt like "fuming and raging," he would calm his mind
by remembering how Mausche had responded to verbal assaults with empathy and kindness. Schweitzer was a paragon of reason who opposed the brutal colonialism and genocides of the twentieth century, but his reason was
built on a strong foundation of hope, empathy, appreciation, and conscience.

To understand the powerful reason exhibited by Schweitzer and others
we first have to understand the psychological foundation, the metaphorical
oxygen, necessary to think rationally. Now let's explore the amazing feats
reason is capable of after it has the oxygen necessary to breathe.

Questioning: A Higher Expression of Reason

Some of the deepest wisdom imparted to me has come not from humans
but from animals. I grew up as an only child in a violent household, and I
also experienced racism in Alabama. But my parents had four dogs that did
not care that I was part Asian, part African American. They loved me un-
conditionally. If it weren't for their love, which helped my brain build the
neural connections necessary for empathy, I would probably either be dead
or a sociopath.

Empathy is awareness, understanding, and wisdom. My dogs, who all
died by the time I was thirteen years old, taught me many lessons about empathy and the mystery of life. I will carry these lessons with me until I die.
In addition to empathy, reason is also a form of awareness, understanding,
and wisdom. But reason is much different from empathy, and it offers us an

understanding that complements empathy. Chimpanzees, gorillas, and other animals have some capacity for reason, but our immense capacity for reason is a uniquely human trait that is necessary to solve our uniquely human problems.

To better understand what reason is and why it is so important for creating a peaceful world, we can compare reason to the human hand. Our multipurpose hands are capable of many tasks. With them we can make tools, start a fire, hunt with a spear, carry objects over long distances, build a shelter, grow crops, play music, paint a portrait, type on a keyboard, eat a burrito, put on clothes, brush our teeth, scratch an itch, drive a car, and manufacture machines. Reason is also multipurpose. With it we can invent tools, understand cause and effect, solve problems, plan for the future, do math, cure diseases, perform organ transplants, detect a lie, and build rockets that travel to the moon.

One of reason's most important functions is to help us question and understand the world around us. Questioning is a higher expression of reason vital for solving our national and global problems. Just as miners panned for gold by using a process that separated gold from sand, we can use reason to pan for truth by using critical thinking to separate truth from deception.

Reason allowed me to question the myths of war and human nature. Throughout my childhood society taught me human beings are naturally violent and warlike. But society's message did not correspond with the reality I witnessed growing up. If we are naturally violent, why did war drive people like my father insane? If we are naturally violent, wouldn't being in war improve our mental health rather than destroy it? In *On Combat* Lt. Col. Dave Grossman discusses the research conducted by Roy Swank and Walter Marchand, who both served as medical doctors in the military during World War II:

> Worst of all were those rare situations in which soldiers were trapped in continuous combat for 60 to 90 days. In those cases, 98 percent became psychiatric casualties. Fighting all day and all night for months on end is a twentieth century phenomenon. The Battle of Gettysburg in 1863 lasted three days, and they took the nights off. This has been the case throughout history. When the sun went down, the fighting stopped, and

the men gathered around the campfire to debrief the day's fight.
It was not until the twentieth century, beginning with
World War I, that battles went day and night, for weeks and
months without end. This resulted in a huge increase in psychiatric casualties and it got vastly worse when soldiers were
unable to rotate out of the battle. On the beaches of Nor-
mandy in World War II, for example, there were no rear lines,
and for two months there was no way to escape the horror of
continuous fighting, of continuous death. It was learned then
that after 60 days and nights of constant combat, 98 percent
of all soldiers became psychiatric casualties.

What about the other two percent? They were aggressive
sociopaths. They were apparently having a good time.[6]

In *Will War Ever End?* I debunk the myth that human beings are naturally violent by exploring military history and human nature. In *The End of
War* I show we are not naturally violent by also examining human aggression.
But those two books only scratch the surface. The second chapter of this
book reveals that every country in history has had to dehumanize the enemy
in order to wage war. Dehumanization is necessary to convince a civilian
population to support a war, but it is not the most effective way to condition
soldiers to kill. Many police officers and martial artists, for example, are
taught to kill without being trained to dehumanize.

What makes soldiers effective killers is *reflex training*. To explain how it
works, I will provide an example from martial arts. If I spend an hour a day
hitting a punching bag I will develop power in my strikes. But a punching
bag does not hit back. When someone tries to hit us, our natural reaction is
to flinch and cover our face. Reflex training, which involves realistic simulations and a lot of repetition, allows us to overcome this natural reaction.

An example of reflex training is having a training partner simulate a punch
to which I respond by evading the strike and counterattacking. After I practice
this many times it becomes a reflex. Then if someone tries to
hit me in a street fight I will evade and counterattack instead of flinching and
covering my face. Another example of reflex training is realistic sparring, which
gives martial artists an opportunity to condition themselves for combat.

Hitting a punching bag is similar to shooting at a round paper target, because no one has ever been hit back by a punching bag and a country has never been attacked by round paper targets. For World War II soldiers trained by shooting at round paper targets, studies show that when they actually had an opportunity to fire at the enemy in combat, only 15 to 20 percent took a shot.[7]

After World War II, army rifle ranges began using human-shaped targets that pop up from behind concealed positions, simulating what happens in combat. When this realistic simulation was combined with a lot of repetition, soldiers became conditioned to shoot without thinking, just as martial arts conditions people to evade and counterattack as a reflex. Studies show this new training method increased the number of soldiers who fired in combat during the Vietnam War to 90 percent.[8]

As I explained in the last section, fear impairs the part of our brain responsible for critical thinking. Since combat is an environment filled with fear, most people do not think well under these stressful life-and-death circumstances. This is why reflex training, which does not require thinking, is so useful in combat. Reflex training is so powerful that it can even condition people to do things that threaten their survival. Lt. Col. Grossman explains:

> We can teach warriors to perform a specific action required for survival without conscious thought but, if we are not careful, we can also teach them to do the wrong thing . . . One example of this can be observed in the way police officers conducted range training with revolvers for almost a century. Because they wanted to avoid having to pick up all the spent brass afterwards, the officers would fire six shots, stop, dump their empty brass from their revolvers into their hands, place the brass in their pockets, reload, and then continue shooting. Everyone assumed that officers would never do that in a real gunfight . . . Well, it happened. After the smoke had settled in many real gunfights, officers were shocked to discover empty brass in their pockets with no memory of how it got there. On several occasions, dead cops were found with brass

in their hands, dying in the middle of an administrative procedure that had been drilled into them . . .

One police officer gave another example of learning to do the wrong thing. He took it upon himself to practice disarming an attacker. At every opportunity, he would have his wife, a friend or a partner hold a pistol on him so he could practice snatching it away. He would snatch the gun, hand it back and repeat several more times. One day he and his partner responded to an unwanted man in a convenience store. He went down one isle, while his partner went down another. At the end of the first isle, he was taken by surprise when the suspect stepped around the corner and pointed a revolver at him. In the blink of an eye, the officer snatched the gun away, shocking the gunman with his speed and finesse. No doubt this criminal was surprised and confused even more when the officer handed the gun right back to him, just as he had practiced hundreds of times before . . .

Whatever is drilled in during training comes out the other end in combat. In one West Coast city, officers training in defensive tactics used to practice an exercise in such a manner that it could have eventually been disastrous in a real life-and-death situation. The trainee playing the arresting officer would simulate a gun by pointing his finger at the trainee playing the suspect, and give him verbal commands to turn around, place his hands on top of his head, and so on. This came to a screeching halt when officers began reporting to the training unit that they had pointed with their fingers in real arrest situations . . .

You do not rise to the occasion in combat, you sink to the level of your training. Do not expect the combat fairy to come bonk you with the combat wand and suddenly make you capable of doing things that you never rehearsed before. It will not happen.[9]

These examples show why the army uses the motto "Train like you fight." Training must be as realistic as possible because bad habits in training will get you killed in combat.

Lt. Col. Grossman says combat is an environment toxic to the human mind, and people have to be trained to perform effectively in combat. Military training and martial arts confirm this. But if human beings are naturally violent, why is combat toxic to the human mind? If we are naturally violent, why does exposure to violence decrease rather than improve our mental health? The assumption that human beings are naturally violent is actually a myth. In their study on combat trauma, Swank and Marchand write: "One thing alone seems to be certain: Practically all infantry soldiers suffer from a neurotic reaction eventually if they are subjected to the stress of modern combat continually and long enough."[10]

Isn't it common sense that living in intensely violent conditions for prolonged periods of time will harm our mental health? But this was not common sense several hundred years ago, and many people today still believe the myth that human beings are naturally violent. Seventeenth-century philosopher Thomas Hobbes believed that because human nature is so violent a primary purpose of society is to stop people from killing each other. But if this is true, why do most people have to be *programmed* to kill other human beings through realistic simulations and a lot of repetition?

Contrary to Hobbes' negative view of human nature, killing human beings is not as easy as he assumed. Lt. Col. Grossman states: "You may think that it is easy to kill, that a person only has to walk onto the battlefield and he will become a killer simply because he has been ordered to. The truth is that it is hard to get people to kill. Consider the murder rate, which is only six per 100,000 per year. Millions of people bump against each other every day, many of them depressed, angry, hostile and full of hate, but only six out of 100,000 will kill."[11]

Unless we are exposed to extreme situations such as trauma, betrayal, and abuse (which we will explore in the next chapter), most people have to be conditioned to kill other human beings. The conditioning used in modern military training has increased casualties not only in the opposing army, but also in the opposing civilian population. After World War II, soldiers went from shooting round paper targets to firing at anything that looks like a human being. But unlike soldiers, police officers are trained to distinguish between armed attackers and unarmed civilians.

Lt. Col. Grossman explains: "Today the body of scientific data supporting realistic training is so powerful that there is a federal circuit court decision which states that, for law enforcement firearms training to be legally sufficient, it must incorporate realistic training, to include stress, decision making, and shoot-don't-shoot training. This is the Oklahoma v. Tuttle decision (1984, 10th Federal Circuit Court), and today many law enforcement trainers teach that a law enforcement agency is probably not in compliance with federal circuit court guidance if they are still shooting at anything other than a clear, realistic depiction of a deadly force threat."[12]

During my time at West Point and in the army, I never received "shoot-don't-shoot training" that distinguishes between armed combatants and unarmed civilians, nor was I trained to shoot only at a "clear, realistic depiction of a deadly force threat." Instead I was put on an army rifle range and conditioned to fire at anything that vaguely resembles a human being. This training is still common in the military today, even though many soldiers are performing police actions overseas.

Everything discussed in this section involves using reason to question popular myths about war and human nature. When anyone claims we are natural-born killers of our own species, we can question their assumption if we understand the importance of reflex training in the military. Reason also tells us human beings, far from having a natural urge to commit violence against each other, actually have a phobia of violence when it is up close and personal.

Lt. Col. Grossman calls this the *universal human phobia* because although a small percentage of people are afraid of snakes, spiders, and heights, around 98 percent will have a phobic-level reaction to human aggression. In fact, this is one reason fear of public speaking is so common: we might say something that evokes an audience's aggression. What if the worst-case scenario happens and the audience shouts at us angrily or laughs cruelly at our expense?

Fear of human aggression can be even more terrifying than fear of death. For example, every year in America hundreds of thousands die from the effects of smoking, but every day millions of people smoke without worrying.

Every year in America tens of thousands die in car accidents, but every day millions of people drive casually to work. However, a few murders by a serial killer will cause a city to go on alert, striking terror in many of its citizens. One terrorist attack in America created so much fear that our country has never been the same since.

What makes terrorism so dangerous is not the terrorist act itself, but our reaction to it. If Osama bin Laden had asked us to betray our democratic ideals by sanctioning torture, spying on U.S. citizens, and infringing on our civil liberties, we would never have agreed. But by attacking us on 9/11, many Americans willingly betrayed our democratic ideals because Osama bin Laden ignited the universal human phobia. Why is the universal human phobia so frightening? Why is our reaction to terrorism often more dangerous than the terrorist act?

Lt. Col. Grossman asks us to consider two scenarios. Imagine that a tornado knocks down your house, destroys everything you own, and causes injuries severe enough to put you and your family in the hospital. Next imagine that a gang breaks into your house, beats you and your family so badly that you all end up in the hospital, and then burns down your house. In both cases the result—your house and possessions destroyed and your family in the hospital—is the same, but which scenario is more traumatic?

Is it more traumatic to fall off a bicycle and break your leg, or for a group of attackers to hold you down and break your leg with a baseball bat? In both cases the result—a broken leg—is the same, but which scenario is more traumatic? Obviously, when people hurt us the trauma is much more severe. But why? Lt. Col. Grossman explains:

> The *Diagnostic and Statistical Manual of Mental Disorders* (*DSM-III-R*), the bible of psychology, states that in post-traumatic stress disorders "the disorder is apparently more severe and longer lasting when the stressor is of human design." We want desperately to be liked, loved, and in control of our lives; and intentional, overt, *human* hostility and aggression—more than anything else in life—assaults our self-image, our sense of control, our sense of the world as a meaningful and comprehensible place, and ultimately, our mental and physical health.

The ultimate fear and horror in most modern lives is to be raped or beaten, to be physically degraded in front of our loved ones, to have our family harmed and the sanctity of our homes invaded by aggressive and hateful intruders. Death and debilitation by disease or accident are statistically far more likely to occur than death and debilitation by malicious action, but the statistics do not calm our basically irrational fears. It is not fear of death and injury from disease or accident but rather acts of personal depredation and domination by our fellow human beings that strike terror and loathing in our hearts.

In rape the psychological harm usually far exceeds the physical injury . . . far more damaging is the impotence, shock, and horror in being so hated and despised as to be debased and abused by a fellow human being.[13]

This is one reason people created legends of werewolves, vampires, wendigos, and other monsters. Centuries ago if a mutilated human body was discovered in a town, believing an inhuman monster was responsible was less disturbing for many people than acknowledging a fellow human was capable of such horrors. According to these legends, people can also be transformed into werewolves, vampires, and wendigos. This portrays a murderous psychopath as someone who has changed into a monster and lost his humanity.

Furthermore, monsters similar to werewolves—such as werehyenas in Africa—can be found in many cultures around the world. But do we have any evidence the werewolves of legend might have actually been ancient serial killers? When we compare the behavior of mythical werewolves to some modern serial killers, the similarities are startling. For example, some serial killers take part in murder, cannibalism, a pattern of violence that frightens the local population, the mutilation of bodies, and they kill secretly, which makes them difficult to catch. This is the same type of behavior attributed to werewolves. Without skilled law enforcement officers capable of capturing serial killers, and without our modern understanding of serial killers, perhaps we would still believe in werewolves today.

Soldiers, martial artists, and peaceful warriors must learn to confront and overcome the universal human phobia. When Martin Luther King Jr. challenged the status quo, for example, he had to face the aggression of those hostile to change. From the age of twenty-six until his death at thirty-nine, King's life was constantly threatened. But if fear of human aggression affects around 98 percent of the population, why do we seem so fascinated with violent television shows, movies, and video games? Although most people have a phobia of violence, we are actually biologically hardwired to stare at violence. This might seem like a contradiction, but the muscle of reason can help us look deeper and understand what is really going on.

If a bear burst into your room right now, would you stare at it? It is difficult to imagine someone who would not. Perhaps you might try to frighten it away or phone for help, but that bear would have your full and undivided attention. The reason you would stare at a bear that burst into your room is simple: to protect yourself. As long as you can see a threat you can protect yourself from it. In martial arts there is a saying: "The punch that knocks you out is the one you don't see coming."

Just as we are biologically hardwired to stare at a predator that threatens our survival, zebras are biologically hardwired to stare at lions. When a lion is spotted in the distance, that lion has the full and undivided attention of the herd. However, there is a creature on this planet far more dangerous than a bear or lion—a violent human being. When people behave violently toward each other, we must stare at it for the same reason we must stare at a bear that enters our living space, and a zebra must stare at a lion. Because it threatens our survival.

Violence between people is extremely destructive to a community, since we rely heavily on cooperation to survive. Reactions to violence vary. Sometimes people will cheer a fight on. Often they will try to break it up or call the police. And sometimes they will simply stare and do nothing. But nearly everyone stares, whether they are five-year-old children seeing a fight on the playground or adults witnessing an attack on the street. Being biologically hardwired to stare at violence is one factor contributing to the popularity of violent television shows, movies, and video games, but there is another and more dangerous element involved.

In *On Killing* Lt. Col. Grossman explains that we live in a society that represses the reality of death. Many of us in America pretend we will never grow old and die; some even get expensive plastic surgery to create the illusion of youth. In many cultures the elderly are respected and admired, but our elders are often put in nursing homes and ignored by their families. We no longer have to kill to eat. And most of us have never seen a corpse in real life; if we have, it was likely embalmed at a funeral home and made to look as though the person was merely asleep. Just as sexual repression during the Victorian era led to strange sexual fetishes and an obsession with sex, the repression of death in our culture has led to bizarre death fetishes and an obsession with our most feared mechanism of death: violence. Lt. Col. Grossman explains:

> [During the Victorian era] sex became hidden, private, mysterious, frightening, and dirty. The era of sexual repression in Western civilization had begun. In this repressed society, women were covered from neck to ankle, and even the furniture legs were covered with skirts, since the sight of these legs disturbed the delicate sensitivities of that era. Yet at the same time that this society repressed sex, it appears to have become obsessed by it. Pornography as we know it blossomed. Child prostitution flourished. And a wave of sexual child abuse began to ripple down through the generations.
>
> Sex is a natural and essential part of life. A society that has no sex has no society in one generation. Today our society has begun the slow, painful process of escaping from this pathological dichotomy of simultaneous sexual repression and obsession. But we may have begun our escape from one denial only to fall into a new and possibly even more dangerous one.
>
> A new repression, revolving around killing and death, precisely parallels the pattern established by the previous sexual repression.
>
> Throughout history man has been surrounded by close and personal death and killing. When family members died of disease, lingering injury, or old age they died in the home. When they died anywhere close to home, their corpses were

brought to the house—or cave, or hut, or hovel—and prepared for burial by the family . . .

In that world each family did its own killing and cleaning of domestic animals. Death was a part of life. Killing was undeniably essential to living. Cruelty was seldom, if ever, a part of this killing. Mankind understood its place in life. And respected the place of the creatures whose deaths were required to perpetuate existence. The American Indian asked forgiveness of the spirit of the deer he killed, and the American farmer respected the dignity of the hogs he slaughtered . . .

Yet at the same time that our society represses killing, a new obsession with the depiction of violence and brutal death and dismemberment of humans has flourished. The public appetite for violence in movies, particularly in splatter movies such as *Friday the 13th*, *Halloween*, and the *Texas Chainsaw Massacre*; the cult status of "heroes" like Jason and Freddy; the popularity of bands with names like Megadeth and Guns N' Roses; and skyrocketing murder and violent crime rates—all these are symptoms of a bizarre, pathological dichotomy of simultaneous repression and obsession with violence.

Sex and death are natural and essential parts of life . . . It seems that when a society does not have natural processes (such as sex, death, and killing) before it, that society will respond by denying and warping that aspect of nature.[14]

Our society's obsession with media violence does not show that human beings are naturally violent. Instead, it demonstrates that our society is ill.

One of the most common arguments I hear in support of the myth that we are naturally violent is "Children like to wrestle, and young boys like to play in ways that mimic violence, such as pretending that sticks are swords." The muscle of reason can help us question this assumption and clear up the misunderstanding.

Children like to wrestle, but so do the young of most other mammals. Why? Wrestling and other forms of play nurture a child's development, because they build the connections in our brain necessary for balance and coordination. When we are wrestling and someone tries to push us down, the part of our brain that controls balance and coordination gets stimulated as it tries to keep us standing. Wrestling also increases muscular strength and can serve as a form of social bonding.

Puppies like to bite with minimal force when playing, not because they are trying to hurt the person or animal they are playing with, but because it helps develop crucial connections in their brains. The difference between play and violence is that the purpose of play is to bond socially, develop muscular strength, and build the connections in our brain necessary for balance and coordination. The purpose of violence is to harm. If a child gets poked in the eye and starts crying during pretend swordplay, the game stops.

The muscle of reason allows us to question the myths of war and human nature that prevent us from realizing how remarkable we truly are. The stronger our muscle of reason, the stronger our ability to question. When we use the power of reason to ask the right questions, we become more difficult to deceive and politicians will have a much harder time manipulating us. In our struggle to end war, reason allows us to question and refute the myths that keep the war machine running. If we believe the myth that human beings are naturally violent, then peace is viewed as a naive dream and war seems inevitable. Reason tells us this could not be further from the truth.

Building: The Highest Expression of Reason

When I was a child, the television series Star Trek changed my life. If not for that show this book probably would not have been written, because Gene Roddenberry, its creator, made me consider the possibility of world peace for the first time. Star Trek: The Next Generation debuted when I was seven years old in 1987, and it planted a seed of hope in my young mind. In Roddenberry's vision of the future, humanity has solved the problems of poverty, injustice, and war on Earth.

Good science fiction provides commentary on social and political problems such as war, oppression, prejudice, and exploitation. Accordingly, when a Star Trek episode is about a conflict between humanity and a species from another planet, it is a metaphor for the conflicts between people on this planet. What struck me most about the show was how humanity had moved beyond its petty differences to end the wars on Earth and unite as a global family. During the 1980s, an era when people feared a nuclear holocaust and science fiction films often depicted apocalyptic futures, Roddenberry's vision made me question, think, and hope. But was his vision of a peaceful future possible? Or was his dream of an end to war, poverty, and injustice simply a fantasy?

To explore these questions, I must discuss what I admire most about *Star Trek*. According to Roddenberry's vision of the future, what saves humanity from destroying itself is not its technology, but its ideals. In *Star Trek* the military has been renamed Starfleet, and its mission is not waging war, but promoting peace, providing humanitarian aid, and exploring the galaxy. In one episode Captain Jean-Luc Picard discusses an important ideal upon which Starfleet is based: "The first duty of every Starfleet officer is to the truth, whether it's scientific truth, or historical truth, or personal truth. It is the guiding principle on which Starfleet is based."[15]

Other Starfleet ideals are respect for other cultures, protecting the dignity of life, living in harmony with the environment, serving others, fairness, justice, and liberty. When reason serves these ideals we gain the power to build a global civilization of peace and prosperity. But when reason separates from these ideals we step closer and closer toward self-destruction.

A hundred years ago human beings were developing automatic machine guns. Now we have enough nuclear weapons to destroy the world several times over. For much of the twentieth century two nuclear superpowers held our planet hostage. But we could face a far more dangerous situation in the twenty-first century, where a nuclear arms race escalates not between two superpowers but among many countries, and nuclear weapons fall into the hands of terrorists.

As technology continues to evolve, who can predict how destructive weapons will be a hundred years from now? Because war has become so devastating, ending it is no longer just a moral issue, but an issue that will determine the survival of humanity. Consequently, the question "Will war ever end?" can be reworded to "Will humanity survive or will we destroy ourselves?" We can better understand the benefits and dangers of technology by exploring the legend of Thor. In Nordic mythology, the god Thor was a great warrior and the guardian of Asgard—the city of the gods. What made Thor so formidable was his hammer—a pinnacle of technology created by dwarves for the purpose of defending the world.

With his mighty hammer in hand, Thor was called the World's Defender. Like Thor's hammer, our technology can also protect our survival and the world that is our home. Technology gave our ancestors the ability to create tools, control fire, build shelters, and grow crops. Just as Thor's hammer protected Asgard, technology protected our ancestors against predators, cold, the elements, and starvation. In the modern era, technology can protect us even further by fighting diseases, healing life-threatening injuries, and allowing us to harness forms of energy that do not destroy our environment.

However, technology not only gives us the power to protect. It also gives us the means to destroy. With the force of a nuclear weapon, Thor's hammer could crush mountains and devastate the world. He could use his hammer to protect the helpless, but he could also use it to slaughter the innocent. Thor's hammer represents the *blessing and curse of technology*.

Technology can be a blessing when used responsibly, but it becomes a curse when wielded without compassion. Technology is simply a tool, and how we use any piece of technology depends on our attitude. I can use a hammer to build a house, school, or hospital—or to kill. In a similar way, medical doctors can use their knowledge to heal the sick or torture people. During the 1940s, German citizen Albert Schweitzer dedicated his life to healing the sick in Africa, while Nazi doctors performed cruel medical experiments on human beings.

The difference between them was that Schweitzer used the muscle of reason to be a protector. When reason is given the oxygen that flows from the muscles of our humanity and our highest ideals, we can also become protectors.

When armed with reason, we can protect in many ways. Gandhi and Martin Luther King Jr. used the muscle of reason to wage peace and challenge injustice, oppression, and war. Furthermore, Gavin de Becker's groundbreaking work on violence prediction and prevention shows how we can use reason and intuition to outsmart violence and prevent attacks before they happen. He says that of all human behavior violence is by far the easiest to predict because it gives off the most warning signs. Also, Lt. Col. Dave Grossman is using reason and scientific research to create a revolution in law enforcement training that will better protect our society.

As discussed earlier in this chapter, reason can also protect us against being deceived and manipulated. Because injustice, oppression, exploitation, and war are built on deception and manipulation, reason can help us solve these problems at their root. Although reason gives us the power to build or destroy, its highest expression is building.

When our muscle of reason becomes strong, we can build civilizations, technological marvels, and much more. In the twenty-first century, we must harness the power of reason to build solutions to our national and global problems. We must also build an economic system that values people over profit, a fair society where people are given opportunity, and technology that allows us to live in harmony with our environment. Above all, we must build a global civilization of peace and prosperity that unleashes our full potential as human beings.

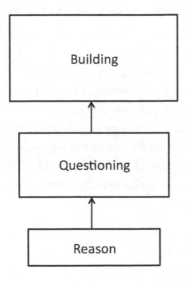

Figure 5.1: The Muscle of Reason

As warriors of peace, we must be armed with reason. But as the Nazi doctors who possessed reason without compassion demonstrated, it will take more than just reason to protect humanity and our planet. Just as our pectoral muscles cannot perform a bench press exercise alone, reason cannot build solutions to our national and global problems without the help of other muscles. Our pectoral muscles require the help of our triceps and deltoid muscles when bench pressing heavy weight, and the muscle of reason requires the muscles of hope, empathy, appreciation, and conscience when trying to solve the problems that threaten to crush us.

Our technology is as mighty as Thor's hammer, and the symbolism of his weapon can help us see our technology in a new way. When the enemies of the gods finally invaded the city Asgard, Thor and his hammer were put to the test. An army of giants and monsters was assembled outside of Asgard, and it was up to him and the other gods to defend their city in the battle of Ragnarök ("Twilight of the Gods"). Realizing they were outmatched, Odin, Thor's father and the leader of the gods, said to them: "We will give our lives and let our [kingdom] be destroyed, but we will battle so that these evil powers will not live after us."[16]

During the battle Fenrir the Wolf, the fiercest of the enemies of the gods, leapt onto Odin and killed him. The giant serpent Jörmungand was about to overwhelm the gods with his venom when Thor came to the rescue and smashed him with his hammer. But as Jörmungand died, he spat his venom all over Thor. Blinded and choking, Thor dropped his hammer and fell lifeless to the ground. The World's Defender was dead. The remaining gods were defeated and Asgard was destroyed.[17]

Star Trek and Nordic mythology contain wisdom that can help us today. In *Star Trek*, our highest ideals, not technology, save humanity. And just as Thor's hammer was not enough to protect his city, all the missiles and bombs in the world cannot save humanity in the twenty-first century.

Frankenstein's Monster

Technology and arrogance are a deadly combination. Thousands of years ago, people foresaw the dangers that arise when technology is corrupted by arrogance. In Greek mythology, Icarus and his father, Daedalus, were imprisoned in a tower, but they had a way to escape. Daedalus had constructed two pairs of wings out of wax and feathers. Although he warned Icarus not to fly too close to the sun, Icarus did not listen. Blinded by his arrogance, he flew higher and higher until the wax holding his wings together melted. Icarus's wings were a technological marvel that gave him a chance at freedom, but his arrogant misuse of this technology caused him to fall into the ocean and die.

Greek mythology also tells us of Phaëton, whose father was the sun god Helios. Phaëton wanted to drive his father's sun chariot, but this arrogant desire led to a disaster. Helios was a mighty deity with the power to drive his sun chariot on a safe path across the sky, but Phaëton was half human and wanted to do what only a god could do. Unable to handle the reins, Phaëton lost control of the sun chariot and could not stop it from plunging toward the earth. Plato writes that "[Phaëton] burnt up all that was upon the earth, and was himself destroyed by a thunderbolt [from Zeus]."[18]

The heat from our sun is generated by a nuclear reaction deep within its core. Our sun's nuclear reaction is at a safe distance of 93 million miles away, but during the 1940s people began creating dangerous nuclear reactions on our planet. Just as Phaëton believed he could control the sun chariot, many believe we can control the thousands of nuclear weapons and nuclear power plants around the world. We have narrowly avoided nuclear annihilation in the past, and in the age of terrorism our grip on the nuclear reins is slipping.

If we lose control of the nuclear chariot we will suffer the same tragedy that befell Phaëton. And if any survive they too will write about how we "burnt up all that was upon the earth." The story of Icarus tells us some technology, like flight, must be used responsibly or we will get ourselves killed. The tragedy of Phaëton reminds us that some technology, like a nuclear weapons arsenal capable of destroying humanity, is a disaster waiting to happen in the hands of fallible human beings.[19]

The theme of our technology turning against us can be found in many stories both ancient and modern. Mary Shelley, author of *Frankenstein*, shed new light on this theme. In her nineteenth-century novel, Frankenstein is not the name of the monster. It is the name of the monster's creator. Victor Frankenstein was a scientist intent on creating life. Piecing together a "man" from the body parts of corpses, he brought his creation to life through his technological brilliance.

But when the monster woke, Frankenstein was so horrified by his creation that he ran away and abandoned it. The monster was left to wander afraid and alone. Like the Nazi doctors during World War II, Frankenstein possessed reason without compassion. He had not considered the well-being of the creature he was bringing into the world, a reckless decision arising from arrogance.

Arrogance leads to recklessness and corrupts technology in several ways. Arrogance caused Icarus to forget caution, Phaëton to forget consequences, and Frankenstein to forget compassion. Frankenstein's creation eventually turned against him, and his life was destroyed by the technology he created. In a similar way, we may be destroyed by nuclear weapons and industrial pollution if we continue to ignore caution, consequences, and compassion.

Joseph Campbell said that science fiction is our modern mythology. In ancient mythology, heroes such as Odysseus explored exotic lands filled with wonder and danger. Since we have mapped the entire surface of the earth, our heroes now explore outer space. According to Campbell, Luke Skywalker of *Star Wars* and other science fiction characters are our modern mythological heroes.

Just as Frankenstein's creation turned against him, modern science fiction films show technology turning against humanity. In the *Terminator* and *Matrix* films, the robots humanity created are waging war against their makers. In the film *Blade Runner*, an artificial life-form kills the man who engineered him by gouging out his eyes. In the film *2001: A Space Odyssey*, a computer attempts to kill the human beings on its ship. And in the new *Battlestar Galactica* television series, human beings are being hunted to extinction by their creations, a race of robots known as the Cylons.

Today we are threatened not only by our technological creations such as nuclear weapons and industrial pollution. We have also constructed other monsters such as an economic system that values profit over people and a military industrial complex that perpetuates fear and violence. The muscles of our humanity give us the strength to dismantle the monsters we have created before they destroy us. What we have made we can also unmake.

In the twenty-first century, will we avoid the disasters born of arrogance and recklessness by listening to caution, consequences, and compassion? Will we use our technology responsibly in ways that serve humanity and protect our planet? Will we choose survival over extinction?

Although we have the technological ability to destroy ourselves, the wisdom from our ancient past gives us insight into our modern problems. Nordic and Greek mythology have something important to tell us about our survival and future. The Old Testament also makes our choices in the twenty-first century very clear: "I call heaven and earth to witness against you today, that I have set before you life and death, blessing and curse. Therefore choose life, that you and your offspring may live."[20]

CHAPTER 6

The Muscle of Discipline

The War Within

Since my childhood, bolts of rage have flowed through me like light-ning. Controlling the rage that urges me to lash out violently is not easy. Sometimes it is like lightning trying to control the sound of its thunder.

Human beings are not naturally violent, yet we can certainly become violent. If a dog is beaten ruthlessly it is more likely to become vicious. In a similar way, the vast majority of violent criminals were abused as children. My personality also has a violent side, and I still struggle to control the storms within me. But I was not born this way. I became this way.

I grew up in Alabama as an only child, and I had almost no contact with my extended family. My mother was Korean and my father was half white and half black, but my parents did not tell me I was part African American until I was in the sixth grade. Because of my father's light skin, it was easy for people to assume he was white. I rarely heard him say anything pos-itive about African Americans, so I too assumed he was white.

Born in 1925, my father grew up in Virginia during segregation. Al-though I was born in 1980, he taught me to think like someone living before the civil rights movement. Like many African Americans conditioned to be-lieve they were inferior to whites, my father did not have a positive view of black people. As I got older, he told me about the racism he had experienced from both white and black people because of his mixed-race heritage.

As a child I was picked on because I looked Asian, and I heard children and adults make racist comments about African Americans. When my par-ents told me I was part black, I couldn't stop crying. It was bad enough being mistreated because I was half Korean. My parents said being part black would further limit my options in life. "People will be nice to you," my father told me, "But when they find out you're part black they will turn on you. The military is the only place that gives black men a chance. You will never be able to get a decent job unless you're in the army." I hoped the army would accept me for who I was, since I did not seem to belong anywhere else.

The place where I felt most like an outsider was not Alabama, but Korea. When I was eleven years old I went there to visit my mother's family. I was excited to be around people who looked like me, but I quickly realized I did not fit in there either. The Korean children made fun of me because I could not speak their language. One boy would mock me and laugh every time I said something in English, until one day my violent temper exploded.

He was sitting on a street corner with my cousin and some other children. We were all about the same age. I said something to my cousin in English; the boy overheard what I said and made fun of me one too many times. Enraged, I grabbed him by the hair. Frozen with fear, he looked up at me with eyes wide and mouth open. I thought, *Is he just going to sit there with his mouth open and let me hit him?* Suddenly my cousin grabbed me. He yelled at me for almost hitting his friend and we quickly left.

When we walked through that neighborhood later in the day, the boy who had made fun of me was hiding behind a wall holding a fishing pole in a defensive posture. He was literally shaking in fear at the sight of me. I walked by without saying anything, but seeing him fearfully clutching an old wooden fishing pole made me feel guilty. I realized he was a poor village boy, and I glimpsed my own fear and vulnerability reflected in him. I learned two things from this experience: those who are abused can become abusers, and I was an outsider in Korea as well as Alabama.

My parents told me white people and Koreans would dislike me for being part black, and African Americans would not accept me because I looked Asian. My parents weren't lying. They were describing reality as they had experienced it and trying to protect me from the cruelty inflicted on them. But sometimes when our parents try to protect us they end up harming us. The fear they instilled in me only added to the trauma of living in a violent household, being bullied at school, and feeling like a racial outcast.

We all yearn to communicate our thoughts and emotions to others, and violence can be a form of expression. When we are happy we want to share our joy with those around us. When we are sad we want people who can listen and empathize with our problems. In my case, words cannot capture the full magnitude of fear and rage I have felt in my life.

If I want others to understand the trauma of a violent upbringing, how can I communicate this experience to them? One way is to speak not with words, but with violence. If I beat someone to the point where he fears for his life, he will begin to understand my fear. Many people commit violence because it is a way to be heard. It is common for abused children to lash out aggressively, and when adults cannot express their fear and rage in productive ways, they will express themselves through violence.

Writing gave me a way to understand and begin healing the fear and rage within me. If my high school English teacher had not encouraged me to become a writer, I would have chosen a path of violence rather than peace. I certainly do not condone murder, but I understand how rage can make people feel like violence is the only way to express themselves, the only way to solve a problem, and the only way to be human.

My childhood experiences are part of our shared human experience. We all sometimes feel like we don't fit in, and we all suffer from varying degrees of fear, humiliation, and pain. But for some the pain is so severe it becomes trauma, and the trauma is so immense it builds up like pressure in a pipe. How can we relieve the pressure before it causes a person to explode?

Kindness is one way, and I was fortunate to receive kindness from some children and adults as I was growing up. There are many in Alabama who do not believe in the old racial stereotypes. But it took time for these acts of kindness to make a lasting impression on me. When people were kind to me I often thought they were being insincere. I was cynical about their kindness. I did not trust their kindness.

When we cannot trust people it is difficult to accept their compassion. I assumed their compassion had strings attached, or they were trying to trick me into trusting them so they could eventually hurt me. If my own father could attack me and make me fear for my life, what reason did I have to trust them?

Even as an adult, trusting people is still a struggle for me. My father would lose control when he beat me, and I received more beatings than I can possibly count. They usually began with him screaming and sometimes threatening to kill me. Panicking, I would run until he caught me. After he knocked me to the ground and began stomping on me, I would curl up in a fetal position and try to protect my head. My mother was raised in a culture where women were subservient to men, but my father's attacks sometimes became so dangerous that she would intervene and barely be able to restrain him.

At the time I did not fully understand how the Korean and Vietnam Wars had traumatized him. All I knew was that people were dangerous and those I trusted would hurt me the most.

The fears we develop in childhood can cause us to behave in ways harmful to others and ourselves. In high school I told racial jokes about African Americans so no one would suspect I was part black. I did it out of fear. I felt like I was carrying a horrible secret within me, and if others realized I had African American blood they would hurt me. My father warned that people would hate me if they discovered I was part black, and the racism I experienced for being half Korean made me believe him.

Eventually I could not carry the secret any longer. At the age of twenty-two, while stationed at my first duty assignment at Fort Bliss in El Paso, Texas, I told a fellow lieutenant I was part black. Even though he was African American, I was worried that my mixed-race background would horrify him.

His reaction was unexpected. He said, "You would probably get along with my father, because he grew up with a lot of racism and doesn't like people who aren't black." *That wasn't so bad,* I thought. All those years of living in fear had been for nothing. As I became less worried about people knowing my racial identity, I told others I was part black, and I realized something surprising. When people found out I was half Korean, a quarter white, and a quarter black, their response was usually positive. They would say things such as "That's a really cool mix."

I am living proof that change happens. My father grew up during an era when being mixed race was something to be ashamed of and interracial marriage was forbidden. He had conditioned me to think like him, but suddenly my eyes were opened. Most people did not hate me because I was mixed race. On the contrary, they thought it was cool. Nevertheless, racism has not disappeared in America. I have experienced its harmful effects on many occasions.

But if as a society we have made progress away from racism, why can't we continue to journey in a positive direction? If we have come so far, why can't we go further? Although I am inspired by the progress I have witnessed, my emotional scars have not fully healed. Suffering is a curse and a blessing. The trauma in my life is a curse that still haunts me, but it is also a blessing that has educated me. Adversity has given me resilience and allowed me to see the world from many perspectives, including the fresh viewpoint of an outsider. Adversity also led me onto the road to peace.

My journey to peace began as a struggle to understand myself. As a child I became obsessed with understanding the war within me and the wars that had hurt my father, but I did not develop the intellectual capacity necessary to answer the difficult questions about life until I became a young adult. As a West Point cadet and officer in the army, I learned how we could use the muscles of our humanity to solve our national and global problems, and I saw the connections between the wars that ravage countries and the war in our hearts.

Adversity has allowed me to see connections that are seldom seen, and I continue to learn from the struggles in my life. Along with my violent upbringing, the struggle of being a racial outcast was also a blessing in disguise. Because I did not fit in as white, Korean, or African American, I began to identify as a member of our global human family. These realizations about our true nature as human beings fill me with hope, but the suffering that led to these insights has taken a heavy psychological toll.

Warrior Discipline

Mike Tyson became the youngest heavyweight champion in boxing history. But at five feet eleven inches, he was a relatively small heavyweight who relied on speed rather than size. When I was growing up during the 1980s, Tyson's nickname was "Kid Dynamite." With explosive punches and unrivaled quickness, he looked unstoppable in the boxing ring. A professional boxer at the age of eighteen, Tyson was only a teenager, but he was knocking out grown men bigger and more experienced than him. In 1986 at the age of twenty, Tyson was heavyweight champion of the world.

During the 1980s this was how the public saw the young Tyson, but there is much they did not see. In the 2009 documentary *Tyson*, the forty-year-old retired boxer reveals what was underneath his intimidating exterior. At the beginning of the documentary, he describes how he was bullied as a child for being short, obese, and wearing glasses:

> I can remember going to school and being bullied and people taking my glasses and putting them in the trunk of a milk cart. I've never had any kind of physical altercation with anybody at that particular time in my life, so I couldn't believe a human being would do that. I never dreamed somebody, an absolute stranger would do that to me. I didn't know why . . . I just ran. I didn't know what happened. I just ran. And I think that's why people like myself become more assertive in life and become more aggressive . . . because they fear that they don't want that to happen to them no more and they don't want to be humiliated in that particular fashion any more. And that's why I believe I'm the person that I am. And people have a misconception that I'm something else, but I'm just afraid of being that way again, of being treated that way again, of being physically humiliated in the streets again . . . And I just wish I knew how to fight back then . . . I was afraid to fight . . . I was so afraid.[1]

Although he was afraid of fighting, a traumatizing incident led to Tyson's first street fight. Growing up in one of the most violent sections of Brooklyn, he loved raising pigeons. They gave him the sense of security and comfort all children need and provided a sanctuary from his abusive surroundings. Unlike people, his birds were loyal and did not hurt him.

One day a group of bullies found his pigeons and took one. He shouted, "Give me my bird back!" The bully holding the bird responded by ripping off its head and throwing the dead bird at Tyson, saying, "There, you can have it." Enraged, Tyson beat up the larger boy. It was his first fight but would not be his last.

By the time he was thirteen Tyson had been arrested thirty-eight times. Like many people who become violent, he was the product of the kind of abuse, fear, and humiliation that breeds violence. As an adult he continued to struggle with legal problems and difficulty controlling his aggression.

Tyson became famous for his legendary boxing career and infamous for his trouble with the law, but he is also widely known for biting off part of Evander Holyfield's ear during a boxing match in 1997. This incident can teach us a lot about violence, rage, and the muscle of discipline.

During their first match in 1996, Holyfield headbutted Tyson multiple times. Headbutts are illegal in boxing but the referee believed they were accidental. One of the headbutts cut Tyson above the eye and the referee called a time-out. The match resumed and Tyson lost in the eleventh round when Holyfield unleashed a barrage of punches. During their 1997 rematch, Holyfield again headbutted Tyson several times, again cutting him above the eye. The referee called a time-out, but soon after the fight resumed Holyfield headbutted Tyson yet again. Tyson talks about what happened next:

> He butts me again. He's taller than me. What is his head doing underneath my head? I received a cut eye. He started looking at the eye. He butts me again. I complain to the referee. The referee doesn't do anything. I become ferocious . . . I'm mad. I get so mad I want to kill him . . . At the moment I'm enraged and I lose all composure and discipline. I fight and fight and fight and I want to choke him. I bit him . . . I wanted to just kick him right in his groin . . . I got so mad I wanted to just choke him. I wanted to kill this guy. I couldn't believe he butted me. And I just lost my cool. I lost my composure. The worst thing a warrior, a soldier could ever do is lose his discipline. I was depressed with myself not because I bit him, but just because I lost my discipline and composure . . . And I'm insane at the moment. I'm a good person, but at that moment I went insane. I was enraged . . . he butted me with his head intentionally to hurt me and my eye, so I wanted to intentionally hurt him, and so when I bit him again and [referee] Mills Lane came and disqualified me, I didn't really care. I wanted to inflict as much pain as possible on that man, because I was totally insane at that moment.[2]

Tyson describes his urge to inflict as much pain as possible on another human being as insanity. There have been times when I was so enraged that I wanted to beat someone to death, and it is the most insane and painful experience I have ever felt. So when I say that human beings are not naturally violent, I am citing not only abundant evidence but also personal experience. Kindness fills us with joy, but the compulsion to inflict violence out of rage feels like insanity. As a teenager I wondered, *If human beings are naturally violent, why does rage feel so terrible and empathy so wonderful?*

As a child I almost drowned in a swimming pool, and when I am consumed by rage it also feels like drowning. Just as a person submerged in water has difficulty hearing and seeing, a person drowning in rage has trouble hearing his conscience and can no longer see with the clarity that empathy gives us. A drowning person's lungs ache desperately for oxygen, and an enraged person's mind aches desperately to inflict violence.

When I am enraged I not only feel like I am drowning. I am also filled with panic and terror. My rage promises to protect me if I agree to obey it, but it tries to convince me that hurting others is the only way I can find safety and comfort. With the same desperation as a person gasping for air, sometimes I sink so deeply into rage that inflicting pain seems like the only way to breathe.

Many people express their anger by yelling, crying, or even breaking things. But rage is a radioactive form of anger that wants to inflict as much pain as possible on another human being. Rage is an infection that festers in deep psychological wounds, and to create a more peaceful world we must learn how to heal these wounds. There is perhaps no infection more dangerous than rage.

Because it warps our perception of reality, rage can cause us to forget about consequences and even personal safety. Just as spilling coffee on a computer can short-circuit its electronic components, rage can short-circuit our conscience, empathy, and reason. Rage can spill into our minds for many reasons. In my case, rage erupts when psychological wounds from my childhood are reopened.

Several years after my father died I had a dream where he called me on the phone to apologize. He said, "I'm so sorry I did all those things to you. I never meant to hurt you. I'm deeply sorry. But I want you to know that when you were in high school I stopped beating you." I found the dream surprising for two reasons: the apology itself and how I reacted.

Instead of forgiving him I started screaming: "The only reason you stopped hitting me in high school was because I started lifting weights and got stronger. You knew if you attacked me I would kill you. Well, I wish you would hit me now so I could beat the shit out of you."

My father used to beat me to the point where I feared for my life, and when I lose my temper I feel the urge to inflict the same violence onto others. But our past experiences only shape us. They do not define us. Instead of committing violent crimes, I have been able to control my urges to attack people thus far in my adult life. Rather than beating someone to death, I have pursued a path of peace that has increased my awareness, empathy, understanding, and determination to create a less violent world. How have I been able to do this?

Although a traumatic upbringing, a mind clouded by rage, and other circumstances can severely impair our ability to make good decisions, inflicting violence on others is always a choice. When explaining why he bit Holyfield's ear, Tyson expressed disappointment in the way he handled the situation: "I lost my composure. The worst thing a warrior, a soldier could ever do is lose his discipline. I was depressed with myself not because I bit him, but just because I lost my discipline and composure."[3]

The muscle of discipline allows us to control our impulses. Soldiers require discipline to control impulses such as hunger, fear, and even rage. In *The Art of War*, Sun Tzu says one of the most dangerous flaws a general can have is "a hasty temper, which can be provoked by insults."[4] Sun Tzu knew that when people are enraged, they cannot think clearly and will make poor decisions. He also said: "If your opponent is of choleric temper, seek to irritate him."[5] According to Sun Tzu, one of the worst things a general can do in war is lose his temper, and one of the best things he can do is make his opponent lose his temper. A general filled with rage becomes reckless and careless, losing concern for consequences. This makes him more likely to fall into his opponent's trap.

The same is true in boxing and mixed martial arts. One of the biggest mistakes boxers or mixed martial artists can make in a fight is losing their temper. Rage clouds their judgment, inhibiting their ability to think clearly and make strategic decisions. Tyson said the most proficient boxers are those who are most relaxed in the ring. Rage is dangerous whether we are boxing, competing in mixed martial arts, waging war, or waging peace.

The muscle of discipline helps us make good decisions in many ways. When I lose my temper, discipline helps me calm down and maintain my composure. If I am so enraged I cannot calm myself down, discipline allows me to control the impulse to lash out by giving me the strength to walk away. When I am on the verge of making a decision out of anger, discipline allows me to control the impulse long enough to "sleep on it" and wait until the next morning. After a good night's sleep I am usually much calmer.

Discipline gives us many options. When I was drowning in rage and felt an overwhelming impulse to explode, discipline always threw me some kind of lifeline. On one occasion, I was so enraged that I went to an emergency room. I was incoherent and barely able to communicate, but discipline gave me the strength to seek medical help rather than act on my impulse to attack someone.

One of my goals in life is to continue healing the wounds that are the source of my rage. So far on my journey of inner healing, discipline has allowed me to make good decisions that kept me from harming others and myself. Nonetheless, I cannot judge those overcome by their violent impulses, because there have been numerous times when my discipline nearly failed me.

Discipline is not just for soldiers, boxers, mixed martial artists, or people trying to control their rage. Discipline is like gold. Just as gold is a universal currency in the world of economics, discipline is a universal currency in the world of achievement. Gold can be exchanged for goods and services in every country, and discipline can be exchanged for hard work and perseverance in every endeavor.

Every word in this book was paid for with discipline. Without discipline I could not have committed the enormous time and effort necessary to research, write, and edit. Many start a project but do not have enough discipline in their psychological bank account to finish. Many finish a project but lack the discipline to polish their work until it shines. For every hour I spent writing this book, I dedicated at least ten to editing and sharpening every sentence. Just as people can convert gold into cash to pay for goods and services, we can convert discipline into the hard work and perseverance that allow us to achieve our full potential.

To succeed in any pursuit, we must have discipline. For example, artists are often stereotyped as being lazy and undisciplined, but the most capable of them have incredible discipline. They spend thousands of hours honing their craft, and the same is true of athletes who endure hours of grueling training nearly every day. Nor can a person become effective at any profession without discipline. Civil rights activist James Lawson said people working for peace must have "fierce discipline" in order to succeed.

In addition to helping us in our profession, discipline can also improve our personal lives. Without it we cannot exercise, maintain a healthy diet, or keep up with our daily responsibilities. Discipline gives us order in our lives. Every day the sun's gravitational pull keeps the planets in orbit. In a similar way, discipline ensures our daily activities and responsibilities do not spiral out of control.

For me discipline is a lifeline that allows me to make good decisions when my mind is drowning in rage. For people trying to achieve anything worthwhile, discipline is gold that can be converted into hard work and perseverance. For people trying to have a happy and healthy life, discipline can shine like the sun. In the next section we will explore how discipline, especially in the twenty-first century, is also a key ingredient in the recipe for human survival.

Self-Control: A Higher Expression of Discipline

There never has been, and cannot be, a good life without self-control.

—Leo Tolstoy[6]

In Greek mythology, Orpheus was the greatest musician who ever lived. When people heard him play his harp, their hatred faded and love conquered their hearts. When he wandered through the forest strumming his haunting melodies, wild animals became enchanted by his songs and followed him. His music gave him the power not only to charm, but also to protect. When

Jason and the Argonauts journeyed to retrieve the Golden Fleece, Orpheus used his music to save them from the Sirens.

The Sirens killed sailors passing by their island. Possessing a woman's head and bird's body, they lured people to their deaths by hypnotizing them with their magical singing voices. When Odysseus, the hero of Homer's epic the *Odyssey*, sailed by the island where the Sirens lived, he ordered his sailors to plug their ears with beeswax. Because he wanted to hear the Sirens' beautiful music, however, he did not plug his ears and instead had his crew tie him to the ship's mast.

The Sirens quickly hypnotized Odysseus with their magical song, calling him to them. He tried desperately to break free from the ropes, but they were tied too tightly. So he begged his crew to untie him, but the sailors knew he would be killed if allowed to visit the Sirens. Eventually his ship passed beyond the reach of the Sirens' hypnotic voices, and Odysseus survived.

Jason and the Argonauts were not as well prepared as Odysseus and his crew. When Jason's ship passed by the island, the Sirens called out with their enchanting melody. All of the men on the ship would have been hypnotized and killed, but Orpheus saved them when he began playing his harp. Orpheus' music was more beautiful than the Sirens' song, and his talent as a musician overpowered their hypnotic voices.

When Orpheus returned from his journey with Jason and the Argonauts, he suffered a painful loss. His wife Eurydice died when a poisonous snake bit her. Stricken with grief, he journeyed to the underworld to retrieve her soul. To rescue his dead wife, Orpheus needed to persuade Hades, the god of the underworld, to release her soul to the world of the living. It would be a difficult task, because Hades had a hardened heart and felt little empathy.

Orpheus descended into the depths of the underworld where Hades resided, a place where few mortals dared to visit. When he finally stood before the god who ruled the dead, he pleaded for the return of his wife not with words, but with music. As Orpheus played his harp, the residents of the underworld were stirred to tears. Even the souls of the damned wept when hearing his moving song.

Hades, who was not easily persuaded, was so deeply touched by the music that he agreed to let Eurydice return to the world of the living with

Orpheus. But on one condition. She must walk behind him, and he must not look at her until they exit the underworld and reach the surface. If he looked at her before leaving the underworld, Hades warned that she would disappear and be gone forever.

Orpheus played his music as they ascended toward the world of light. With Eurydice following closely behind him, he could barely restrain his desire to turn around and see her. During every moment that passed, he could not stop thinking about how much he missed her, and how badly he wanted to hold her in his arms again. After a long journey through the underworld's winding caverns, Orpheus saw the exit ahead.

With the surface world in sight, the thought of seeing his wife again caused his heart to beat faster and his desire to overwhelm him. When he came within a few steps of the exit, he could no longer restrain himself. At the last moment, he surrendered to his impulse to look at Eurydice. He turned around and saw her smiling face, but only for a moment. Within seconds, she disappeared and was gone forever, just as Hades had warned.

Orpheus never recovered from the grief of losing his wife again. This time a snake did not kill her. He did. If only he had restrained his impulse to turn around for a few more moments, she would be alive. The tragic story of Orpheus reveals a vital truth about human nature. One of the most important life skills we can have is the ability to delay gratification. This requires self-control, a higher expression of discipline that allows us to make short-term sacrifices for long-term gains. Because Orpheus lacked self-control, he lost his wife a second time.

During the 1960s Walter Mischel, a Stanford University professor of psychology, performed a groundbreaking experiment that demonstrated the importance of self-control. Four-year-olds were asked to select a treat from a tray of marshmallows, cookies, and pretzel sticks. When a child chose a marshmallow, Mischel would make an offer. The child could either eat one marshmallow immediately or wait until Mischel returned after leaving the room and receive two marshmallows as a reward. If the child could not wait for the second marshmallow, he or she could ring a bell and Mischel would come back and dispense one marshmallow. A New Yorker article written by Jonah Lehrer explains the results:

Footage of these experiments, which were conducted over several years, is poignant, as the kids struggle to delay gratification for just a little bit longer. Some cover their eyes with their hands or turn around so that they can't see the tray. Others start kicking the desk, or tug on their pigtails, or stroke the marshmallow as if it were a tiny stuffed animal . . . [Most of the children] struggled to resist the treat and held out for an average of less than three minutes. "A few kids ate the marshmallow right away," Walter Mischel, the Stanford professor of psychology in charge of the experiment, remembers. "They didn't even bother ringing the bell. Other kids would stare directly at the marshmallow and then ring the bell thirty seconds later. About thirty percent of the children . . . successfully delayed gratification until the researcher returned, some fifteen minutes later. These kids wrestled with temptation but found a way to resist it . . .

Starting in 1981, Mischel sent out a questionnaire to all the reachable parents, teachers, and academic advisers of the six hundred and fifty-three subjects who had participated in the marshmallow task, who were by then in high school. He asked about every trait he could think of, from their capacity to plan and think ahead to their ability to "cope well with problems" and get along with their peers. He also requested their S.A.T. scores.

Once Mischel began analyzing the results, he noticed that low delayers, the children who rang the bell quickly, seemed more likely to have behavioral problems, both in school and at home. They got lower S.A.T. scores. They struggled in stressful situations, often had trouble paying attention, and found it difficult to maintain friendships. The child who could wait fifteen minutes had an S.A.T. score that was, on average, two hundred and ten points higher than that of the kid who could wait only thirty seconds . . .

For decades, psychologists have focused on raw intelligence as the most important variable when it comes to predicting success in life. Mischel argues that intelligence is largely at the mercy of self-control: even the smartest kids still need to do their homework.[7]

Later in the article Lehrer tells us:

> Angela Lee Duckworth, an assistant professor of psychology at the University of Pennsylvania . . . first grew interested in the subject after working as a high-school math teacher. "For the most part, it was an incredibly frustrating experience," she says. "I gradually became convinced that trying to teach a teenager algebra when they don't have self-control is a pretty futile exercise." And so, at the age of thirty-two, Duckworth decided to become a psychologist. One of her main research projects looked at the relationship between self-control and grade-point average. She found that the ability to delay gratification—eighth graders were given a choice between a dollar right away or two dollars the following week—was a far better predictor of academic performance than I.Q. She said that her study shows that "intelligence is really important, but it's still not as important as self-control."[8]

To predict how well people will perform in life, the best indicator is not intelligence, but self-control. To make the most of our intelligence and talent, we must have self-control. In Greek mythology Orpheus was the greatest musician who ever lived, but his failed attempt to save his wife shows that all the talent in the world does not matter if we lack self-control.

Mischel's research shows that self-control not only contributes to successful careers. It is also vital to successful relationships. Someone who constantly surrenders to impulses and immediate gratification has trouble investing the hard work and patience that friendships, families, and marriages require in order to flourish.

Additionally, Ozlem Ayduk, assistant professor of psychology at the University of California at Berkeley, found that people who lack self-control are more likely to suffer from drug addiction and health problems caused by overeating.[9] These studies show that a lack of self-control can hurt not just our careers. It can also harm our friendships, families, marriages, and physical health.

To create a more peaceful world, we must recognize that self-control improves the health of our society along with the well-being of our personal lives. In chapter 2, I noted that a characteristic of psychopaths is lack of empathy. Another attribute common to psychopaths is an inability to control their impulses. Both are reasons they are capable of causing so much harm.

Individual lack of self-control also harms a community by diminishing cooperation among its members. Research into chimpanzee behavior shows they lack much of the self-control that human beings are capable of developing. Because they have difficulty controlling their impulses, chimpanzees cannot cooperate as well as people. Referring to an experiment where two chimpanzees had to cooperate to obtain food, the narrator in the documentary *Ape Genius* states: "A series of trials shows that this teamwork doesn't come easily. The helper must be a friend, and the food divided into separate dishes."

When the experiment was performed with bonobos (an ape closely related to chimpanzees), they were able to share food from the same dish.[10] Because bonobos have a more congenial temperament and are less aggressive and impulsive than chimpanzees, they are better able to cooperate.

In the army I learned that the power to control impulses and delay gratification gives leaders the ability to sacrifice for their subordinates. As mentioned earlier, on army field exercises the highest-ranking soldiers eat last. The army taught me that self-control is a necessary leadership skill that allows us to make short-term sacrifices for long-term rewards. As General Patton said: "A pint of sweat saves a gallon of blood."[11]

The fact that short-term sacrifices can produce long-term rewards is true not only in war, but in any endeavor. Musicians know serious practice and rehearsal are key to an exceptional concert performance. Athletes know hard work and sacrifice during training pay off significantly during competition. My writing coach Jo Ann Deck always tells me: "Hard writing produces easy reading." The more hard work and sacrifice I put into writing this book, the easier it will be for people to read.

Many fables reveal the value of making short-term sacrifices. In Aesop's

"The Grasshopper and the Ant," a lazy grasshopper plays while a disciplined ant saves enough food to last through the winter. In "The Three Little Pigs," one pig puts in the effort to build his house out of bricks while the other two merely use straw and sticks. When a wolf blows down the straw and stick houses, the two lazy pigs seek safety in the hard working pig's house of bricks. I put a lot of hard work and sacrifice into my writing because I want this book to be a brick house, not a house of straw easily blown down.

Because Orpheus lacked self-control, he was unable to make the short-term sacrifice of not looking at Eurydice for the long-term reward of bringing her back to life. This tragedy reminds us that a lack of self-control ultimately hurts those around us. Today it is imperative that humanity make decisions with long-term gains rather than immediate gratification in mind, or we will perpetuate our problems and increase suffering around the world.

Self-control is necessary to solve problems such as war, environmental destruction, overpopulation, and the threat of nuclear weapons, but where these problems are concerned we are not choosing between the immediate gratification of one marshmallow and the long-term reward of two. We must choose between nearsighted decisions that will lead to our extinction or long-term planning that will protect our survival. In an article about the lack of long-term thinking in politics, Brian Merchant says:

> If there's one fundamental principle that people of all po-
> litical ideologies could agree upon, it'd have to be this basic con-
> cept: We should be striving to make the nation a good place to
> live in the long term, with an eye to what things might be like
> in 20, 50, 100 years, rather than merely after 2, 4, or 6 years.
>
> But it seems difficult to get US politicians to adhere to the
> long view when their goals are pegged to the election cycle.
> Certainly, popular opinion of our representatives, senators and
> presidents holds that each are more concerned with their own
> reelection than long-term thinking . . . If we are going to make
> concrete progress in moving society towards loftier aims, it
> means not only demanding our politicians tackle some of the
> bigger, unpopular questions, but that they start taking a longer
> view as well.[12]

By helping us restrain our impulses and delay gratification, self-control allows us to plan strategically for the long-term. If humanity is going to survive in the twenty-first century and beyond, we must make the kinds of short-term sacrifices that will pay off years from now. Parents do this every day when they make sacrifices that will contribute to their children's future, and entire countries can be persuaded to make short-term sacrifices for long-term gains.

During World War II when food, gas, and other resources were low, Americans saw it as their patriotic duty to conserve these valuable commodities. They planted vegetables in their backyards, known as "victory gardens," to help contribute to the food supply. When the nation's survival was at stake, Americans took pride in their sacrifices and saw them as a service to their country. Today we must shift attitudes in America, and throughout the world, toward the importance of long-term planning. I believe this is possible, because if I could develop self-control, anyone can.

As a child, I was impatient and had great difficulty restraining my impulses. In 1980 I was born into the "instant gratification generation"; we were conditioned by television and other societal influences to have short attention spans. Throughout childhood I had trouble paying attention in class and exhibited many of the same behavioral problems as the children who performed poorly in Mischel's marshmallow test. Like many young people I had impulses to procrastinate, cut corners when doing my work, and seek immediate gratification instead of long-term rewards.

Although I still struggle at times, training in the art of living has greatly increased my self-control, and I continue to train every day. The patience and perseverance I have developed through discipline are necessary for my peace work. The civil and women's rights movements show us meaningful change may require decades and even generations of hard work. How have I been able to strengthen my muscle of discipline into its higher expression of self-control, and why am I so hopeful that others can develop the discipline necessary to work for peace? To answer these questions we must explore the benefits that arise when we unlock the highest expression of discipline.

Inner Freedom: The Highest Expression of Discipline

In some ways West Point is like a monastery. Cadets are punished if they are caught having sex on campus, and alcohol use is severely restricted. A hundred "hours"—walking back and forth in uniform with a rifle on your shoulder—is the usual punishment for these violations. When I was there if you missed a class, or were late for class three times, you were given ten hours. To pay off ten hours a cadet would walk five hours on Saturday and another five on Sunday. A hundred-hour punishment could take months to fulfill.

Many other standards were also enforced. During my first two years at West Point, I wasn't allowed to have civilian clothes in my room and I could leave campus only a couple of times during a semester. I had to wake up early and make my bed every morning, be in my room by 11:30 p.m. during the school week, and play an intramural sport or attend parade practice following my afternoon classes. My room was inspected nearly every day. Had I failed one of the many drug tests I would have been kicked out. West Point also had an honor code, and expulsion was common for cadets caught lying, cheating, or stealing. I had to take eighteen to twenty-one credit hours every semester and minor in engineering no matter what my major was, and summer vacations lasted only a few weeks due to mandatory military training in the summer.

Although I was miserable during most of my four years there, I think Gandhi would have loved West Point. Because he understood the importance of having a strong muscle of discipline when working for peace, his lifestyle was similar to that of a cadet. Tenzin Kacho, a Tibetan nun ordained by the fourteenth Dalai Lama, served as a Buddhist chaplain at the U.S. Air Force Academy for six years. When she first arrived at the academy, which is similar to West Point in many ways, she was surprised by how much she had in common with the cadets. She got along with them very well and never imagined that a military academy shared similarities with a Buddhist monastery.

According to West Point, Gandhi, and Buddhist philosophy, we cannot overcome significant obstacles unless discipline becomes part of our daily life. Gandhi said: "I regard myself as a soldier, though a soldier of peace. I know the value of discipline and truth."[13]

West Point instilled in me something else of great value: it taught me to think critically. Many of my professors encouraged me to question and think for myself, and West Point's guest speakers also challenged how I thought. In 2006 (a few years after I graduated in 2002) West Point invited Noam Chomsky, a well-known critic of American foreign policy, to give a lecture to the sophomore class on just war theory and whether the Iraq War was just. Introducing Chomsky, West Point philosophy professor Dr. Robert Tully said: "Let this discussion be what all philosophical debate aims to be: objective, open, respectful, fair, well-argued. In one word—rational."[14]

In an interview with *Journal News*, Lieutenant Colonel Casey Neff, who works at West Point's commandant's office, said free speech is one of the rights the military is here to defend, and he enjoyed Chomsky's debate-provoking lecture.[15] In the same year West Point also invited Bill Moyers, another critic of American foreign policy, to give a lecture on the meaning of freedom. Moyers said:

> Finally, and this above all—a lesson I wish I had learned earlier. If you rise in the ranks to important positions—or even if you don't—speak the truth as you see it, even if the questioner is a higher authority with a clear preference for one and only one answer. It may not be the way to promote your career; it can in fact harm it. Among my military heroes of this [Iraq] war are the generals who frankly told the President [Bush] and his advisers that their information and their plans were both incomplete and misleading—and who paid the price of being ignored and bypassed and possibly frozen forever in their existing ranks: men like General Eric K. Shinseki, another son of West Point. It is not easy to be honest—and fair—in a bureaucratic system. But it is what free men and women have to do. *Be true to your principles*, General Kosciuszko reminded Thomas Jefferson. If doing so exposes the ignorance and arrogance of power, you may be doing more to save the nation than exploits in combat can achieve.[16]

I did not appreciate the many gifts West Point gave me until after I graduated. When I reflect upon my experiences at the academy, I realize how the
adversity strengthened my character and taught me valuable life lessons. Because I wasn't allowed to party and get drunk on weekends, I learned how
to savor life's simple yet profound pleasures, like having a stimulating conversation, reading a book, and enjoying the company of friends. West Point
taught me many leadership skills that help me wage peace, and its challenging lifestyle taught me a lot about myself. After four years at West Point, the
indescribable sense of accomplishment I felt upon graduating was convincing
proof that short-term sacrifices lead to long-term gains.

We don't have to attend West Point or live in a Buddhist monastery to
strengthen our muscle of discipline. We can begin in childhood. In the
Lehrer article mentioned earlier he says:

> He [Mischel] knows that it's not enough just to teach kids
> mental tricks [for self-control]—the real challenge is turning
> those tricks into habits, and that requires years of diligent prac-
> tice. "This is where your parents are important," Mischel says.
> "Have they established rituals that force you to delay on a daily
> basis? Do they encourage you to wait? And do they make wait-
> ing worthwhile?" According to Mischel, even the most mun-
> dane routines of childhood—such as not snacking before
> dinner, or saving up your allowance, or holding out until
> Christmas morning—are really sly exercises in cognitive train-
> ing: we're teaching ourselves how to think so that we can out-
> smart our desires. But Mischel isn't satisfied with such an
> informal approach. "We should give marshmallows to every
> kindergartner," he says. "We should say, 'You see this marsh-
> mallow? You don't have to eat it. You can wait. Here's how.'" [17]

Many physical exercises allow us to improve our body's health, and numerous psychological exercises can help us increase our mental discipline.
Meditation is one technique for strengthening the mind. When we lift
weights regularly, we can hold an object that once seemed heavy with little
effort. In a similar way, when we practice meditation on a daily basis, we

can easily control impulses that once seemed overpowering.

We will explore the secrets of meditation in future books. For now we must stay focused on our current mission, which is to understand why discipline is an integral part of our humanity that can improve our lives and the world around us. During every step of this mission we have revealed truths about discipline that allow us to break stereotypes.

One stereotype we must shatter is the image, generated in the 1960s, of peace activists as hedonistic, irresponsible, drug abusing, sexually promiscuous hippies who have no discipline or self-control. We need a more realistic depiction of what it looks like to work for peace. To heal the causes of conflict in the twenty-first century, humanity requires a disciplined approach to peacemaking and a new army of peace activists. The soldiers of peace in this new army will be well prepared to solve our human problems. They will be highly trained in leadership skills and the art of waging peace. They will be disciplined, determined, resilient, compassionate, and strategically brilliant. They will be able to persuade people with opposing viewpoints, rather than just preach to the choir.

Martin Luther King Jr. called civil rights leader James Lawson "the leading theorist and strategist of nonviolence in the world." Lawson said, "The difficulty with nonviolent people and efforts is that they don't recognize the necessity of fierce discipline and training, and strategizing, and planning, and recruiting."[18]

This new army begins with a peaceful revolution in people like you and me and spreads from there. We can all become soldiers of peace in our daily lives, and we can all contribute to a peaceful revolution in the lives of others.

West Point is not a perfect institution, but it taught me many skills and life lessons that help me wage peace today. One lesson is that true discipline does not mean obeying an authoritarian system out of fear of punishment. According to West Point, discipline must be internalized, and those with discipline deeply embedded in their character will behave ethically not because they are worried about being punished, but because it is the right thing to do. During my four years at the academy, I internalized enough discipline to serve me for the rest of my life. That was West Point's intent.

By restricting my freedom West Point also gave me enormous appreciation for the gift of freedom, which helps me understand why it is worth defending. Many people in America do not appreciate their freedom because it has never been taken from them. After spending four years at West Point, I will never take my freedom for granted again.

Although many people take their freedom for granted, far more people do not appreciate or even think about inner freedom. What is inner freedom?

Inner freedom means being released from the prison of uncontrollable impulses. True discipline does not cause us to repress our impulses, but to have a new relationship with them. Instead of being a slave to every whim, discipline allows us to master our desires. As I explained in the last section, when the muscle of discipline grows strong it becomes self-control: a higher expression of discipline that allows us to make short-term sacrifices for long-term gains. When the muscle of discipline reaches its highest expression, we achieve inner freedom.

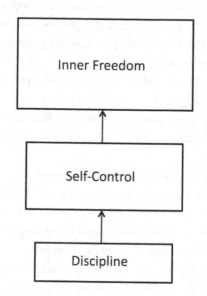

Figure 6.1: The Muscle of Discipline

In the Bhagavad-Gita, a Hindu text that greatly influenced Gandhi, the warrior Krishna says: "Constant self-control is the real and perpetual happiness."[19] According to Hinduism and many other religions, self-control creates happiness by freeing us from the prison of our desires. When we are no longer slaves to our impulses, we gain the joy of inner freedom.

As each of us journeys through life, the human mind is like a ship. When the captain and crew consist of empathy, conscience, reason, and the other muscles of our humanity, the ship is best prepared to endure storms, overcome adversity, and sail to beautiful shores. Standing in the way of our happiness are unrestrained impulses, which act like a thick fog. When people are enslaved by their desires and imprisoned by immediate gratification, the fog blocks their vision and a shipwreck becomes more likely. But discipline is sunlight that burns through the fog. It allows us to see clearly. It allows us to navigate safely. It allows us to live freely.

Sir Gawain and the Green Knight

Sir Gawain was King Arthur's nephew and a knight of the Round Table. According to Arthurian legend, Gawain was a disciplined warrior and Arthur's bravest knight, who was duty bound to accept challenges on behalf of his king. One day the massive Green Knight, riding a green horse and carrying a menacing green axe, came uninvited to Arthur's castle. As Arthur and his knights stared in wonder, the Green Knight proposed a challenge. He wanted one of Arthur's knights to cut off his head and fulfill an oath to meet him one year later at a green chapel, where he in turn would decapitate his killer. It seemed impossible for the Green Knight to return from the dead, and Arthur and his knights were intrigued by this strange challenge. The only one brave enough to accept it was Gawain.

The Green Knight got off his horse, handed Gawain his axe and knelt down. In one swift motion Gawain removed the Green Knight's head. A few moments later, everyone watched in shock as the Green Knight's body picked up its head and held it at arm's length by the hair. The head opened its eyes, smiled calmly, and reminded Gawain to meet him in a year. Then the Green Knight mounted his horse and rode off.

A year later, Gawain kept his oath by riding into the woods toward the green chapel. But the deeper he journeyed into the forest the less certain he became of the chapel's location. As the sun began to set one evening, he saw a small cabin in the distance and decided to ask for directions. A hunter cheerfully greeted him and listened intently as he explained why he must be at the green chapel in three days. The hunter pointed the way to the chapel, which was nearby, and kindly asked Gawain to spend the next three days at his small cabin to rest.

The hunter and his wife fed Gawain well and treated him with the utmost kindness. But every day while the hunter was away hunting, his beautiful wife tried to seduce Gawain. Although the hunter's wife offered him an opportunity to have sex one last time before he died and was also one of the most beautiful women he had ever seen, he could not betray the kind hunter by sleeping with his wife. Every day the hunter's wife tried more aggressively to seduce Gawain, but he used his discipline to resist temptation.

After three days had passed, he thanked the couple and rode to the green chapel. Approaching cautiously, he saw the Green Knight sharpening his axe. Gawain greeted the Green Knight respectfully, and the magical creature responded by asking him to lower his head and prepare for death. Gawain knelt on both knees and closed his eyes.

As the Green Knight lifted his axe high into the air, Gawain flinched. Ridiculing him for his cowardice, the Green Knight told him to stretch out his neck a little more. Gawain used his discipline to summon his bravery and overcome his fear. Again the Green Knight raised his axe high into the air, but he brought it down with just enough force to leave a tiny cut on Gawain's neck.[20]

Sparing his life, the Green Knight revealed he was the hunter. He had used his magic to create the cabin, hunter, and hunter's wife to test Gawain's discipline and bravery. Because Gawain resisted the temptation to sleep with the hunter's wife and showed courage in the face of death, the Green Knight let him live. Joseph Campbell explains the meaning behind this story: "Here's a knight [Sir Gawain] who really transcended the two great temptations— the fear of death and lust for sex . . . And the moral is that the realization of your bliss—your true being—comes when you have put aside the passing moment with its terror and with its temptations."[21]

In the previous section I discussed how discipline does not restrict our happiness. On the contrary, it increases our joy by freeing us from the prison of uncontrollable impulses. If we are undisciplined, we will be enslaved by laziness and gluttony. When our muscle of discipline is strong, however, we have the willpower necessary to work hard for what we believe in and live life to its fullest. The willpower created by discipline gives us patience and persistence, a powerful combination. This willpower also gives us the strength to resist temptation.

As we struggle to create the change our world so desperately needs, we must resist many temptations. In addition to temptations such as fear and greed, we must resist the temptation to remain silent when witnessing injustice. When experiencing adversity, we must resist the temptation to become cynical. As we strive to solve our human problems, we must resist the temptation to settle for easy answers that do not address the root causes of our problems. When obstacles seem to block our progress toward peace, we must resist the temptation to give up.

Lt. Col. Dave Grossman offers the simplest definition of what it means to be a warrior. He says that after the terrorist attacks on September 11, 2001, most people thought, "Thank goodness I wasn't on those hijacked planes." However, a warrior's response to hearing about the September 11 attacks would have been, "I wish I could have been on those planes. Maybe I could have made a difference."[22] Being on a hijacked plane would frighten almost anyone. What defines a warrior is not whether a person feels fear, but his or her response to it.

Warriors are brave, not fearless, and there is a big difference between the two. A fearless person feels no fear, but a brave person is afraid and overcomes the temptation to surrender to fear. People can be fearless due to ignorance or insanity, but warriors must be intelligent enough to understand the dangers they face and brave enough to overcome fear despite the risks. Sir Gawain felt enormous fear when the Green Knight first lifted his axe high into the air, but he was brave enough to overcome his fear of death, which is what all warriors must do.

In *Will War Ever End?* I explained that in combat our flight response is far more powerful than our fight response. The vast majority of people prefer to run when a sword is wielded against them, a spear is thrust in their direction, a bullet flies over their head, or a bomb explodes in their vicinity. Most people do not want to be maimed or die a violent and painful death. General Patton said: "Every man is scared in his first battle. If he says he's not, he's a liar."[23] Even Mike Tyson was frightened during his first boxing match. He explains:

I was so scared in my first amateur fight that I went
downstairs and said . . . "I'm going to the store," to my trainer.
And I went downstairs and I said [to myself], "Man, I should
get on this train and just never come back." I wanted to get
on the train and just leave. I was so scared. I didn't want to
fight anybody. It's just such a different dynamic than fighting
somebody in the ring than it is fighting somebody in the
street. And I never thought I could fight somebody. Even after
all the training, I was totally intimidated fighting somebody
in the ring. But I pulled myself together with the discipline I
learned from Cus [Tyson's trainer], and I went in the ring and
scored a third-round knockout.[24]

A warrior's ability to overcome the fear of injury and death is best
represented by the Trojan hero Hector. In Homer's *Iliad*, he is the most ad-
mirable character, a loving family man who dislikes war but fights courageously to protect his people. Like all true warriors, Hector is not fearless,
but he is brave. Confronted by the Greek warrior Achilles, Hector is so overwhelmed by fear that he runs away. Achilles chases him around the city of
Troy three times. Eventually Hector stops running and faces Achilles. To
protect his homeland from the invading Greek army, Hector has to overcome
his fear of death. He fights Achilles and dies defending his people.

On September 11, brave firefighters ascended the stairs of the burning
Twin Towers to rescue those who needed help. These firefighters were not
fearless. Like Sir Gawain and Hector, they were aware of the risks involved
and brave enough to overcome their fear of death. Grossman says a warrior's
response to hearing about September 11 would be: "I wish I could have been
on those planes. Maybe I could have made a difference." But he is not saying
warriors have a death wish. Warriors come in all shapes and sizes, and physical bravery is only one manifestation of the warrior spirit.

True warriors are willing to make a difference, even if it means putting
themselves at risk. From the age of twenty-six until his assassination at thirty-
nine, Martin Luther King Jr.'s life was constantly threatened. Jens Pulver,
a mixed martial artist and former champion of the Ultimate Fighting
Championship, says: "To be remembered is one thing, to be remembered

and *appreciated*—that's Martin Luther King Jr. . . . To be a protector. That's what Martin Luther King Jr. was. He was a mentor. He was a motivator. But above that he was a protector."[25]

Warriors are protectors, and there are many ways to be a protector. Albert Schweitzer went to Africa to help the sick, and Mother Teresa went to India to help the suffering. But often where we are needed most is right here at home. Every day in the United States unsung heroes help those who are struggling in their own neighborhoods. Grossman calls these people "peace warriors."

The toughest peace warriors are similar to boxers. A punch is most likely to knock someone unconscious if it strikes the jaw, because getting hit on the chin causes our head to rotate so quickly that the human brain has trouble withstanding the whiplash. A boxer who is easy to knock out is said to have a glass jaw, while one who is difficult to knock unconscious has an iron jaw. Like peace warriors who never give up, boxers with iron jaws keep pushing forward no matter how hard they are hit.

The film *Iron Jawed Angels* shows the incredible bravery and discipline demonstrated by women activists. During the struggle for women's rights, Alice Paul and other female peace warriors had metaphorical iron jaws. Although physically beaten, imprisoned, and tortured for protesting against gender inequality, they never gave up. They kept pushing forward until they achieved a constitutional amendment granting women the right to vote. Possessing bravery similar to warriors such as Sir Gawain and Hector, they did not allow their fear of injury or death to defeat them.

A strong muscle of discipline is essential for all warriors, because when we are imprisoned by uncontrollable impulses and the need for immediate gratification our capacity to make a positive difference becomes impaired. According to Joseph Campbell, the two great temptations that prevent warriors from achieving their full potential are fear of death and uncontrollable lust for sex. In the army I learned the importance of overcoming these and other temptations, because warriors are often put in situations where they can take advantage of people.

As a battery commander I was responsible for the well-being of over a hundred soldiers. Consensual sex with a female soldier under my command would likely have resulted in my court-martial. In the army I learned why this standard is necessary to maintain cohesion and trust in a unit. When a leader has control over a subordinate's well-being, a power imbalance is created, which puts the leader in a position to take advantage of that person. Authority figures often abuse their power to obtain sex. To prevent such abuses, an army leader is supposed to be disciplined, respectful, and professional.

As an army captain, I was in a position to take advantage of women under my command, and this is true for someone in any leadership role. Due to the power imbalance that results when people are placed in positions of authority, professors can take advantage of their students sexually, and bosses can exploit their employees in a similar way. Sexual harassment is a problem in universities and workplaces around America because many people lack warrior virtues such as discipline, respect, and professionalism.

The army taught me that a leader's job is to serve as a mentor, and mentoring and flirtation do not mix. Michael Nguyen, an officer I served with, says his pet peeves are "flirtation poorly disguised as mentorship; selfishness poorly disguised as selflessness." Leaders unable to resist temptation can harm the people they are supposed to help. Unfortunately, not every army leader lives up to these warrior virtues, and abuses of power do happen in the army.

Outside the army, peace warriors also have opportunities to take advantage of people. To show how humanity can achieve peace, my books must explore and provide new insights into the most compelling questions ever asked. What does it mean to be human? How can we live together in harmony? How can we survive and create a brighter future? To be effective, my message must be expressed in a way that uplifts the human spirit, and offers hope and meaning.

When we offer people inspiration and ways of achieving peace and joy in their lives, there are opportunities to take advantage of their vulnerabilities. Many people who offer hope have scammed others out of their money, and many men who offer inspiration have taken sexual advantage of young women. The importance of resisting these temptations, especially if we are struggling for peace, is not based on Christian dogma. It is a timeless warrior ideal that transcends cultures. Commenting on the legend of Sir Gawain and the Green Knight, Joseph Campbell says: "Do we not see what the tests are of this young knight Gawain? They are the same as the first two of Buddha. One is of desire, lust. The other is of the fear of death."[26]

Siddhartha Gautama, who became known as the Buddha, was a spiritual warrior who journeyed to discover the awakened state of enlightenment. After six years of fruitless searching, he sat under a Bodhi tree, vowing not to rise until he attained enlightenment. As he descended into deep meditation, he began to understand the highest truths of the human condition.

The demon Mara, who represented illusion, tried to distract Gautama from his mission by offering him a harem of beautiful women. When that failed, Mara used an army of demons armed with bows and arrows. With thousands of arrows falling from the sky toward him, Gautama did not move. The illusion was broken and the fearsome arrows transformed into flowers.

Eastern and Western philosophy both agree that the power to resist temptation allows us to achieve our full potential as human beings. The Western spiritual warrior Socrates was admired for his ability to resist temptations such as fear of death, lust for sex, and greed. The Greek general Alcibiades admired Socrates' impressive sexual restraint[27] and also compared him to the mighty Greek warrior Ajax: "I admired his character, his self-control and courage. Here was someone with a degree of understanding and tough-mindedness I'd never expected to find . . . I knew well that he was more completely invulnerable to the power of money than Ajax was to weapons."[28]

Socrates, Buddhism, West Point, the U.S. Army, and Eastern and Western philosophy agree that discipline is one of our greatest human powers. Throughout history, discipline and the ability to resist temptation were also viewed as signs of manliness and strength. Sara Lipton, an associate professor of history at the State University of New York, tells us: "We tend to accept the idea that power accentuates the lusty nature of men. This conception of masculinity is relatively new, however. For most of Western history, the primary and most valued characteristic of manhood was self-mastery. Late antique and Roman writers, like Plutarch, lauded men for their ability to resist sexual temptation and control bodily desire through force of will and intellect . . . A man who indulged in excessive eating, drinking, sleeping or sex—who failed to 'rule himself'—was considered unfit to rule his household, much less a polity [political organization]."[29]

Discipline is a cherished ideal in the East and West, and it is crucial for the well-being of all people. But it is even more important for warrior protectors, because those in need of help are often in vulnerable situations. Warriors who have a strong muscle of discipline will resist the temptation to take advantage of vulnerable people.

When we feel the temptation to take advantage of people, it is often caused by greed, lack of empathy, and psychological wounds that cause us to hurt others. By healing our psychological wounds and strengthening the muscles of our humanity, we can reduce our temptations at their root. To become peace warriors we must be committed to this kind of self-improvement, which allows us to achieve our full potential as human beings. This path is not without struggle, but like all things worth achieving, it is more than worth it.

As I journey toward healing my psychological wounds, the discipline I learned at West Point and in the army does not restrict me. It liberates me. Discipline lets me spend time away from the prison of uncontrollable impulses, the need for instant gratification, and temptation. It gives me the persistence and patience necessary to accomplish my goals and live fully. Most important, it gives me the strength to serve as a peace warrior to the best of my ability. In *The Little Prince*, Antoine de Saint-Exupéry encourages each of us to be disciplined peace warriors. "'It's a question of discipline,' the little prince told me later on. 'When you've finished washing and dressing each morning, you must tend your planet.'"[30] The survival of humanity and fate of our planet depend upon it.

CHAPTER 7

The Muscle of Curiosity

Madness and Redemption

The darkest periods of my life were not the times when I felt unloved, but when I was unable to love. It can be difficult to trust people when they have repeatedly hurt us, betrayed us, and let us down. To protect ourselves from pain and disappointment we can refuse to give others our trust. If we lose our ability to trust, however, we also lose our capacity to love.

Human beings require connection as much as plants need sunlight. Trust and love are sources of light that allow us to experience deep connection with each other. When we give trust and love, we cross the abyss of isolation that separates us, and the bonds of friendship and family become possible. A person able to trust and love never feels truly alone.

My father ruptured my ability to trust, and I have spent years trying to heal that wound. Fear tells me that trust makes me vulnerable to betrayal, but hope has convinced me that I can become strong enough to survive betrayal. To heal myself and build this strength, the road to peace has been my salvation. The more progress I make on this journey, the more grateful I am to my father. Every hopeful idea in this book is a product of childhood trauma, but that is not the only reason I appreciate my father. When people see compassion in me, they are seeing a reflection of him. He conditioned me to be violent, but he also taught me how to be gentle. My father showed me how to be both a destroyer and a protector.

In elementary school, one of my favorite Nintendo games was *Mike Tyson's Punch-Out!!* When I was in third grade, a friend from school visited my house and we played the game together. If you knew the password, you could skip to the last level, which involved a boxing match with Mike Tyson. As my friend entered the password that he had on a small piece of paper, I asked if he would share it but he refused, and it was too long for me to memorize.

My father had been standing in the back of the room and saw what happened. Unknown to us, he had quickly copied the password onto a piece of paper when he saw it displayed on the screen. After my friend left, my father surprised me by handing me the paper. I was so excited I could barely contain my emotions. In the depths of my heart, it was not the password that mattered, but that he had looked out for me. It is one of the fondest memories I have of my father.

But by the time I was in sixth grade, my father's paranoia had become so severe that he no longer wanted me to have friends. Growing up with him was like living with two different people. He could be violent and paranoid but also compassionate and gentle. He loved to garden and feed the birds in our backyard, and he treated animals kindly. When I was an infant, he adopted a sick puppy that was going to be euthanized. She was so ill nobody else wanted her, but he gave her a home and paid for the medical treatment to get her healthy. He told my mother, "I couldn't stand to see the poor little thing suffer."

My father rarely talked about war, but I remember him telling me about the countless suffering children he had seen during his service in the Korean War. He said his heart broke when he saw little boys and girls "shivering in the cold with frozen snot hanging from their noses." As a young soldier, fighting in a war decades before I was born, he had wanted to protect the Korean people. When I was a child I wanted to be like my father.

By observing my father's protective and destructive qualities, I learned an important truth about human nature. Whether we are male or female, black or white, rich or poor, every human being is similar to a burning flame. Imagine being lost in a forest during winter. The sun has set, and you are shivering uncontrollably in the subzero temperature. After wandering for hours in icy darkness, you walk by a log cabin. A kind person invites you to come inside and warm yourself by the fireplace. As you sit by the fire, its peaceful glow comforts and protects you. It feels like bliss.

Compassionate people are like a fireplace in the middle of winter. A flame can provide light during the darkest night, comforting and protecting us when we are most vulnerable. Our ancestors relied on fire to protect them not only from cold but also from predators. Fire is a great protector, but it can also be a great destroyer. The flame that warms a house can also burn it to the ground. Fire can maim, kill, and turn cities into ashes.

Every human being is similar to a flame, because we all have the potential to be protectors or destroyers. But unlike fire, which has no choice in what effect it will create, we each must make a decision. Will we strive to be a light that comforts and protects or will we be a raging inferno that wounds and destroys? As a child I witnessed both extremes in my father's behavior. Every day I work to fan the flames of compassion within me, but I know the embers of rage still smolder in the scars of my psychological wounds.

When I was a child, my father seemed like a walking contradiction, the embodiment of gentleness and rage. I loved and admired him as a protector but feared and hated him as a destroyer. For most of my life he felt like a stranger to me, yet after his death I have begun to feel closer to him. Because he is so much a part of me, the more I learn about myself the better I understand him. His rage is my rage. His madness also belongs to me.

Much of who we are is a reflection of our parents or a reaction against the way they tried to mold us. My father told me the army was the only place where an African American had a fair chance to succeed. As a result, West Point was the only college I applied to. He threatened to commit suicide if I didn't get accepted. I now understand that this was his way of motivating me and trying to protect me from the disappointments he had suffered, but putting that much pressure on a child leaves painful wounds that do not heal easily. Forgiveness has helped me heal, but when others have hurt us deeply, forgiveness is a gradual process.

On the path to forgiveness, I realized that my father raised me as best he could. It's not easy being human, let alone raising humans. When someone has survived the horrors of war, as my father did, being human is not only difficult. It can be intolerable. I have often felt that life is intolerable, and I have resisted the urge to commit suicide, but just barely. Childhood trauma creates a maddening emptiness in those who survive its wrath. The emptiness within me is so vast that all the money and fame in the world cannot fill it. I am still alive because the road to peace offers us a kind of wealth more fulfilling than fame or fortune, and it gives us what human beings need most.

As human beings, we all want to be happy. We all want connection. We all want to be acknowledged. We all want to feel worthy of love. When these psychological hungers are not satisfied, we ache with emptiness and struggle with madness. I have not surrendered to the madness that urges me toward destruction. I have fought it with every ounce of my being. By walking the road to peace, I will continue to fight the madness caused by violence in the home, and I will work with others to end the madness of war.

My Drug of Choice

Many people who experience severe childhood trauma become alcoholics and drug addicts. When we cannot bear the pain of our psychological wounds, we can medicate our agony with excessive alcohol and drug use. But this form of treatment has more in common with poison than medication, because it magnifies our agony and multiplies our problems instead of healing our suffering and helping us to live well. When people abuse alcohol and drugs to medicate their psychological wounds, it is like throwing gasoline on a furnace.

Because of the trauma in my life, I could have easily slipped into the downward spiral of drug addiction that shatters families and leaves people homeless, in prison, or dead. At West Point my obsessive behavior resembled the illness of addiction, and I became addicted to an unusual drug. Rather than craving cocaine or heroin, I was addicted to philosophy.

I grew up hating school, and I also hated reading books. But at age fifteen I fell in love with writing not because I liked reading, but because the creative process allowed me to explore and express the pain within me. Even though I wrote a lot during high school, I still saw books as those boring things my teachers made me read.[1] It was not until West Point that I realized how incredible books truly are. Once I understood their power, I became obsessed with them.

As I mentioned in chapter 3, a book is one of the most powerful things in the world. If you doubt this, consider why it was illegal to teach slaves how to read.[2] Also think about why the Nazis burned books and why dictators throughout history have banned books. One of the biggest threats to slavery, the Nazis, dictators, or any unjust system is books. Slave owners knew this. The Nazis knew this. Dictators know this today. Yet despite this, so many people take books for granted, just as I did when I was a teenager.

The daily demands of academics and military duties allowed for little spare time at West Point. Because drugs and alcohol were prohibited and the privilege of leaving campus was restricted, spare time had to be used creatively. I was fortunate to have good friends at West Point that I looked up to. They spent much of their recreational time exercising and reading books, and I thought of them as athletic intellectuals. Because I wanted to be more like them and didn't have anything better to do with my spare time, I started reading. Gradually I began to enjoy it more and more.

If someone who hated books as much as I did could learn to love reading, almost anyone can. My attitude changed when I found books that interested me and saw reading's positive benefits. Reading a book is one of the best investments a person can make. The philosopher Francis Bacon said "knowledge is power," and West Point taught me the mind is the most powerful weapon in the world. A dull mind is as useful as a dull sword; reading is one of the best ways to sharpen the mind.

An author may spend years, sometimes a lifetime, researching and writing a book, and reading it allows us to reap the rewards in a matter of hours. Nevertheless, how much a person benefits from a book depends on the receptiveness of the reader as well as the talent of the author. This is because people are like windows and the wisest books are similar to fresh air. The amount of fresh air that enters a room depends on how open the window is, just as the amount of wisdom a person absorbs from a book depends on how open their mind is to new information.

For example, taking advanced English for all four years of high school, I was required to read over fifty books, but I read only two: *Siddhartha* by Herman Hesse and *The Good Earth* by Pearl S. Buck. For every other book I read Cliffs Notes or a similar study guide. I read *Siddhartha* because it was short, not much longer than the Cliffs Notes. I found it boring, but when I read it again at the age of twenty-one it became one of my favorite books. I had also tried reading *The Grapes of Wrath* in high school but stopped due to boredom. At the age of twenty-six I took a copy with me to Iraq and thought it was one of the best books I had ever read. In my twenties these books filled me with excitement and seemed completely different from the boring novels I remembered from high school.

What changed? Many factors can make us more receptive to the wisdom contained in books, and several influences contributed to opening my mind's window. During my twenties I gained a lot more life experience. I also matured and grew as a human being due to the character education at West Point, the positive influence of my friends, the wisdom I absorbed from books, and many hours spent in quiet contemplation. As West Point taught me to be more idealistic about life and the world, I became less cynical and more receptive to the idea that I must take an active role in creating a brighter future.

Life experience, maturity, personal growth, the positive influence of friends, contemplation, and idealism are some of the factors that can open our mind's window. As the fresh air of wisdom pours into our being, a book that once seemed boring can fill us with hope and excitement. Widening our mind's window not only makes us more receptive, but also more perceptive. When our mind's window is open and we let in the fresh air of wisdom, we are not only able to see the full depth of great books, but it is easier to recognize when certain books lack depth. As we mature and grow as human beings, we sometimes realize that the books we used to like are actually very shallow.

I owe much of my strength as a writer to the fact that I grew up hating school. When I write, I want to reach and awaken the bored student I used to be. I have far more in common with the student that teachers think will never amount to anything than the one voted most likely to succeed, and I try my best to write books that would have interested the person I was in high school.

At West Point I became addicted to reading books on history, psychology, religion, and many other subjects, but my primary addiction was philosophy. People become drug addicts often to heal their psychological wounds and cope with life, and I pursued philosophy for the same reasons. Early philosophers such as Socrates, Buddha, Lao Tzu, Confucius, and Jesus explored how we can become happy, live well, coexist peacefully with others, and achieve our full potential as human beings. This was the kind of philosophy that I became obsessed with.

Like drug addiction, my addiction to philosophy was so severe at times that it negatively impacted my life. Instead of doing my homework at West Point, I would stay up late reading philosophy. I did the minimal amount of work necessary to pass most of my classes in order to have more time to read and write. I did not feel like I had any other choice. In my mind, I was in a life or death situation. If I did not find a way to heal my rage and suffering, I was going to die and perhaps hurt others in the process.

Our muscle of reason becomes weak under the debilitating influence of alcohol, cocaine, heroin, and other drugs, but for me philosophy was a drug that strengthened reason. Philosophy also strengthened my muscles of hope, empathy, appreciation, conscience, and discipline in long-lasting ways. No other drug is capable of doing this. Instead of healing our psychological wounds and helping us cope with life, cocaine and heroin drag people into a downward spiral of self-destructive behavior, but philosophy leads us through an upward spiral of personal growth that increases our emotional well-being and mental health.

Philosophy strengthened the muscles of my humanity, especially my muscle of curiosity. As I explained in *The End of War*, human beings are natural explorers, and it is not true that people always fear the unknown. Thousands of years ago we humans were nomads who traversed and populated the great unknown regions of Africa, Asia, Europe, Australia, and even the Americas. We explored the mysterious unknown not only of fire, but the entire natural world. During the past thousand years we sailed the dangerous oceans that led into the great unknown; we peered into the great unknown with telescopes; we looked deeply into the great unknown with microscopes. Eventually we set foot on the great unknown that was the moon.

If you give kindergarteners magnets to play with, are they terrified of the great unknown—the invisible forces at work within these mysterious objects—or are they deeply curious? Our large brains would be of little use without this inherent curiosity, which is why all explorations, innovations, and scientific breakthroughs are the offspring of humanity's love affair with the great unknown.

When astrophysicist Neil deGrasse Tyson was asked, "What should be done about the fact that our kids lag woefully far behind children in other countries in the areas of physics and mathematics?" he said, "My first reply is—as a parent—get out of their way. You are born a scientist. What does a scientist do? We look up and say, 'I wonder what that is. Let me go find out. Let me poke it. Let me break it. Let me turn it around.' . . . That's what kids do . . . We prevent that. We prevent these depths of curiosity from revealing themselves."[3]

When I was in preschool I asked questions about everything. Why does it rain? Why is the sky blue? Why does water turn into ice when it gets cold? What is lightning? What is the sun? What are the stars? Sometimes my parents and teachers got annoyed and told me to stop asking so many questions. Thousands of years ago our ancestors asked similar questions. To satisfy their curiosity, they created stories about gods to help them understand the sun, stars, and other mysteries of the universe.

When my father started attacking me and I witnessed his enormous suffering, my questions began to change. What is happening to my father? Why is he in so much pain? Why does he complain about nightmares of war? What is war?

As I grew older and my intellectual capacity developed throughout middle and high school, my questions continued to evolve. Are human beings naturally violent? Why does war happen? Is war inevitable? Will war ever end? At West Point and in the army, my thinking was pushed in new directions. This caused my questions to progress even further. How can we end war? How can we stop oppression and injustice? How can we live in harmony with our planet? How can we create a peaceful revolution that will give us the strength to solve our national and global problems?

Curiosity has fueled every question, discovery, and solution in human history, taking us into the deepest mysteries of life and the universe. Curiosity was vital to the survival of our ancestors, because it allowed them to explore and begin to understand their world. It enabled them to ask the right questions and find the best solutions. A strong muscle of curiosity is just as vital for our survival in the twenty-first century, and philosophy can help us strengthen this muscle.

Philosophy is the art of questioning, discovering, and solving. In these ways, philosophy exercises our muscle of curiosity. At heart, every philosopher is a curious child wanting to explore the great questions, discover the secrets of life and the universe, and solve the problems that prevent us from being happy and coexisting peacefully.

Equating my obsession with philosophy to drug addiction might seem like an exaggeration, but this comparison reflects how psychotic and out of control I used to feel. Although philosophy gave me the fulfillment that people hope to find in drugs, there are certainly differences between philosophy and addictive chemical substances. When we exercise our muscle of curiosity through philosophy, we not only gain the strength to serve humanity and our planet. We also achieve a sense of bliss more potent than the "high" produced by any other drug.

Adventure: A Higher Expression of Curiosity

For most of recorded history, people believed the sun revolved around the earth. In the second century, the astronomer Ptolemy reinforced this popular view by creating a model of the universe where the sun and stars orbit our tiny blue planet. The majority of people believed this myth for nearly fifteen hundred years, until a new viewpoint began to emerge.

During the sixteenth century, Copernicus proposed a new model of the universe where the earth revolved around the sun. After him, other astronomers such as Galileo Galilei and Johannes Kepler supported Copernicus' theory with convincing evidence. By challenging popular assumptions and refuting widely believed myths, they ignited a scientific revolution that changed how people saw the universe. We are living during an exciting time in human history, because we have an opportunity to witness and participate in an even greater revolution.

The peaceful revolution is a revolution of mind, heart, and spirit. But it is also a scientific revolution. To explain the importance of hope, empathy, appreciation, conscience, reason, discipline, and curiosity, I am relying on facts instead of my opinions. Without these muscles of our humanity, we cannot coexist peacefully as a global community or solve the greatest problems that threaten humanity. This is not a statement of opinion, but fact.

The peaceful revolution goes much deeper than this, and these chapters have only begun to scratch the surface. Copernicus, Galileo, and Kepler helped people understand how the universe works, and the peaceful revolution will help us understand how our internal universe functions. In our society, human nature and the muscles of our humanity are a mystery to most people. Hope, empathy, and appreciation are clichés, and the true power of conscience, reason, and discipline is rarely talked about. The peaceful revolution will create a paradigm shift that changes how we see war, peace, our responsibility to the planet, our kinship with each other, and what it means to be human.

Just as the revolution that Copernicus began refuted the myth that the universe revolves around us, the peaceful revolution will dispel many myths—like the myth that human beings are naturally violent. As the peaceful revolution grows stronger during the coming years, helping more of us understand the truth of our humanity, saying we are naturally violent will sound as absurd as saying the sun revolves around the earth.

Our ancestors believed the sun revolved around the earth, and many of them also thought the world was flat.[4] Although incorrect, they were far from stupid. If I had lived a thousand years ago, I would have believed the same misconceptions. To better understand this, imagine going back in time and trying to convince someone the earth revolved around the sun. An intelligent person may have responded like this: "Are you crazy? If we're orbiting the sun, why don't we feel a sense of motion? If you look up at the sky, it's obvious the sun and stars are circling around us. If our world was moving, we would feel it."[5]

Furthermore, imagine going back in time and trying to convince someone the world was round. An intelligent person may have responded like this: "Are you crazy? If you look around, isn't it obvious the world is flat? But if the earth is shaped like a ball as you suggest, then where am I located on this ball? Am I on the bottom? If so, why haven't I fallen off? Do you expect me to believe I'm upside down? And if I'm on its side, what is stopping me from sliding off? Maybe I'm standing on the very top of this ball, but in that case the rest of the world would be uninhabitable. Everyone on the sides and bottom would fall off."

Just as intelligent people used to believe the sun revolved around the earth and the world was flat, I have met intelligent people who believe human beings are naturally violent. When I suggest we are not, they sometimes say: "Are you crazy? If human beings aren't naturally violent, why have we had so many wars throughout history? Why do people commit murder and genocide? Think of all the horrible things we do to each other. You expect me to believe human beings aren't naturally violent?"

According to Thomas Hobbes and other theorists, we have a natural urge to hurt and kill each other that must be repressed. However, this book along with my first two demonstrate that we have a natural urge to coexist peacefully, but we can become violent through conditioning and other causes.

The earth revolving around the sun, the world being round, and humanity not being naturally violent are ideas that seem counterintuitive at first glance. If we are revolving around the sun, why don't we experience a sense of movement? It seems to defy common sense at first, but once we understand the laws of physics it makes complete sense. If the world is round, why don't people on the bottom and sides fall off? It seems to defy common sense at first, but once we understand the law of gravity it makes complete sense. If human beings aren't naturally violent, why have there been so many wars throughout history? It seems to defy common sense at first, but once we understand the laws of human nature it makes complete sense.

As I studied military history at West Point, I realized there is a deeper and more intriguing story to the history of warfare, and that everything is not as it first appears. Although war is common throughout history, the greatest problem of every army has been this: When a battle begins, how do you stop soldiers from running away? Where our fight-or-flight response is concerned, the vast majority of people prefer to run when a sword is wielded against them, a spear is thrust in their direction, a bullet flies over their head, or a bomb explodes in their vicinity.

Convincing soldiers to risk their lives and fight courageously is a problem even more urgent than defeating the opposing army, because if a general can't get his soldiers to remain on the battlefield there is no chance of victory. Many techniques can be used to make soldiers fight and not retreat. In the U.S. Army, a complex system of conditioning trains soldiers to stay and fight, but the ancient Greeks discovered a more effective method still used today.

At first glance the Greeks' solution might seem like a contradiction, because the most powerful motivator that convinces people to stay and fight is not a natural propensity for violence or killing, but their capacity for love and compassion. Halfway around the world, Lao Tzu acknowledged this fundamental truth about human nature when he said, "By being loving, we are capable of being brave."[6] This is why the most effective armies have a strong sense of brotherhood and camaraderie.

When our lives are threatened by lethal violence, our flight response tends to be more powerful than our fight response. This is a law of human nature. But when we see our loved ones in danger, our instinct to protect them, which I call fury, tends to be more powerful than our flight response. This is also a law of human nature.

In this book and *The End of War*, I explain some of the factors that can interfere with these laws. For example, I sometimes feel so much rage that I can barely restrain my urge to assault someone, but this is not natural. I was not born this way. Through abuse and a violent upbringing, I was conditioned to be this way.

People have understood the power of empathy and discipline for thousands of years, and both Eastern and Western religions express this awareness. Socrates, Buddha, Jesus, and Gandhi taught others to be compassionate and disciplined, but they did not have the scientific evidence to back up their claims. In the twenty-first century, we are gathering enough evidence to transform our understanding of empathy and discipline from moral ideals into scientific truths.

As I explained in the preface of this book, we are living during an information revolution that has dramatically changed our understanding in many ways. We discovered more about physics during the twentieth century than every previous century of recorded history combined. In the twentieth century we also made more advances in medical technology than during all the preceding centuries put together.

A bright new era is dawning that will push our understanding even further. During the peaceful revolution we will discover a wealth of convincing evidence and scientific knowledge about what it means to be human, how we can coexist peacefully as a global community, and how we can solve our national and global problems.

I experienced a revolution in my own way of thinking in 1998. When

I first learned about Lt. Col. Dave Grossman's revolutionary ideas as an eighteen-year-old West Point cadet, it was like being introduced to the work of Copernicus. This is not an exaggeration, because Grossman's book *On Killing* gave me a radically new view of the universe, just as Copernicus offered people a new perspective on the cosmos. No other single book has so completely changed how I see the world.

I had grown up believing that human beings have a natural desire to destroy each other. As a child I saw action movies where the hero casually killed hundreds of people without feeling fear or remorse. Grossman's revelations, like the work of Copernicus, gave me a new understanding that helped me make sense of the universe. According to *On Killing*, human beings are not natural killers, soldiers require training to perform effectively in battle, and every war requires dehumanization. One difference between Copernicus and Grossman is that Grossman offers a lot more evidence to support his claims than Copernicus did.

Although there are similarities between the peaceful revolution we are a part of and the scientific revolution led by Copernicus, Galileo, and Kepler, there are also significant differences. By shattering Ptolemy's earth-centered model of the universe, Copernicus, Galileo, and Kepler proved that virtually everyone before them had been incorrect about their understanding of the cosmos. In order to build a new house of understanding, the previous one had to be torn down. This shook the Christian world, which had an earth-centered view of the universe. But instead of tearing down the house where our traditional values reside, the peaceful revolution will build on its foundation and take our understanding to the next level.

Unlike Copernicus, Galileo, and Kepler, I am showing that many of those who came before us were not wrong, but right. Have you noticed that the ideas in this book sound very similar to the philosophy of Buddha and Jesus? I discuss the importance of unconditional love, for example, but not from a religious standpoint. Instead I assert the importance of unconditional love within the context of human survival and happiness. Unconditional love is vital for our survival, especially in the twenty-first century, and it also gives us a sense of meaning, purpose, connection, and fulfillment that leads to the highest peaks of bliss. This is not a coincidence.

Eating fresh fruit promotes our survival, and this is why it tastes good to most people. Eating animal dung and rotting meat does not promote our survival, and this is why it makes most people want to vomit. In a similar way, being hopeful, having close friendships built on strong bonds of empathy, appreciating life's many gifts, living without a guilty conscience, being calm and rational instead of angry and irrational, embracing the inner freedom of discipline, and being curious instead of closed-minded are all experiences that promote our survival. This is why they feel so damn good.

But what about candy and junk food? They taste good, but aren't they also bad for us? In nature, fruit contains a lot of sugar and nutrients. Junk food simulates fruit's high sugar content, tricking our brain into thinking we are eating something nutritious. Humanity is hungry for nutritious ideas that create unity and peace instead of junk food ideologies that promote apathy, division, and conflict.

There is another major difference between the revolution created by Copernicus, Galileo, and Kepler and the peaceful revolution we are involved in. Although they refuted the misconceptions of nearly every previous thinker, Grossman and I not only affirm but also rely heavily on the discoveries of many previous thinkers. Carl Sagan said: "If we see far, it is because we stand on the shoulders of giants."[7] Grossman's work is built on his own research but also on the contributions of many others. In the same way, my books stand on the shoulders of countless people. Without them my books would not exist.

This book confirms much of what these giants taught us. Socrates, Buddha, Lao Tzu, Thoreau, and Gandhi did not have the scientific evidence to back up their teachings about humanity, yet they were correct about many things. Nevertheless, I have met people who believe such wisdom is nonsense. When I discuss ideals like unconditional love and service to others, I have heard responses such as "Unconditional love and service to others? Those are silly moral ideals based on fantasy. That's the kind of crap Jesus talked about."

The peaceful revolution is building momentum as I write this, but it did not begin with me and it will not end with me. I am simply a link in a chain. I am one thread in a tapestry, and we can all become threads in the fabric of peace and justice. This book has started to uncover the laws of human nature, and a lot more work has to be done not just by me, but others who want to create a scientific foundation for our understanding of love, peace, and what it means to be human.

Copernicus, Galileo, Kepler, and other scientists used theories, equations, and observations to create a paradigm shift in human understanding. However, it took time for them to gather enough evidence to confirm this new understanding of the universe, and their realizations did not become common knowledge overnight. In a similar way, it will take time before neuroscience is able to gather enough evidence to confirm the ideas in this book. What has been revealed about human nature in these chapters will also not become common knowledge overnight.

Just as astronomers used telescopes to see the structure of our solar system, I have seen the structure of human nature as clearly as they saw the orbits of the planets. Meditation and contemplation have functioned as a metaphorical telescope allowing me to look deep within myself. Instead of a telescope that gazes at the stars, meditation and contemplation work together to create a telescope that looks within. I have seen the features of hope, empathy, appreciation, and rage with my mind's eye as clearly as Galileo saw the features of the moon.

Looking deep within myself has allowed me to know that human beings aren't naturally violent and peace is possible. Learning this for myself was a great challenge, but convincing others is an even greater challenge. It is easy for authors to write in an academic style that few can understand, but transforming complex concepts into simple ideas that people can easily comprehend is the biggest obstacle that every author, thinker, philosopher, and scientist must overcome. Making complex ideas sound simple without dumbing them down is a mission that I have tried to accomplish to the best of my ability.

Many years ago I heard an adage: "If you can't explain something complex in a simple way, then you don't understand it well enough." And Schweitzer said, "The value of any philosophy is in the last resort to be measured by its capacity, or incapacity, to transform itself into a living philosophy of the people. Whatever is deep is also simple."[8]

By revealing the truth of human nature in ways that convey simplicity and depth, the peaceful revolution will reach the masses during the coming years. The peaceful revolution will give people everywhere a new understanding that allows us to solve our national and global problems and heal the root causes of our conflicts rather than merely addressing their symptoms. War, oppression, injustice, and environmental destruction are symptoms of much deeper problems, and we must cure the virus.

To solve our problems at their root, we must strengthen our muscle of curiosity. Without it, we cannot face the challenges ahead with courage. When our muscle of curiosity becomes strong, we can approach life with a sense of adventure. This attitude allowed our nomadic ancestors to journey into unknown lands in search of greener pastures. A sense of adventure led to the greatest scientific discoveries in history, a man walking on the moon, and the social movements that have increased peace and justice around the world.

When people worked to abolish state-sanctioned slavery, the supporters of slavery fearfully argued that society would collapse if slavery were made illegal. But the abolitionists were brave pioneers, possessing a sense of adventure that came from knowing they were working to reshape the world in a positive way. They abolished state-sanctioned slavery, and the world did not end. When women wanted equal rights, the supporters of gender oppression said that society would collapse if women were allowed to vote and own property. Women achieved their rights, and the world did not end. When the civil rights movement struggled to end segregation, the supporters of segregation argued that society would collapse if white and black people lived together and intermarried. The segregation laws were defeated. Again the world did not end.

In the twenty-first century, humanity must end war, protect our environment, and create societies filled with fairness and opportunity if we are going to survive as a global community. I have heard fearful people say that society will collapse if we spend more money on helping people than manufacturing bombs, develop clean forms of energy that allow us to live in harmony with our environment, and stop the methods of exploitation that endanger fairness and opportunity. However, if we solve these problems the world will not end. It will survive.

Helen Keller said: "Life is a daring adventure or nothing."[9] Like the peaceful pioneers who preceded us, we must embrace the sense of adventure that comes from knowing we are reshaping the world in a positive way.

Adventure is a higher expression of curiosity that gives meaning to life, and the peaceful revolution is an adventure unlike any other in human history. During this critical time, we have the opportunity to shape our civilization in positive ways that would not only make our ancestors proud, but will give our descendants a chance to live full and productive lives.

In my next book, *The Art of Waging Peace*, we will explore how we can put the muscles of our humanity into action. We will also learn the tools that make positive change possible, and apply the principles of strategy and tactics to the mission of peace. *The Art of Waging Peace* will journey even deeper into my personal experiences and the heart of darkness in order to take our understanding of peace to the next level. I have a lot more to say about the peaceful revolution, as will many others. This book is just a beginning. There is so much more to discover and do. It will be an adventure.

Awe: The Highest Expression of Curiosity

I am alive today largely due to luck. For every person who rises from the underworld of trauma to ascend the road to peace, countless others end up addicted to drugs, homeless, in prison, or dead. A few acts of kindness and a handful of rare opportunities saved my life, and I hope this book has helped you see the least fortunate among us in a new way. We all share the same human spark that yearns for a meaningful life, and I am not so different from the people who have chosen violence over peace. If my high school English teacher had not encouraged me to be a writer and I had not attended West Point, I might have become a person who wants to destroy humanity, rather than someone working to protect it.

It is confusing to be human, and the messages I heard from society compounded my confusion. Growing up in the 1980s, I heard that greed is good, selfishness is a virtue, human beings are naturally violent, and peace is naive. In a society filled with so many confusing messages, I did not begin to understand the full potential of peace until I attended the United States Military Academy at West Point. Ironic, isn't it?

Not only is life in our society confusing, but we are taught so little about how to truly be happy, how to heal our suffering, and how to be human.

Herman Hesse said: "You knew so little, so desperately little about other people. You had learned a hundred dates of ridiculous battles and the names of ridiculous old kings in school; you daily read articles about taxes or about the Balkans; but you knew nothing of people. If a bell failed to ring, if a stove smoked, if a wheel on a machine stuck, you knew at once where to look and did so with alacrity; you found the defect and knew how to cure it. But the thing within you, the secret mainspring that alone gave meaning to life, the thing within us that alone is living, alone is capable of feeling pleasure and pain, of craving happiness and experiencing it—that was unknown. You knew nothing about that, nothing at all, and if the mainspring failed there was no cure. Wasn't it insane?"[10]

Since my childhood I have wanted to understand "the secret mainspring that alone gave meaning to life, the thing within us that alone is living, alone is capable of feeling pleasure and pain, of craving happiness and experiencing it." To unlock the secrets within us, I had to look below the shallow surface of the world around me. So many of the actors, athletes, politicians, and rock stars the media exposed me to were not ideal role models. They did not tell me what I wanted to know about life, happiness, peace, and what it means to be human.

What does it mean to be human? To understand this, I first had to remember what it meant to be a child. When I look back to my earliest childhood memories, I can recall many happy experiences. Before my father began descending into madness when I was four, the world seemed magical and mysterious, almost like a fairy tale. In the fairy tale world of my childhood, every day was an adventure with so much to explore, and everything seemed miraculous to me.

When I saw birds gliding through the air and trees towering over me, I was filled with wonder and awe. Smelling the inviting aromas of my mother's cooking, seeing the full moon and countless stars illuminate the haunting night sky, tasting the first sip of cool lemonade on a hot summer day, hearing the soothing rhythm of rain, and touching the soft fur of a dog were experiences that filled me with joyful calm. I felt truly alive. I felt connected to nature and united with the universe.

But then my perception of the world began to change, and the beauty and bliss of childhood gradually faded away. As I grew older and people mistreated me, my heart began to harden. Instead of experiencing wonder and awe when I looked at the mysterious world around me, I felt numb. The blissful calm within me was replaced by urges to commit violence and cruelty. The cold knife of cynicism severed my connection to nature, and the heavy weight of mental anguish shattered my sense of unity. I felt isolated and alone, and the world became a very frightening place. Herman Hesse said that when we are young, we all experience the beauty, adventure, magic, wonder, and awe that arise from the mystery of childhood. He explained:

> All children feel this way, although they do not feel it with the same intensity and sensitivity. And with many of them all of this is already gone, as if it had never existed, even before they begin to learn how to read the alphabet. For others, the mystery of childhood remains close to them for a long time, and they take a remnant and echo of it with them into the days of their white hair and weariness. All children, as long as they still live in the mystery, are continuously occupied in their souls with the only thing that is important, which is themselves and their enigmatic relationship to the world around them. Seekers and wise people return to these preoccupations as they mature. Most people, however, forget and leave forever this inner world of the truly significant very early in their lives. Like lost souls they wander about for their entire lives in the multicolored maze of worries, wishes, and goals, none of which dwells in their innermost being and none of which leads them to their innermost core and home.[11]

The universe is indeed a mystery, and scientific discoveries lead us deeper and deeper into this mystery. For example, the ancient Greeks were unable to explain the mystery of lightning, so they created stories of the Greek God Zeus hurling lightning bolts across the sky. When scientists discovered that lightning is electricity, this led to an even deeper mystery. What is electricity? When scientists discovered that electricity is caused by charged particles at the subatomic level, this led to an even deeper mystery. Why do the laws of physics work in this way? When scientists suggested that the laws of physics were created during the Big Bang—this led to even deeper mysteries. Where did the Big Bang come from? Why did it happen? What existed before the Big Bang?

Many of our ancestors looked at lightning with a sense of curiosity and wonder. To them it was a mysterious and miraculous force of nature. Although our scientific discoveries have allowed us to harness the power of electricity, it still remains a mystery to us. We understand how the laws of physics cause lightning, but we don't know where these laws came from or why they are arranged in such a precise way that makes lightning possible. If the laws of physics were slightly different, lightning and every other phenomenon in the universe, including life itself, would cease to exist.

The mystery we perceive during our youth is not a child's fantasy but a glimpse of reality, because the universe is actually a vast mystery, and every scientific discovery leads deeper into this mystery. According to Joseph Campbell, God is a metaphor for the great mystery of the universe. Cultures throughout history have created gods to explain not just lightning, but the sun, moon, stars, and deeper phenomena that ultimately cannot be explained.

When some animals see themselves in the mirror they are unable to comprehend their own reflection, and they respond as if the reflection is another animal. In a similar way, there are some things the human mind may never be able to grasp. Science is a remarkable demonstration of our intelligence that can benefit humanity in many ways, but where the universe came from may be beyond our comprehension, just as a reflection is beyond the comprehension of many animals.

Albert Einstein believed the human mind cannot fully comprehend the ultimate mystery of the universe. But experiencing this mystery and striving to unlock its secrets make us feel truly alive. He said: "The most beautiful thing we can experience is the mysterious. It is the fundamental emotion that stands at the cradle of true art and true science. He who does not know it and can no longer wonder, no longer feel amazement, is as good as dead, a snuffed-out candle."[12]

Many adults lose this sense of amazement. Because they have forgotten how to feel wonder and awe, they are no longer able to marvel at the profound mysteries of nature. Every major religion has teachers who acknowledge the deep mystery of the universe. Buddhist monk Thich Nhat Hanh, whom Martin Luther King Jr. nominated for the Nobel Peace Prize, says that existence itself is a mystery. A miracle is a mystery that cannot be fully explained, and by recognizing the mystery of existence, Thich Nhat Hanh saw human beings, the blue sky, and even the act of walking as miracles. He explains:

> I like to walk alone on country paths, rice plants and wild grasses on both sides, putting each foot down on the earth in mindfulness, knowing that I walk on the wondrous earth. In such moments, existence is a miraculous and mysterious reality. People usually consider walking on water or in thin air a miracle. But I think the real miracle is not to walk either on water or in thin air, but to walk on earth. Every day we are engaged in a miracle which we don't even recognize: a blue sky, white clouds, green leaves, the black, curious eyes of a child—our own two eyes. All is a miracle.[13]

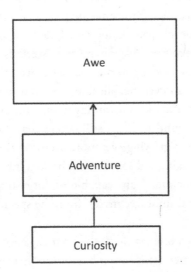

Figure 7.1: The Muscle of Curiosity

When our curiosity causes us to marvel in amazement at the great mystery of the universe, we experience awe, which is the highest expression of curiosity. Schweitzer realized that young children who perceive the great mystery of the universe are seeing the world more realistically than adults who lack a sense of amazement. When children, with their eyes wide with awe, look at human beings or animals, they are seeing their true nature—mysteries and miracles that cannot be fully explained. Schweitzer said:

> [In elementary school] the instruction in nature studies held something strangely exciting for me. I could not escape the feeling that we were not told sufficiently how little is really understood of what is going on in nature . . . It seemed ridiculous to me that wind, snow, hail, rain, the formation of clouds, the spontaneous ignition of hay, the trade winds, the Gulf Stream, thunder, and lightning were supposed to have been explained. For me a special enigma was the formation of the rain drop, the snowflake, and the hailstone. It wounded me that the ultimate mysteriousness of nature was not recognized and teachers confidently claimed to have an explanation where only a more deeply penetrating description had been achieved; this made the mysterious only more mysterious. Already then it had become evident to me that what we call "force" and "life" remains forever inexplicable to us in its essence.[14]
>
> Thus I drifted into dreaming about the thousand wonders that surround us . . . I still dream that way today, and this dreaming is growing ever more overpowering. When I sit at the dinner table and see the light broken into rainbow colors in a water jug, I am capable of forgetting everything around me. I cannot free myself from the spectacle.[15]

As we grow older, one reason we lose our capacity to look at the world with wonder, amazement, and awe is because an increase in weight requires an increase in muscle. As children we can be carefree because we are not fully aware of life's difficulties. The awareness of life's struggles adds weight to our soul, and we must strengthen our muscle of curiosity in order to carry this extra weight. If we do not strengthen it, our capacity to experience awe will be crushed, just as a person required to carry a heavy weight on his shoulders will collapse if he has not strengthened his legs.

Herman Hesse and Erich Fromm both described three stages of human life. The first is *innocence*, which involves the wonder, beauty, magic, and awe of childhood. The second is *innocence lost*, which occurs when the fairy-tale world of our childhood fades and we begin to feel shame, worry, numbness, and cynicism. The third is *innocence regained*, which few people achieve. What is innocence regained? To understand this it is important to explore what it means to be an adult.

Someone once told me, "You become an adult when you're able to take care of yourself." I disagreed and said, "You become an adult when you're able to take care of others." What distinguishes adults from children and adolescents is that adults are able to take responsibility for the well-being of their community.

Being an adult is a matter of attitude, not age. I have met people in their forties who behave like spoiled children, and most of us have seen parents who act like adolescents. Unfortunately, not all parents have developed the level of responsibility necessary to take proper care of their sons and daughters. Unlike children, adults take responsibility for their actions and work for the well-being of their community. In early human tribes, children asked questions such as "When can I eat next?" But adults asked questions such as "How can I best feed my tribe?"

Gandhi, Thich Nhat Hanh, Archbishop Desmond Tutu, the Fourteenth Dalai Lama, and other pioneers of peace are known for their positive child-like qualities. Innocence regained involves recapturing the awe of childhood that does not see people through the narrow lens of judgment and condemnation, but rather through the open heart of wonder and compassion. When I was three years old and looked at people with my wide-eyed curiosity, I did not see myself as superior or inferior. I did not judge, condemn, or hate. Everyone was beautiful, miraculous, and worthy of awe.

Gandhi and the other pioneers of peace combine the strength of childhood (ability to experience awe) with the strength of adulthood (ability to take responsibility). They see the world with the awe of a child, but are also able to take responsibility not only for themselves but humanity and our planet. On the other hand, I have met those who combine the weakness of childhood (irresponsibility) with the weakness of adulthood (vulnerability to cynicism). Like children who have not yet matured, they are unable to take responsibility for their actions, and they blame others for their problems. Like adults who have lost their connection with the beauty and magic of childhood, they adopt a cynical attitude toward life.

We must not judge people who are irresponsible and cynical, but help them. We must look at them not with condemnation, but with compassion. Recapturing the joy of childhood requires a lot of hard work, and few receive the proper guidance. And we all have bad days from time to time. On a good day I feel at peace with myself and connected to humanity; the world is full of magic, beauty, and awe. Some days I experience so much awe that I achieve a oneness with the universe that is blissful beyond description. On a bad day my old psychological wounds reopen and the suffering is so unbearable I sometimes wish for death.

My life has been full of contradictions. I have experienced the extremes of love and rage, along with the mountains of hope and valleys of despair. As long as I am alive, I will never cease my struggle to heal my psychological wounds and overcome the agony within me. I will never stop working for the peaceful revolution humanity needs to survive. But because I am realistic, I know the madness I inherited from war and my father may eventually destroy me. Because I am realistic, I also know that a peaceful revolution built on powerful ideas will be strong enough to succeed with or without me.

The Rising Phoenix

This book is a love song to humanity. During my thirty-one years on our fragile blue planet, I have lived through so much that could lead me to hate and despair. But I have experienced far more that allows me to love and hope.

It has been ten years since I struggled to unlock the mysteries of human nature in a barracks room at West Point, yet in some ways the journey is just beginning. As soldiers of peace, we must work together to create a transformation, a revolution, and a rebirth in human thinking if our species is going to survive.

The phoenix is a mythical bird that represents the power of rebirth. Because rebirth is an idea that transcends cultures, the legend of the phoenix can be found in places as diverse as Greece, Korea, Egypt, Rome, and China. The phoenix is a symbol of rebirth, because it is born from fire. According to ancient legends, when a phoenix dies it erupts in a burst of flame, and its offspring is born from the smoldering ashes it leaves behind. The phoenix symbolizes our human capacity for spiritual rebirth in the fire of hardship. Like an inferno that gives birth to a phoenix, the flames of suffering and adversity can give birth to strength and understanding.

According to the Greek historian Herodotus, the mythological phoenix must bury its father after rising from the burning ashes of its dead parent. He explained: "They say that the bird [phoenix] sets out from its homeland in Arabia on a journey to the sanctuary of the sun, bringing its father sealed in myrrh, and buries its father there."[16]

I was born from the fire of my father. Like the phoenix that voyages to bury its father in the sanctuary of the sun, I am also journeying to make peace with my past. The phoenix is a metaphor that lives within all of us, because it represents our human capacity for spiritual growth and transformation. When we experience the flames of adversity, we can be reduced into a charred heap of bitterness and cynicism, or we can experience a spiritual rebirth that makes us kinder and more compassionate. Healing can rise from the fire of trauma. Understanding can rise from the fire of suffering. Gentleness can rise from the fire of rage.

From every fire, a phoenix can be born. The civil rights movement rose from the fire of segregation. The women's rights movement rose from the fire of gender oppression. Today the world is burning with war, oppression, injustice, and environmental destruction. But as we strengthen the muscles of our humanity, a peaceful revolution will rise like a phoenix from the fire of our national and global problems. As we walk together on the road to peace, humanity will be reborn.

DESTROY THIS MAD BRUTE

"Destroy this mad brute" is the caption of this World War I propaganda poster for enlistment in the U.S. Army. A dribbling, ape-like German wielding a club bearing the word "kultur" and wearing a pickelhaube helmet with the word "militarism" is walking onto the shore of America while holding a half-naked woman in his grasp (possibly meant to depict Liberty). This is a US version of an earlier British poster with the same image. Picture from http://web.viu.ca/davies/H482.WWI/poster. Text from http://www.learnnc.org/lp/multimedia/10612.

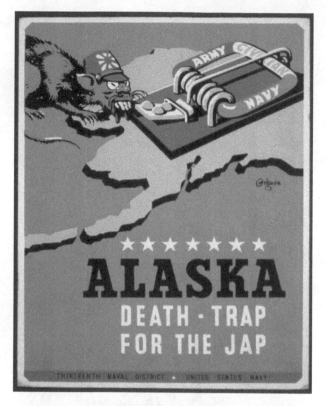

DEATH-TRAP FOR THE JAP

Racist depictions of Japanese and other Asian immigrants were common well before World War II. Since immigration from Japan began increasing in the 1880s, Japanese were described as an invading horde or "yellow peril," a threat to white society. After the bombing of Pearl Harbor, the U.S. government mass-produced propaganda posters showing racist stereotypes of a subhuman Japanese enemy — fanged, slit-eyed, devious creatures. The Japanese enemy was often pictured in the form of ugly and frightening animals, such as rats, bats, and other vermin. The decision to incarcerate all individuals of Japanese ancestry living on the West Coast in 1942 was influenced by widespread assumptions that people of Japanese descent were perpetually foreign and untrustworthy by virtue of their race. Picture from http://www.loc.gov/pictures/resource/cph.3b48885/. Text from http://historymatters.gmu.edu/d/8332.

WOLF BOY

This Japanese leaflet was dropped on the Chinese troops allied with the British. It shows a wolf-faced British soldier leading a Chinese soldier to a cliff where he will surely fall off and into massed Japanese bayonets depicted below. The text on the front is: "Do you really want to sell your soul to the British white ghost and see the Liao Zhai tragedy befall you?" Why does the British soldier have the face of a wolf? In China the wolf represented rapacity and greed or an official who exacted money unfairly from the people in the shape of unauthorized taxation. In fact, Chinese propaganda sometimes showed the Japanese as wolves. The term "white ghost" was an insult used for Caucasians. Picture and text from http://www.psywarrior.com/JapanPSYOPWW2b.html.

A MAN AND A BROTHER

The most infamous word in American history used to dehumanize a group of people is the racial slur "nigger." We cannot understand how African Americans were enslaved, lynched, and segregated unless we also understand how dehumanization blocks empathy. To confront dehumanization and assert their humanity, the sanitation workers that protested for equal rights during the civil rights movement wore a sign that read: "I am a man." And during the peaceful movement to abolish state-sanctioned slavery in Europe, an image of an enslaved African became a symbol of the movement. Underneath the image were the words: "Am I not a man and a brother?" Picture from http://www.loc.gov/rr/print/195_copr.html.

APPENDIX B

Let a man begin to think about the mystery of his life and the
links which connect him with life that fills the world, and he
cannot but bring to bear upon his own life and all other life
that comes within his reach the principle of reverence for life.
— Albert Schweitzer[1]

To show what makes us human, I had to discuss the differences between human
beings and other mammals. The road to peace, however, requires us to understand not only what makes us unique as human beings, but also what we share
with the other creatures on the earth. These myth-busting films show how much
we have in common with other animals, and that other species also have rich
emotional lives.

- *A Murder of Crows* *
- *Buck*
- *Chimpanzees: An Unnatural History*
- *Clash: Encounters of Bears and Wolves* **
- *Conversations with Koko*
- *Dogs Decoded*
- *The Dolphin Defender*

*This is a PBS Nature documentary, not to be confused with a film of the same name.
** This documentary illustrates several points from my books.
1. Animals demonstrate physical fury to protect their young.
2. Instead of fighting with the intention to kill, buffalos ram horns. When bears fight, the victorious
bear—instead of killing the other bear—usually turns its back, signaling the fight is over. These re-
strictions during combat minimize fatalities within species, although animals sometimes die after-
ward from injuries sustained during such confrontations.
3. In *Will War Ever End?* and *The End of War* I discuss how warning aggression, also known as pos-
turing, is used to deter violence. *Clash* shows that conflicts between mammals are more often resolved
through warning aggression than through lethal violence. Our society holds the misconception that
animals in nature rely heavily on violence and are constantly at war with each other. When not
hunting out of necessity animals are far more risk averse than many people realize.

NOTES

Preface

1. *General MacArthur: Speeches and Reports: 1908–1964*, Edward T. Imparato, ed. (Paducah, KY: Turner Publishing, 2000), 237, 240.

2. This is a commonly used alternate translation of Hugo's statement *"On résiste à l'invasion des armées; on ne résiste pas à l'invasion des idées."* Victor Hugo, *The History of a Crime* (Boston: Little, Brown, and Co., 1909), 627.

3. Address by General of the Army Douglas MacArthur to the Corps of Cadets on accepting the Thayer Award. General MacArthur incorrectly attributed this quotation to Plato. www.westpoint.org/real/macarthur_address.html.

4. George S. Patton Jr., "The Secret of Victory," http://www.pattonhq.com/pdffiles/vintagetext.pdf.

Chapter 1

1. The notion that lemmings commit mass suicide is a myth.

2. *Native American Wisdom*, ed. Kristen Marée Clearly (Barnes and Noble Books: New York, 1996), 14.

3. Ibid., 10.

4. Will Durant, *The Story of Philosophy* (New York: Simon & Schuster, 1933), 171.

5. Wording confirmed by Woody Guthrie Foundation in an email dated July 19, 2011.

6. Woody Guthrie, *Library of Congress Recordings*, CD, 1940.

7. Wording confirmed by Woody Guthrie Foundation in an email dated January 19, 2011.

8. Nick Spitzer, *This Land Is Your Land*, http://www.npr.org/templates/story/story.php?storyId=1076186.

9. Rabbi Michael Shire, *The Jewish Prophet* (Woodstock, VT: Jewish Lights Publishing, 2001), 121.

10. Dwight D. Eisenhower, address at the Columbia University National Bicentennial Dinner, New York City, May 31, 1954; http://www.presidency.ucsb.edu/ws/index.php?pid=9906.

11. Howard Zinn on *Bill Moyers Journal*, PBS, December 11, 2009.

12. Albert Schweitzer, *Memoirs of Childhood and Youth*, trans. Kate Bergel and Alice R. Bergel (Syracuse: Syracuse University Press, 1997), 90.

13. Ibid., 94.

14. Albert Schweitzer, *Out of My Life and Thought*, trans. Antje Bultmann Lemke (Baltimore: John Hopkins University Press, 1998), 92.

15. *The Expanded Quotable Einstein*, trans. Alice Calaprice (Princeton: Princeton University Press, 2000), 99.

16. Schweitzer, *Out of My Life and Thought*, 82.

17. Ibid., 92.

18. *The Words of Albert Schweitzer*, Norman Cousins, ed. (New York: New Market Press, 1984), 8–10.

19. Ibid., 69.

20. General Douglas MacArthur, farewell speech given to the Corps of Cadets at West Point, May 12, 1962, http://www.nationalcenter.org/MacArthurFarewell.html.

21. Thomas Paine, *The Rights of Man*, 1791.

22. Schweitzer, *Memoirs of Childhood and Youth*, 93.

23. Joseph Campbell, *Myths to Live By* (New York: Penguin, 1972), 46.

24. Erich Fromm, *The Art of Loving* (New York, Perennial Classics, 2000), 107–08.

25. *The Expanded Quotable Einstein*, 82.

26. Mohandas Gandhi, *Autobiography: The Story of My Experiments with Truth* (New York: Dover Publications, 1983), 4, 17.

27. Ibid., 22.

28. Louis Fischer, *Gandhi: His Life and Message for the World* (New York, Mentor, 1982), 90.

29. Lucius Annaeus Seneca, *Letters from a Stoic*, trans. Robin Campbell (New York: Penguin, 1969), 40.

30. Erich Fromm, *The Sane Society* (New York: Rinehart & Co., 1959), xiv.

31. State of Maine: Department of Education, http://www.maine.gov/education/ml/.

32. Pandit Satyakam Vidyalankar, ed., *The Holy Vedas*, (Delhi: Clarion Books, 1983), 100.

33. Antoine de Saint-Exupéry, *A Guide for Grown-ups* (New York: Harcourt, 2002), 51.

Chapter 2

1. Albert Schweitzer, *The Philosophy of Civilization* (New York: MacMillan, 1959), 6, 7.

2. Also known as the *Bushido Shoshinshu. Code of the Samurai*, trans. Thomas Cleary (Boston: Tuttle Publishing, 1999), 46.

3. Martin van Creveld, *The Art of War: War and Military Thought* (New York: Harper Collins, 2002), 76.

4. *Sun Tzu on the Art of War: The Oldest Military Treatise in the World*, trans. Lionel Giles (El Paso Norte Press: El Paso, 2005), 49. Actual authorship of *The Art of War* is still subject to debate.

5. General George Patton, speech to the Third Army, June 5, 1944, http://www.pattonhq.com/speech.html.

6. Floyd H. Ross and Tynette Hills, *The Great Religions by Which Men Live* (New York: Beacon Press, 1956), 80.

7. http://www.wickedlocal.com/salem/features/x2022452645/Doctor-to-receive-Salem-Award-for-study-of-PTSD-in-Vietnam-vets#axzz1WeFPTvsO.

8. Commandant, U.S. Marine Corps Trust Study—Final Report, Appendix E: Cohesion Essay, 2000.

9. van Creveld, *The Art of War*, 124.

10. William Shakespeare, *Henry V*, act 4, scene 3.

11. Peter Brock, *Gandhi's Nonviolence and His War Service, Peace and Change: A Journal of Peace Research*, March 5, 2009, 72; http://onlinelibrary.wiley.com/doi/10.1111/j.1468-0130.1981.tb00428.x/abstract.

12. Ibid.

13. Ibid., 76.

14. Medal of Honor Recipients, listing for Private First Class Ross McGinnis, http://www.history.army.mil/html/moh/iraq.html.

15. *The Power of Music: Jack Leroy Tueller*, http://www.youtube.com/watch?v=aQzRxGuBn0k.

16. Rudyard Kipling, "The Law of the Jungle," *The Jungle Book*, http://www.poetryloverspage.com/poets/kipling/law_of_jungle.html.

17. Fromm, *The Art of Loving*, 44.

18. A January 2002 interview with Gene Knudsen Hoffman, http://www.peaceheroes.com/PeaceHeroes/jeanknudsenhoffman.htm.

19. NCO Creed, http://www.armystudyguide.com/content/army_board_study_guide_topics/nco_history/nco-creed.shtml.

20. Dave Grossman, *On Killing* (Boston: Little, Brown and Company, 1995), 1–2.

21. Dave Grossman with Loren W. Christensen, *On Combat* (Milstadt, IL: Warrior Science Publications, 2008), xiii.

22. In some mammal species such as lions, there is an aversion to killing adult males, but less of an aversion to killing the young. For example, adult male lions will sometimes kill the helpless young of other adult males, but fights between adult male lions are usually not to the death. This behavior promotes the survival of lions as a species. In some mammals that rely more heavily on cooperation to survive (e.g. human beings), there is an aversion to killing both adults and babies. This promotes our survival as a species.

23. *Life in Cold Blood*, narrated by Richard Attenborough (BBC Warner, 2008), DVD.

24. Grossman, *On Killing*, 164–65.

25. Ibid., 99–130.

26. Klaus P. Fischer, *Nazi Germany: A New History* (New York: Continuum, 2006), 503.

27. Richard Breitman, *The Architect of Genocide* (University Press of New England: NH, 1991), 196–97.

28. Fischer, *Nazi Germany*, 502.

29. *Earth Made of Glass* (Sparks Rising, LLC, 2011), DVD.

30. Friedrich Nietzsche, *Beyond Good and Evil*, trans. Walter Kaufmann (New York: Vintage, 1966), 89.

31. Erich Fromm, *On Being Human* (New York: Continuum, 2003), 27–28.

32. David Henderson, *Who Is 'We'?*, http://original.antiwar.com/henderson/2005/11/03/who-is-we/.

33. George Orwell, *Homage to Catalonia* (Boston: Houghton Mifflin Harcourt, 1980), 65.

34. This poem is an interpretation by Daniel Ladinsky of how Hafiz saw love. *The Gift: Poems by Hafiz the Great Sufi Master*, trans. Daniel Ladinsky (New York: Penguin, 1999), 34.

35. Living the Army Values: Selfless Service, http://www.goarmy.com/soldier-life/being-a-soldier/living-the-army-values.noFlash.html#selfless.

36. Fromm, *The Art of Loving*, 43.

37. Mother Teresa, *In My Own Words*, comp. José Luis González-Balado (New York: Barnes and Noble Books, 1996), 89.

38. Henry David Thoreau, *Civil Disobedience and Other Essays* (Stilwell, KS: Digireads.com Publishing, 2005), 147.

39. New International Version,http://www.biblestudytools.com/ecclesiastes/4.html.

40. *Seven Samurai*, commentary disc (Criterion Collection, 1954), DVD.

41. Phone conversation with Jonathan Shay.

42. Lucius Annaeus Seneca, *Letters from a Stoic*, trans. Robin Campbell (New York: Penguin, 1969), 49, 51. I took out the reference to Epicurus.

43. Ralph Waldo Emerson, *The Complete Works of Ralph Waldo Emerson* (Houghton and Mifflin Co.: Boston and New York, 1904), 212.

44. Carl Jung, *The Undiscovered Self* (New York: New American Library, 1959), 117–18.

45. *The Words of Albert Schweitzer*, 81.

46. Mother Teresa, *In My Own Words*, 45.

47. Boethius, *The Consolation of Philosophy*, trans. Richard Green (Indianapolis: Bob Merrill Co., 1976), 29.

48. *The Sayings of Leo Tolstoy*, ed. Robert Pearce (London: Gerald Duckworth and Co. 1995), 33.

49. *The Most Brilliant Thoughts of All Time*, ed. John M. Shanahan (New York: HarperCollins, 1999), 172.

50. Discussion with James Lawson, November 2010.

51. Albert Einstein, *Bite-Size Einstein*, collected and edited by Jerry Mayer and John P. Holmes (New York: Gramercy Books, 1996), 10 (I added quote marks around the word universe.)

52. Schweitzer, *Memoirs of Childhood and Youth*, 95–96.

Chapter 3

1. Owen Morris, *I Figured Out the Meaning of Life*, http://www.removed-from-reality.blogspot.com/.

2. *The Words of Albert Schweitzer*, 67.

3. Thich Nhat Hanh, *Peace Is Every Step*, ed. Arnold Kotler (New York: Bantam Books, 1991), 26–27.

4. Interview with historian Eric Foner, http://www.pbs.org/wgbh/amex/reconstruction/schools/sf_postwar.html.

5. John Milton, *Paradise Lost*, bk. 1, lines 254–55, http://www.dartmouth.edu/~milton/reading_room/pl/book_1/.

6. *Native American Wisdom*, ed. Kristen Marée Clearly (Barnes and Noble Books: New York, 1996), 18.

7. Joseph Campbell, *Pathways to Bliss*, ed. David Kudler (Novato, CA: New World Library, 2004), 27.

8. John F. Kennedy's inaugural address, January 20, 1961.

9. *The Words of Albert Schweitzer*, 20.

10. Credit for this idea belongs to Erich Fromm; I don't recall the source.

11. *The Autobiography of Martin Luther King Jr.*, ed. Clayborne Carson (New York: Warner Books, 1998), 105.

12. Schweitzer, *Out of My Life and Thought*, 90.

13. Nathan Irvin Huggins, *Slave and Citizen* (London: Pearson, 1980), 49.

14. Alice Walker, *The World Has Changed* (New York, New Press, 2010), 80.

15. Albert Einstein, *Ideas and Opinions*, ed. Cal Seelig (New York: Three Rivers Press, 1982), 13.

16. *Cosmos: Carl Sagan* (Cosmos Studios, 2002), DVD.

Chapter 4

1. Peter Brock. "Gandhi's Nonviolence and His War Service." *Peace and Change: A Journal of Peace Research*, March 2009, 78, http://onlinelibrary.wiley.com/doi/10.1111/j.1468-0130.1981.tb00428.x/abstract.

2. Ibid., 74.

3. Ibid., 75–6.

4. *The Words of Martin Luther King Jr.*, selected by Coretta Scott King (New York: Newmarket Press, 1996), 23.

5. *Stay On the Job Until Every Murdering Jap Is Wiped Out!*, 1941–1945. http://arcweb.archives.gov/arc/action/ExternalIdSearch?id=515483&jScript=true.

6. Transcript of speech given in Cincinnati, Ohio, http://www.guardian.co.uk/world/2002/oct/07/usa.iraq.

7. Nell Greenfieldboyce, "Dogs Understand Fairness, Get Jealous, Study Finds," National Public Radio. http://www.npr.org/templates/story/story.php?storyId=97944783.

8. Michael Garrett and J. T. Garrett, *Native American Faith in America*, ed. J. Gordon Melton (New York: Facts on File, 2003), 98.

9. J. F. C. Fuller, *The Generalship of Alexander the Great* (New Brunswick: Da Capo Press, 1960), 304–5.

10. West Point Bugle Notes, http://www.west-point.org/academy/malo-wa/inspirations/buglenotes.html.

11. Henry David Thoreau, *Walden and Civil Disobedience* (New York: Penguin, 1986), 30.

12. Ibid., 386.

13. *The Autobiography of Martin Luther King, Jr.*, 197–98.

14. Interview with Martin Luther King Jr., 1957, http://www.youtube.com/watch?v=-Ll4QmvnGcU.

15. Ibid.

16. After Shakespeare and the Enlightenment, many people still believed kings and queens were different from "commoners" not for divine reasons, but genetic ones. The notion of having royal blood asserted the belief that those in the royal family were somehow different from other human beings and therefore deserved special treatment.

17. *The Autobiography of Martin Luther King, Jr.*, 128.

18. F. W. Bogen, *The German in America* (New York: Koch and Co., 1851), 7, 41, 57.

19. *The Autobiography of Martin Luther King, Jr.*, 197–98.

20. Saul Friedländer, *Nazi Germany and the Jews*, (New York: HarperCollins, 1997), 98.

21. After the Show: How the Gift of Fear Can Save Your Life, http://www.oprah.com/spirit/After-the-Show-How-the-Gift-of-Fear-Can-Save-Your-Life.

22. U.S. Army Medical Department, Office of Medical History, http://history.amedd.army.mil/MOH/womackb.html.

23. *The Autobiography of Martin Luther King, Jr.*, 365–66.

24. The Poetry of Pablo Neruda, ed. Ilan Stavans (New York: Farrar, Straus, and Giroux, 2003), 233.

25. Fischer, *Gandhi*, 39.

26. *In Depth with Noam Chomsky* (C-SPAN: Booknotes, 2006), DVD.

27. Arundhati Roy, *Power Politics* (Boston: South End Press, 2001).

Chapter 5

1. Gavin de Becker, *The Late Late Show with Craig Ferguson*, http://www.youtube.com/watch?v=BgI1MQ47H5c&feature=related.

2. Grossman, *On Combat*, 44.

3. G. M. Gilbert, *Nuremberg Diary* (Cambridge: Da Capo Press, 1995), 278.

4. http://horebinternational.com/2010/01/31/the-power-of-empathy/.

5. Schweitzer, *Memoirs of Childhood and Youth*, 13–14.

6. Grossman, *On Combat*, 12–13.

7. Ibid., 78.

8. Ibid.

9. Ibid., 75–76.

10. Roy L. Swank and Walter E. Marchand. "Combat Neuroses: Development of Combat Exhaustion." American Medical Association: Archives of Neurology and Psychiatry, 1946, 243.

11. Grossman, *On Combat*, 77.

12. Ibid., 79. See Grossman's *Stop Teaching Our Kids to Kill* for an explanation of how violent first-person video games provide the same kind of conditioning.

13. Grossman, *On Killing*, 77.

14. Ibid., xvii–xx.

15. "The First Duty," *Star Trek: The Next Generation*, Season 5 (Paramount, 1992).

16. Padraic Colum, *Nordic Gods and Heroes* (New York: Dover Publications, 1996), 280.

17. Ibid., 280–81 (paraphrased).

18. Plato, *Timaeus*, http://classics.mit.edu/Plato/timaeus.html.

19. In his commentary Plato seems to miss the symbolism of Phaëton. He interprets the story of Phaëton in the most literal way possible by saying that it is an explanation for astronomical events. However, the stories of Icarus and Phaëton are clearly about hubris, a concept that the Greeks understood well. Hubris means arrogance and an overestimation of one's abilities that leads to one's ruin. The Greeks probably could not foresee weapons as destructive as nuclear weapons, but they were well aware of human fallibility. Our fallibility as human beings is what ultimately makes nuclear weapons so dangerous. According to John F. Kennedy, nuclear holocaust can result from accident, miscalculation, or madness, which are all products of human fallibility. Also, weapons such as the bow and arrow (the Persians were said to have so many archers that they could blot out the sun with their arrows) and "Greek fire" gave the Greeks some awareness of technology's dangers.

20. Deuteronomy 30:19, English Standard Version.

Chapter 6

1. *Tyson*, (Sony Picture Classics, 2009), DVD.
2. Ibid.
3. Ibid.
4. Sun Tzu, *The Art of War*, 37.
5. Ibid., 5.
6. Laurence G. Boldt, *Zen Soup* (New York: Penguin, 1998), 114.
7. Jonah Lehrer. "Don't!: The Secret of Self-Control." *New Yorker*, May 18, 2009, 1–2, http://www.newyorker.com/reporting/2009/05/18/090518fa_fact_lehrer?currentPage=1.
8. Ibid., 5.
9. Ibid., 2.
10. *Ape Genius* (PBS Nova, 2008), DVD.
11. George S. Patton, *War As I Knew It* (Boston: Houghton Mifflin Company, 1995), 108.
12. Brian Merchant. "How Far Ahead Do Politicians Really Think?" *Utopianist*, http://utopianist.com/2011/02/how-far-ahead-do-politicians-really-think/.
13. Gandhi, speech at Victoria Hall, Geneva, Switzerland, December 10, 1931.
14. Noam Chomsky, *Failed States* (C-SPAN Book TV, April 2006), DVD.
15. Alice Gomstyn, *Journal News*, http://www.infoshop.org/inews/article.php?story=20060531004125659 (paraphrased).
16. Bill Moyers, Message to West Point speech, http://www.tompaine.com/articles/2006/11/29/message_to_west_point.php.
17. Lehrer, "Don't!: The Secret of Self-Control," 6, http://www.newyorker.com/reporting/2009/05/18/090518fa_fact_lehrer?currentPage=1.
18. *A Force More Powerful* (A Force More Powerful Films, 2002), DVD.
19. Sri Chinmoy, *The Three Branches of India's Life Tree* (New York: Aum Publications, 1996), 179.
20. I based most of this interpretation of the story on Joseph Campbell's research, but focused only on the parts integral to the themes of discipline and resisting temptation.
21. Joseph Campbell and Bill Moyers, *The Power of Myth* (PBS, Athena, 2010), DVD.
22. Dave Grossman, *The Bulletproof Mind* (Dave Grossman and Gavin de Becker, 2008), DVD.
23. Patton's speech to the Third Army, June 5, 1944, http://www.pattonhq.com/speech.html.
24. *Tyson*, DVD.
25. *Driven* (Lovely Machine, 2011), DVD.
26. Campbell, *The Power of Myth*, 190.
27. Plato, *The Symposium*, trans. Christopher Gill (New York: Penguin Books, 1999), 83.
28. Ibid., 59.
29. Sarah Lipton. "Those Manly Men of Yore." *New York Times*, June 16, 2011, http://www.nytimes.com/2011/06/17/opinion/17lipton.html?_r=1&ref=opinion.
30. Antoine de Saint-Exupéry, *The Little Prince*, trans. Richard Howard (New York: Harcourt, 1943), 15.

Chapter 7

1. In high school I attempted to read books on my own because I knew that I had to read more to become a good writer, but it was a struggle. I did not begin loving to read until I was at West Point.

2. Interview with historian Eric Foner, http://www.pbs.org/wgbh/amex/reconstruction/schools/sf_postwar.html.

3. "10 Questions for Neil deGrasse Tyson," *Time*, http://www.youtube.com/watch?v=wiOwqDmacJo.

4. Some people began to realize the Earth was round over two thousand years ago, and although most people today know this to be true, there are still some people who believe the world is flat.

5. Most of us have been on a plane and felt a sense of complete stillness while we are in motion, so the idea of moving through space without sensing motion is an easy concept for us to grasp. However, two thousand years ago there were no planes that could give people a sense of motion with stillness. People had horses, chariots, and boats, but these were often bumpy rides.

6. Floyd H. Ross and Tynette Hills, *The Great Religions by Which Men Live* (New York: Beacon Press, 1956), 80.

7. Carl Sagan, *Cosmos* (Cosmos Studios, 2002), DVD.

8. Albert Schweitzer, *The Philosophy of Civilization* (New York: MacMillan, 1959), 7.

9. Dorothy Herrmann, *Helen Keller: A Life* (Chicago: University of Chicago Press, 1998), 271.

10. Herman Hesse, *Klingsor's Last Summer*, trans. Richard and Clara Winston (New York: Farrar, Straus and Giroux, 1970), 126.

11. Herman Hesse, *The Fairy Tales of Herman Hesse*, trans. Jack Zipes (New York, Bantam Books, 1995), 248.

12. *The Expanded Quotable Einstein*, ed. Alice Calaprice (Princeton: Princeton University Press, 2000), 295.

13. Thich Nhat Hanh, *The Miracle of Mindfulness*, trans. Mobi Ho (Boston: Beacon Press, 1999), 12.

14. Schweitzer, *Memoirs of Childhood and Youth*, 64–65.

15. Ibid., 65.

16. Herodotus, *The Histories*, trans. Robin Waterfield (Oxford: Oxford University Press, 1998), 123.

Appendix B

1. *Words of Albert Schweitzer*, ed., Cousins, 8–10.

INDEX